WBI DEVELOPMENT STUDIES

Mexico's Transition to a Knowledge-Based Economy

Challenges and Opportunities

Yevgeny Kuznetsov
Carl. J. Dahlman

THE WORLD BANK
Washington, D.C.

Contents

List of Boxes, Figures, and Tables

Boxes

Figures

Tables

Foreword

Knowledge and talent are prerequisites for success in today's global knowledge economy. For developing countries, this increasing importance of knowledge and its productive application has created new challenges as well as new windows of opportunity. This book is about how Mexico can transform itself into a knowledge-based economy by tapping into a number of existing socioeconomic advantages: macroeconomic stability, emerging regional enterprise clusters that combine local talent with a dynamic private sector, geographical proximity to the world's knowledge economy powerhouse—the United States, as well as a rich cultural base that generates a wealth of ideas.

Mexico's Transition to a Knowledge-Based Economy provides a broad assessment of the country's readiness to join the global knowledge economy, highlighting the importance of education and institutional reform, and of creating an environment that is conducive to innovation. This transformation, however, is not only about shaping the reform agenda from the top down. It also means trial-and-error experimentation to test what works and what doesn't in the Mexican context, and then taking successful bottom-up initiatives to scale. The book takes a dual approach in its analysis and recommendations. It tackles both the strategic long-term agenda, which entails many difficult changes and choices, while also proposing a diversity of pragmatic, short- and medium-term entry points to initiate and promote the transition within the current institutional structure.

The World Bank looks forward to working with Mexican stakeholders in devising practical initiatives to help the country realize its full potential in the global knowledge economy of the twenty-first century.

Rakesh Nangia
Acting Vice President
World Bank Institute

Acknowledgments

The report was prepared by a team led by Carl Dahlman and Yevgeny Kuznetsov of the World Bank Institute's Knowledge for Development Program (WBIKD). Team members included Guillermo Abdel Musik (Instituto Tecnológico Autónomo de México, Mexico City), Aimilios Chatzinikolaou (International Finance Corporation), Joost Draaisma (World Bank, Latin America and Caribbean Region, Economic Policy Sector), and Robert Stephens (World Bank–Global Information and Communications Technologies Department, Policy Division). Valuable contributions were made by Clemente Ruiz Duran (Universidad Nacional Autónoma de México, Mexico City), Carlos Mancera (Valora Consultores), Mark Hagerstrom and Harry Patrinos (World Bank, Latin America and Caribbean Region, Human Development), Daniel Crisafulli (IBRD–Global Information and Communications Technologies Department, Policy Division), and Derek Chen (WBIKD). Administrative and editorial assistance was provided by Faythe Calandra (WBIKD).

We express special thanks to participants of a discussion with the government organized by the Presidency of Mexico on January 17, 2005, particularly Alejandro Werner (Secretaría de Hacienda y Crédito Público de México), Guillermo Aguirre (Consejo Nacional de Ciencia y Tecnología), and Bernardo Gonzalez-Arrechiga (Instituto Tecnológico de Estudios Superiores de Monterrey).

Members of the Mexico country team, particularly Krishna Challa and Anna Wellenstein (World Bank, Latin America and Caribbean Region, Finance, Private Sector and Infrastructure), provided guidance and advice. We would also like to thank Peter Scherer and our colleagues in Mexico, particularly Rene Villareal (Centro de Capital Intelectual y Competitividad), Roberto Villareal (Office of the President), Guillermo Fernandez de la Garza (US-Mexico Foundation for Science), and Hector Moreira (Instituto Tecnológico y de Estudios Superiores de Monterrey) for their useful insights.

Peer reviewers are Jose Luis Guasch (Latin America and Caribbean Region, Finance, Private Sector, and Infrastructure), Lauritz Holm-Nielsen (Latin American and Caribbean Region, Human Development, Education Sector), Alfred Jay Watkins (Europe and Central Asia Region, Poverty and Financial Sectors Development), and Fernando Clavijo (Analitica Consultores, Mexico).

Abbreviations and Acronyms

ADIAT	Asociación Mexicana de Directivos de la Investigación Aplicada y el Desarollo
ADSL	Asymmetric Digital Subscriber Line
ARPU	Average Revenue Per User
ATE	Asesores Tecnológicos Empresariales
AVANCE	Apoyo para la Creación de Nuevos Negocios a partir de Desarrollos Científicos y Tecnológicos
CCD	Centros Communitarios Digitales
CFC	Controlled Foreign Corporation
CFE	Comisión Federal de Electricidad
CIATEQ	Centro de Informática Científica y Tecnológica
CIMO	Programa Calidad Integral y Modernización
CMM 3	(certificación) Modelo de Madurez y Capacidad Nivel 3
COFECO	Comisión Federal de Competencia
COFETEL	Comisión Federal de Telecomunicaciones
COMPITE	Comité Nacional de Productividad e Innovación Tecnológica
CONACYT	Consejo Nacional de Ciencia y Tecnología
CONAFE	Consejo Nacional de Fomento Educativo
CONAPO	Consejo Nacional de Población
CONEVYT	Consejo Nacional de Educación para la Vida y el Trabajo
CONOCER	Consejo de Normalización y Certificación de Competencia Laboral
CRE	Comisión Reguladora de Energía
CRECE	Centros Regionales para la Competitividad Empresarial
DF	Distrito Federal
EMS	Environmental Management Systems
ENESTYC	Encuesta Nacional de Empleo, Salarios, Tecnología y Capacitación
ENIGH	Encuesta Nacional de Ingresos y Gastos de los Hogares
FCST	Fondo de Cobertura Social de las Telecomunicaciones
FDI	Foreign direct investment
FEMSA	Fomento Económico Mexicano
FIDECAP	Fondo de Fomento a la Integración de Cadenas Productivas
FIMPES	Federation of private higher education institutions
FTL	Federal Telecommunications Law
GATT	General Agreement on Tariffs and Trade
GDP	Gross domestic product
GE	General Electric
GM	General Motors
GNI	Gross national income
GNP	Gross national product

IBM	International Business Machines Corporation
ICEES	Instituto de Crédito Educativo del Estado de Sonora
ICT	Information and communication technologies
IIE	Instituto Internacional de la Educación
ILAS	Individual learning accounts
IMNC	Instituto Mexicano de Normalización y Certificación
IMP	Instituto Mexicano del Petróleo
IMPI	Instituto Mexicano de la Propiedad Industrial
IMSS	Instituto Mexicano de Seguro Social
INEA	Instituto Nacional para la Educación de los Adultos
INEE	Instituto Nacional de Evaluación Educativa
INEGI	Instituto Nacional de Estadística Geografía e Informática
INFONAVIT	Instituto del Fondo Nacional para la Vivienda de los Trabajadores
ININ	Instituto Nacional de Investigaciones Nucleares
IPN	Instituto Politécnico Nacional
ISCED	Internacional Standard Classification of Education
ISO	Internacional Organization for Standardization
ITESM	Instituto Tecnológico de Estudios Superiores de Monterrey (Tec)
K4D	Knowledge for Development Program
KAM	Knowledge Assessment Methodology
KE	Knowledge Economy
KEI	Knowledge Economy Index
LLL	Lifelong Learning
MEX-EX	Distribuidor directo de productos agrícolas y alimenticios, con servicio complete de exportación
MNC	Multinational Corporations
NAFTA	North American Free Trade Agreement
NAFIN	Nacional Financiera
NGO	Nongovernmental organization
NORMEX	Sociedad Mexicana de Normalización y Certificación
OECD	Organisation for Economic Co-operation and Development
OEM	Original Equipment Manufacturing
PAC	Patronato de Arte Contemporánea
PAIDEC	Programa de Apoyo a Proyectos Conjuntos de Investigación y Desarollo
PATCI	Programa de Asistencia Técnica y Campañas de Imagen
PC	Plaza Comunitarias
PEMEX	Petróleos Mexicanos
PISA	Programme for International Student Assessment
PMT	Programa de Modernización Tecnológica
PROMEP	Programa de Mejoramiento del Profesorado
PRONABES	Programa Nacional de Becas para la Educación Superior
R&D	Research and Development
RCA	Revealed comparative advantages
SAT	Servício de Administración Tributaria
SCT	Secretaría de Comunicaciones y Transportes

SE	Secretaría de Economía
SECTUR	Secretaría de Turismo
SEP	Secretaría de Educación Pública
SEPE	Secretariados de Educación Pública Estatales
SME	Small and Medium Enterprise
SNI	Sistema Nacional de Investigadores
SNTE	Sindicato Nacional de Trabajadores de la Educación
S&T	Science and Technology
SOFES	Sociedad de Fomento a la Educación Superior
STPS	Secretaría del Trabajo y Previsión Social
TFP	Total Factor Productivity
TIMSS	Trends in International Mathematics and Science Study
TSU	Técnico Superior Universitaria
TTAC	Centro de Asistencia Técnica y Entrenamiento
UNAM	Universidad Nacional Autónoma de México
UNCTAD	United Nations Conference on Trade and Development
USPTO	United States Patent Office
VAT	Value-added Tax
WTO	World Trade Organization
WBI	World Bank Institute

Part I
Need for a Transition
to Knowledge-Based Economy

Where does Mexico aspire to be 20 years from now, and what will its industrial structure look like? This question is impossible to answer in any reasonable detail, just as it was impossible to predict, in the wake of the debt crisis, how Mexico would be transformed over the past 20 years. Today Mexico needs to embark on a no less dramatic transformation. This transformation will be based on the North American Free Trade Agreement (NAFTA) economic model, but it will need to go further. Further reforms within the NAFTA agenda must focus on dramatically improving national capabilities to generate knowledge and transform it into wealth. Such capabilities are largely about flexible and efficient networks of public and private organizations interacting in a concerted way to generate and adopt knowledge. This "national learning capacity" is what permits nations to adopt and innovate in their initial areas of comparative advantage. It also helps create new areas of advantage. To underline continuity with the existing model, and stress the need for a new generation of reforms to tap into the knowledge revolution, we call a knowledge economy agenda for Mexico a "knowledge-driven (second-generation) NAFTA agenda."

Driven by the rapid application of new information and communications technologies (ICT), and the application of scientific discoveries to production in every sector of the economy, the knowledge revolution has created massive opportunities for countries to dramatically increase their competitiveness and to achieve rapid growth. At the same time, it presents great challenges. Knowledge-driven supply chains and markets now dominate the global economy. If countries fail to position themselves properly in this global, knowledge-based marketplace, they will be increasingly unable to compete.

1

New Challenges and Opportunities

Much of the challenge Mexico faces in the global knowledge economy could be retold as a parable of two small, family-owned garment firms, one in Chihuahua and the other in Michoacan. They share the same history and, until very recently, were almost identical in their endowments of human and fixed capital. Yet one is prospering and exporting, while the other is struggling to survive. The successful firm was able to plug into worldwide garment networks. Through this collaboration, it takes advantage of design and marketing capabilities of leading firms in Mexico and the United States. More generally, it learns about product differentiation and the importance of just-in-time delivery. Given the rapidly changing tastes of consumers and clothing designs, and the demanding production and logistics disciplines needed to keep pace with these changes, the successful firm is becoming part of the new, knowledge-processing economy. Its small size and modest resources are not obstacles to success, precisely because manufacturing and marketing skills reside in networks, not individual firms.

In contrast, the struggling firm is at risk precisely because, like so many other Mexican firms, it is trying to survive on its own, largely cut off from leading foreign corporations with direct investments in Mexico, and from other domestic companies. All the knowledge-induced changes that create opportunities for the first firm are threats to its neighbor, because the same disruptions of routine and habit that allow the first firm to convert inexperience into open-mindedness and the ability to take a fresh approach create daunting risks for the second. Worse yet, the first firm is learning how to learn, while the second knows only how much it does not know. The first firm embarks on *a virtuous circle of learning:* success breeds success—inclusion in knowledge networks brings new expertise and makes subsequent learning more productive. The second firm falls into a *vicious circle of poverty:* failure breeds failure—exclusion from knowledge networks diminishes further chances to catch up.

This chapter discusses the knowledge revolution and the exciting opportunities for growth it presents for Mexico. Knowledge, as discussed in this book, is emphatically not just about high technology. By putting knowledge to work, the developing regions of Mexico, small and medium-size enterprises (SMEs), and other less developed actors can improve everyday life and enjoy new possibilities. Mexico's service sector (tourism and health services, for example) provides particularly fertile ground for the application of knowledge.

Knowledge-Based Growth

One proxy for a nation's ability to absorb knowledge is total factor productivity (TFP), a residual in the production function that cannot be explained by inputs. This capability to adopt, adapt, and create knowledge is critically dependent on countries' institutions, particularly investment climate and regulatory framework.

Figure 1.1 *GDP per Capita Growth in the Republic of Korea and Mexico, 1960–2002*

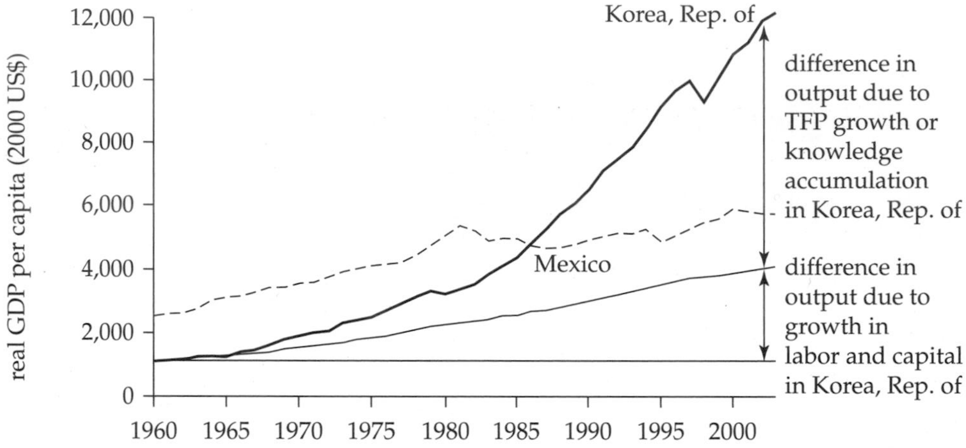

Source: World Bank (1999); see also Annex 1, "Theoretical Framework for Growth Projections."

It is often measured by a so-called residual in the production function that cannot be explained by factor inputs.[1] This ability to put knowledge to work produces a dramatic difference in a country's wealth. Figure 1.1 illustrates the dramatic difference in wealth attributable to national learning capacities. The Republic of Korea developed such a capability in the 1970s and 1980s, whereas Mexico did not. If, in the next 15 years, Mexico embarks on the same trajectory of total factor productivity growth as Korea, per capita gross domestic product (GDP) in the year 2020 is projected to be about $15,000 (see Figure 1.2). Clearly, the stakes are high in the process of transformation to a knowledge-based economy.

While many countries have been able to embark on a path of knowledge-based growth, there is no single path to such transformation. Different countries have found different ways to build on their strengths in order to improve their competitive positions. Three countries illustrate three distinct strategies for upgrading national capabilities: the Republic of Korea, Ireland, and Finland.

Korea represents a growth model based largely on diversified conglomerates. These conglomerates took advantage of the protected domestic market, which allowed them to generate surplus capital for investment. At the same time, these firms started investing in industries, such as shipbuilding or microchips, where the minimum efficient scale was the global market. This private sector strategy was complemented by an excellent education system. When the domestic market was opened, these firms were already world-class companies with significant technological capabilities.

Ireland based its development strategy on the attraction of multinational corporations, particularly in the electronics and software industries. Once the firms had become established in Ireland, the country made a strong effort to create vertical

---

[1] Because TFP is a very imperfect proxy, Figures 1.1 and 1.2 are merely illustrative and serve to outline qualitative scenarios of development.

linkages and develop suppliers, first as product suppliers, and later on higher value-added activities such as software. Here again the government played a very active role in creating training programs to improve abilities specific to the industries.

Finland is a resource-rich country, and not long ago its economy was based on its rich forests. The country started doing research and development (R&D) to further strengthen its strong industries—forestry, pulp, and paper. Based on the knowledge generated from the R&D activities, telecommunications, design, and consulting firms have sprung up. Given the small size of the domestic market, these firms now are leaders on a global scale.

Mexico shares certain elements with each of these examples: large business groups, the presence of multinationals, natural resources. However, the country should find its own strategy given its present conditions and strengths.

At the level of the firm, learning capability can be disaggregated into project execution capability, production capability, and innovation capability (Amsden and Hikino 1994).

- *Project execution capability* refers to the skills required to establish or expand corporate facilities. Included are the skills required for preinvestment feasibility studies (identification of markets for project outputs, and so forth), project management, project engineering (basic and detailed), procurement, construction, and start-up of operations.
- *Production capability* refers to the skills required to operate the facilities once they are established.
- *Innovation capability* refers to the skills for basic and applied research and related engineering, and to the ability to create new products and processes.

In both Mexico and Korea during the period of intense industrialization, major companies' large-scale investment projects were established by means of turnkey technology transfers in the continuous process industries such as soap, cement, and petrochemicals—industries characterized by high capital requirements and little opportunity for reverse engineering. Some of the Korean companies, faced with export pressures, went on to become industrial leaders by quickly developing sophisticated capabilities for project execution and innovation. In contrast, Mexican conglomerates (with some notable exceptions, such as CEMEX) still face relatively undemanding markets and do not innovate aggressively. Technology is actively sought, but innovation capabilities, even in the best firms, are not considered a major competitive asset worth nourishing. Large Mexican conglomerates are some of the best in the world in production and project execution capabilities, which is no small achievement, but like every achievement, this could be a handicap to the extent that it reduces an urgency to develop sophisticated innovation capabilities.

Korean firms, on the other hand, faced the need to pursue more aggressive export strategies than their Mexican counterparts, and they were able to rely on more efficient public innovation organizations that were more responsive to private sector needs. Innovation (and the associated private investment in applied R&D and technology upgrading) thus became the strategic focus of Korean firms, enabling them to compete internationally.

Figure 1.2 presents four different assumptions regarding Mexico's ability to utilize knowledge by the year 2020. As in Figure 1.1, total factor productivity is a proxy for national learning capability. *Projection 1* plots the path of Mexico's real

Figure 1.2 *Four Projections of Mexico's Real GDP per Capita, 2001–2020*

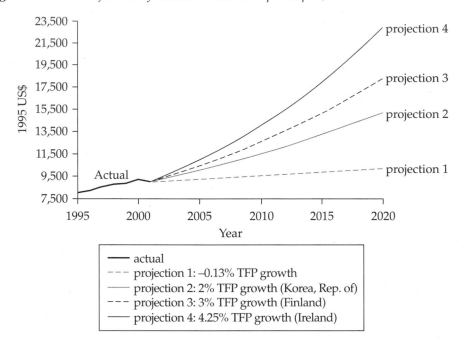

Source: Based on historical data. For more details on the methodology and sources of data, see Annex 1, "Theoretical Framework for Growth Projections."

Note: For all four projections, capital, labor, and human capital were assumed to grow at the 1991–2000 average growth rates for Mexico—3.32 percent, 2.75 percent, and 0.92 percent, respectively.

GDP per capita if the TFP growth rate were to take its 1991–2000 average value (–0.13 percent per year).[3] *Projection 2* plots the path of Mexico's real GDP per capita if the TFP growth rate were 2 percent per year, which is close to the 1991–2000 decade average for Korea. *Projection 3* plots the path that Mexico's real GDP per capita would take if the TFP growth rate were 3 percent per year, which is close to the 1961–1970 decade average for Finland. Lastly, *projection 4* plots the path of Mexico's real GDP per capita if the TFP growth rate were to be 4.25 percent per year—the approximate value of the 1991–2000 decade average for Ireland.

Projection 1 is an inertial scenario, projections 2 and 3 are both realistic scenarios outlining a range of possibilities for Mexico, and projection 4 is a very optimistic yet not altogether impossible scenario. We see that knowledge, quite literally, makes the difference between poverty and wealth. All things being equal, the difference in per capita GDP between the realistically optimistic scenario 3 and inertial scenario by year 2020 is almost twofold.

---

[3] Alternative methodologies to calculate total factor productivity are available. To make sure that our results are robust, Annex 1 develops and compares two methodologies that show consistent results—close to zero TFP growth. Our inertial growth projection uses the most optimistic TFP estimate (i.e., other estimates are even lower). Annex 1 also surveys the literature on TFP estimates for Mexico, which are all consistent with the ones proposed here.

Mexico's Growth Paradox

Glimpses of our high-case scenario—of prosperous knowledge-based Mexico 20 years from now are already in the making. The engineering centers of General Electric (GE), General Motors (GM), and Delphi, employing hundreds of highly skilled knowledge workers, can become springboards for innovation clusters. The provision of health services to retirement communities in San Miguel de Allende or Cuernavaca indicates the potential for high value-added health care service and recreation clusters. (See Box 1.1 on rising health care expenditures in developed countries and the potential of health care tourism.) These two examples may seem worlds apart, but they both rely on efficient knowledge workers and knowledge organizations. The chapters that follow were written to inform the national debate on how to develop a critical mass of knowledge workers and knowledge organizations.

Mexico has already developed many pockets of excellence and high productivity associated with multinationals operating in high-tech and higher middle-tech industries, and with national conglomerates operating in mature industries. These are no longer maquila operations because they employ many professionals and have in-house design and engineering. Yet these pockets of excellence are often enclaves with few linkages to the rest of the economy. This is Mexico's growth paradox: a promise of higher productivity, value added, and wages—a promise that remains largely unrealized.

Box 1.1 *Health Care Services as a Global Opportunity: Lessons from India*

India is a well-known exporter of software and information technology (IT)-enabled services. Health care tourism is poised to be the next significant business for India because of its exceptional expertise, cost advantages, and world-class facilities. Worldwide, health care is a $3 trillion industry, and India is in a position to tap the top-end segment by highlighting its facilities and services, and exploiting the brand equity of leading Indian health care professionals across the globe.

Western Standard Hospitals are likely to generate about $20 billion in annual revenues by 2010, two-thirds of which is expected to come from patients who are not Indian in origin. From the Middle East, Bangladesh, Sri Lanka, Egypt, and Mauritius, patients are beginning to come to these hospitals for cardiac bypass surgery. The procedure costs $5,000 in India compared to $20,000 in the United Kingdom and $30,000 in the United States. Cataract patients from Europe also are choosing to have their cataract operations in India. Afterward they spend two weeks in Goa—an Indian island similar to Hawaii—to recuperate. These patients avoid the long waiting times for European hospitals, and the European insurance companies pay all costs (including the costs of recuperating).

Some Indian radiologists are beginning to read the X-ray charts of U.S. patients and send their preliminary findings to U.S. radiologists, who verify their findings and do a thorough quality check. In this model, the initial 80 percent of the work is in India and the remaining 20 percent in the United States (with proper quality checks by professionals who have U.S. medical licenses).

The provision of health care services for the U.S. and Canadian population, in particular retirees, is a major opportunity for Mexico. High-quality and low-cost health care can become one of Mexico's major attractions, along with its unsurpassed natural beauty and culture.

Source: World Bank staff.

Figure 1.3 *Manufacturing Productivity in Mexico, 1993–99*

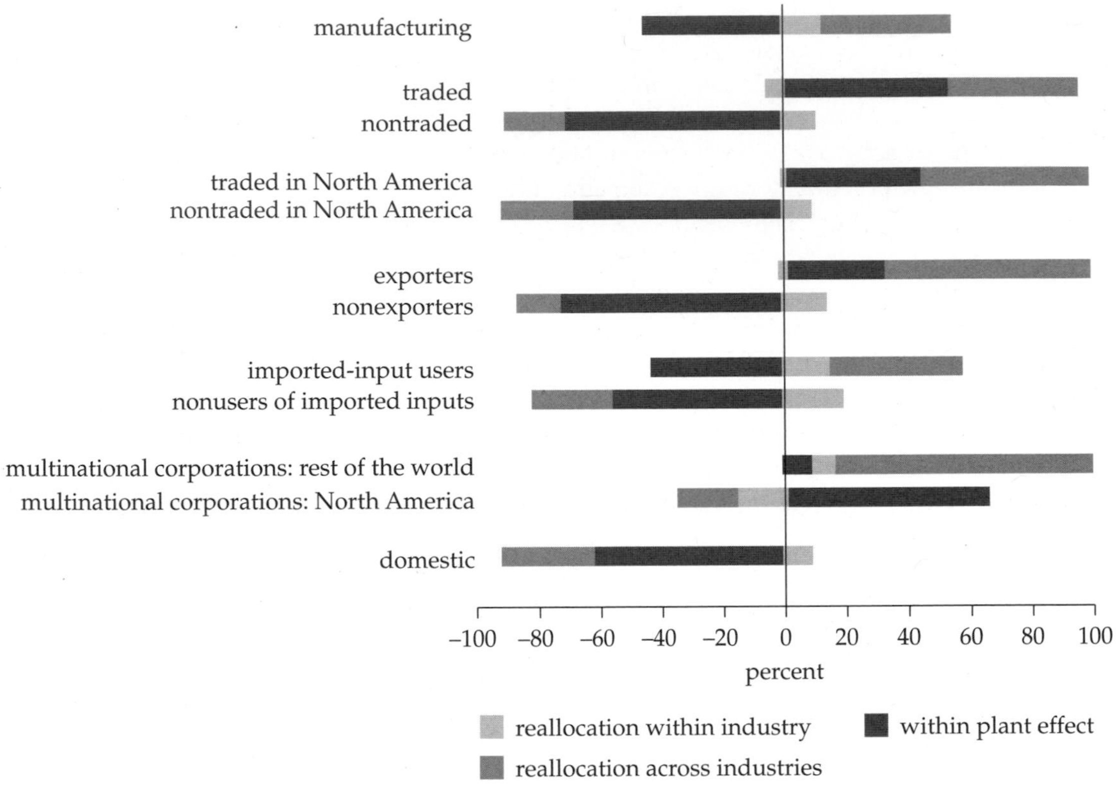

Source: López-Córdova (2002).

A key fact behind the paradox is the scant learning at the firm level, with a related low level of productivity increase. Figure 1.3 captures this by decomposing Mexico's gains in total factor productivity. It shows the "within plant effect" (innovation) and reallocation effect. NAFTA gains are almost exclusively relegated to reallocation between and within sectors, rather than to an increase in technical efficiency (the "within plant effect"). Indeed, this is what economic theory would predict: reallocation effects based on change of relative price followed by micro-level increases in efficiency based on learning and innovation.

One indication of Mexico's new strength is its revealed comparative advantage by technological intensity.[4] Figure 1.4 shows that Mexico has modest but growing

---

[4] We use "contribution to the trade balance" as an indicator of revealed comparative advantage. Mathematically, the contribution to the trade balance is defined as

$$(X_j - M_j) - (X - M)\frac{X_j + M_j}{X + M}$$

where

X_j represents the exports of industry j
M_j represents the imports of industry j
X represents the total exports of the economy
M represents the total imports of the economy.

Figure 1.4 *Manufacturing Industries in Mexico: Revealed Comparative Advantage by Technological Intensity*

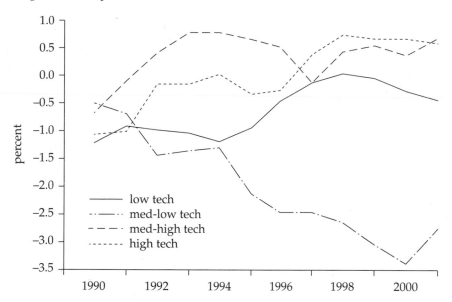

Source: Data for imports and exports at the industry level were obtained from the United Nations COMTRADE database employing ISIC revision 3 industry codes.

advantages in high-tech and medium-high-tech industries (dominated mainly by multinationals), and it is starting to acquire comparative disadvantage in low-tech and medium-low-tech industries, which are normally associated with low-cost labor.

Mexico is now at a crossroads: it cannot yet compete on the basis of knowledge assets (as can the Organisation for Economic Co-operation and Development [OECD] countries), yet its traditional comparative advantage is being eroded by low-cost competitors. Both government and industry leaders are extremely concerned about Asian countries attracting many of the firms now established in Mexico. This was clearly shown when Mexico tried to block China's accession to the World Trade Organization (WTO). However, these leaders seem to understand the problem of lack of competitiveness as a problem arising mainly from differences in labor costs; they ignore the close relationship between the country's performance and its technological capabilities (including adoption, adaptation, and creation of knowledge). Failure to recognize this critical link will result in further loss of productivity.

Underlying the sense of urgency is the fact that Mexico is losing ground in terms of the quality of the competitive environment for firms compared with Mexico's main training partners and competitors. Figure 1.5 illustrates that Mexico's competitive position is quite low for an economy so highly integrated with the United States and Canada, with no signs of consistent improvement.

The Knowledge Revolution

The incredible speed with which knowledge is created, shared, and applied in all parts of the economy and society has led many commentators to talk about the knowledge "revolution." Indeed, this revolution in many ways mirrors past periods

Figure 1.5 *Microeconomic Competitiveness*

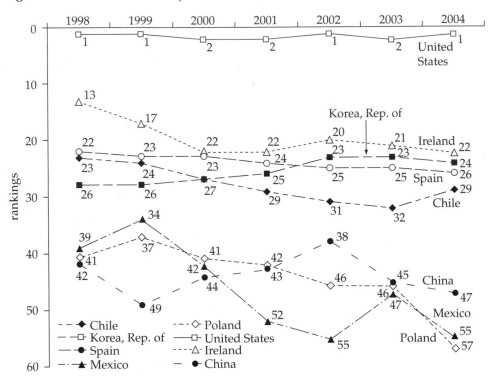

Source: *The Global Competitiveness Report* (2005), World Economic Forum.

of rapid economic and social change. Examples include the changes brought about by the printing press in the 1500s, the harnessing of steam in the 1800s, and the development and expansion of electricity and the automobile industry in the 1900s. However, what is different today from these earlier periods is that rapid and pervasive change is widely diffused. Indeed, it is experienced across almost all technologies and sectors—not only the information and communications technologies (ICT) sector or the high-tech sector. Today new scientific discoveries are everyday occurrences, and, in the marketplace, product life cycles have shortened, reflecting the degree and pace of invention and innovation.

Complementing this, the extent to which scientific discoveries are now being codified and shared—another key enabler of the knowledge revolution—has led to the development and application of new technologies at an unprecedented rate. Closer links between science and business have encouraged faster uptake of the new technologies; indeed, proximity to relevant university research facilities is fast becoming a key locational driver for leading companies. Spurred by increasing levels of demand from more sophisticated consumers than ever before, business has invested heavily in research, design, and development to produce higher quality functionality in products. Massive amounts of knowledge—in the form of design, software, and services—are embedded in even the most basic products.

In this new economy, education and skills enhancement have become increasingly important to business. With the constant changes taking place in production technology and the regular introduction of new products, lifelong learning has become an important policy consideration for governments and a critical investment for businesses.

At the same time, greater policy liberalization, improvements in transport and communications technologies, and pressure on business to find the most cost-effective locations have increased the scale and widened the nature of global activity and competition. International business has growing numbers of supply chains spanning many countries, as businesses balance what each location can contribute to their overall competitiveness. This new global economy provides enormous potential for countries to strengthen their economic and social development by providing more efficient ways of producing and delivering goods and services.

Dynamic networks and new styles of organization and management are also creating new forms of competition. Wealth is created not just by natural resources or production, but also by the ways in which products and services are designed and delivered to the market. The power of ideas and brand names—and the harnessing of knowledge and information to leverage them—are driving the world economy. Keeping up with these new developments requires investments in such intangibles as R&D, software, education, training, marketing, distribution, organization, and networks.

In short, more knowledge is being created and applied around the world than at any previous time in history. One indicator of the accelerating creation of knowledge is the number of new patents registered each year. In the United States, the annual number of patents grew from about 50,000 at the end of the 1980s to nearly 100,000 in 2000–2001 (Figure 1.6). Part of this surge is due to the greater importance of protecting intellectual property—a sign of the awareness of what knowledge means for wealth creation.

Figure 1.6 *Patents of U.S. and Foreign Origin Granted by the U.S. Patent Office, 1981–2001*

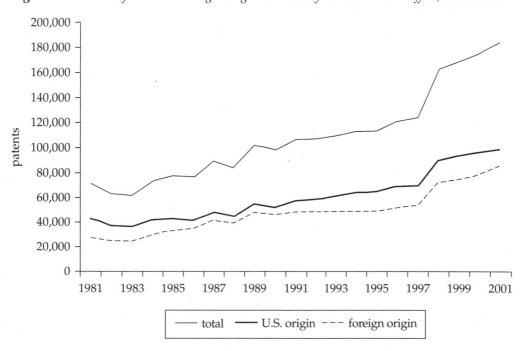

Source: U.S. Patent and Trademark Office, http://www.uspto.gov/.

The rapid development and spread of knowledge are creating a more competitive and interdependent world. The share of world trade (exports and imports) in world GDP, an indicator of globalization and competition in the global economy, rose from 28 percent in 1970 to 57 percent in 2001 (see Table 1.1).[5] Other indicators of greater global interaction include increased foreign direct investment (FDI), international sourcing of production inputs, and interfirm alliances for R&D and technology licensing. Accelerating this process are three factors: the wider availability of information and communications technologies, the deregulation of financial and product markets, and the liberalization of trade, investment, and capital movements. Greater international competition, in turn, spurs firms to create new products and more efficient production processes.

All sectors and industries are being affected by these changes. Even such traditional industries as textiles, cement, and steel are using new technical knowledge and information systems to improve the design and quality of products and production processes, and the efficiency of marketing and distribution. In agriculture, greater understanding of plant reproduction and growth, advances in genetic engineering, and better techniques for harvesting, storage, transportation, and distribution are changing the value and competitiveness of different types of plant and animal products. And such services as transportation, distribution, finance, insurance, health, and education are becoming more sophisticated and more intensive in knowledge and information.

Global Trends in Knowledge

The OECD uses the term "knowledge economy" to draw attention to the importance of knowledge in all economic activities. Once applied only to manufacturing industries that made intensive use of technology, the concept has expanded to include services that are heavily knowledge-based. The knowledge economy now accounts, on average, for roughly half of nongovernment economic activity in the OECD (see Table 1.2).

Increased Spending on R&D

In most OECD countries, spending on R&D has risen faster than GDP, although there have been year-to-year fluctuations (see Table 1.3). Perhaps even more importantly, there has been a shift in the composition of R&D. After 1990 and the end of the Cold War, the share of defense-related R&D declined for some of the largest R&D spending countries—notably the United States, the United Kingdom, and France. Conversely, the share accounted for by nondefense research rose to more than 90 percent of the total. In the OECD, the number of researchers in the economy grew faster than the labor force as a whole.

---

[5] The direct role of technology in this process is reflected in the changing patterns of international trade. Between 1976 and 1996, the share of high-technology and medium-technology products increased from 33 percent to 54 percent of total goods traded. At the same time, the share of other primary commodities fell from 34 percent to just 13 percent, while that of resource-based products remained constant. These trends have major implications for developing countries, which are primarily exporters of primary commodities. Not only the share but also the prices of their exports have been falling over the past five decades.

Table 1.1 *World Trade as a Percentage of Global GDP, by Income Level of Country, 1970 and 2001*

Income level and country	1970	2001
Low income	**21**	**51**
India	8	27
Lower-middle income	**18**	**53**
China	4	49
Upper-middle income	**36**	**69**
Mexico	17	57
High income	**28**	**48**[a]
World	**27**	**57**

Source: World Bank, Statistical Information Management and Analysis (SIMA) database (2005).
Note: World trade is imports plus exports of goods and services.
a. For 2000.

Table 1.2 *Value Added of Knowledge-Based Industries, OECD Countries*

Country	Total	High-technology industries	Medium-technology industries	Post and telecommunication services	Finance, insurance, and other business services
European Union 1998[a]	26.0	1.8	5.8	2.3	15.2
Japan 1998	24.4	3.6	7.2	1.9	11.8
United Kingdom 1999	28.3	2.9	4.9	3.0	17.5
United States 2000	29.6	3.5	4.3	3.4	18.3
OECD[b] 1997	26.2	2.1	5.6	2.6	14.8
China 1997[c]	29.7	4.7	6.0	5.0	8.0
Mexico[d] 1999	18.3	2.2	5.6	1.7	8.8

Source: OECD (2002b, Annex Table 4, p. 286).
Note: This is based on an OECD classification.
a. Estimate. Regroups Austria, Denmark, Finland, France, Italy, Spain, Sweden, and the United Kingdom. For percentage shares of value added, also includes Germany and Ireland up to 1991, and Belgium up to 1995.
b. Estimate. Includes the EU countries, Canada, Japan, Korea, Mexico, Norway, and the United States. For percentage shares of value added, also includes also the Czech Republic up to 1990 and Hungary up to 1992.
c. Estimate. From data in *China's Statistic Yearbook* (1999).
d. HT industries do not include medical, precision, and optical instruments.

Of global R&D, 88 percent is undertaken by high-income countries (see Table 1.4), with 31 percent of global R&D centered in one country: the United States. Multinational companies, now carrying out R&D in countries other than their home countries, are establishing strategic alliances—even mergers and acquisitions—to collaborate on technology and acquire technological assets. Also on the rise is the number of international collaborations in patenting and technical publications. The share of scientific publications with foreign coauthors more than doubled for many OECD countries, reaching an average of 26 percent for 1995–97 (OECD 2000).

Even large countries rely on knowledge from abroad. This is evident from royalty and licensing payments to other countries and from the technology they import in capital goods and components. One study (OECD 1998) found that the R&D implicit in imports was as high or higher than domestic R&D.

Table 1.3 *Gross Domestic Expenditures on R&D as Percentage of GDP, 1981–2000*

	1981	1985	1990	1995	2000
OECD	1.95	2.27	2.29	2.10	2.24
United States	2.34	2.76	2.65	2.51	2.70
Japan	2.11	2.54	2.78	2.69	2.98
European Union	1.69	1.87	1.95	1.80	1.88
Mexico	N/A	N/A	0.22	0.31	0.40[a]

Source: OECD (2002b, Annex Table 7, p. 289).
a. Data for year 1999.

Table 1.4 *R&D Spending in Selected Countries, by Income Level*

	R&D spending as a percentage of GDP (1989–00)	R&D spending as a percentage of world total
World	**2.38**	**100.00**
Low income	0.5[a]	0.67
India	1.23	0.67
Lower-middle income	0.72	3.39
China	1.00	1.02
Upper-middle income	0.99[b]	2.02
Brazil	0.77	0.69
High income	2.61	88.47
United States	2.69	30.83
Europe (Economic and Monetary Union)	2.12	20.43
Japan	2.98	19.39
Mexico	**0.43**	**0.25**

Source: World Bank, *World Development Indicators 2003*.
a. From *World Development Indicators 2001*.
b. From *World Development Indicators 2002*.

An important implication is that knowledge produced outside the country can be as important in the development process as domestically produced knowledge. Therefore, all countries need to focus on these twin challenges: how to create and use domestic knowledge, and how to obtain knowledge produced outside their borders. Indeed, there has been a shift over the past two decades from an almost exclusive focus on generating knowledge to a broader focus on acquiring and disseminating knowledge, especially knowledge acquired from abroad.

Increased Inflows of Foreign Direct Investment

Foreign direct investment is the key agent of globalization. High-productivity and high-value added FDI (the one that generates linkages in local economies and stays in the country, unlike footloose investments, for a long time) are determined mainly by the desire to exploit knowledge assets on a global scale—technology, management, access to markets, and access to such special resources as finance, labor, and natural resources. Knowledge does not depreciate with use, so once it is developed, there is a strong incentive to exploit it over the largest scale possible.

Table 1.5 *Investment in Tangibles and Intangibles, Selected OECD Countries, 1998*
Investment in tangibles and intangibles as a percent of GDP 1998

	Gross fixed capital formation as percent of GDP	Of which: investment in machinery and equipment	Investment in intangibles as percent of GDP	Of which: public spending on education[a]	R&D	Software
OECD	**21.0**	9.0	8.6	5.2	2.2	**1.2**
United States	19.2	9.1	9.1	5.0	2.6	1.5
European Union	19.9	8.0	8.0	5.2	1.8	1.0
Japan	26.8	10.5	7.6	3.5	3.0	1.1
United Kingdom	17.4	8.6	7.8	4.7	1.8	1.3
Mexico	20.9	11.1	5.0	4.2	0.4	0.4

Source: OECD (2002b, Annex Table 3, p. 285).

a. From the World Bank, Statistical Information Management and Analysis (SIMA) database. Public spending on education includes public spending on public education plus subsidies to private education at the primary, secondary, and tertiary levels. The total investment in intangibles is calculated based on the indicated data on education spending.

Foreign direct investment inflows increased fifteenfold between 1982 and 1999, during which period its share of world gross fixed-capital formation rose from 2.6 percent to 14.3 percent. In 1997 the estimated value added of home and overseas production by transnational corporations was $8 trillion—more than 27 percent of world GDP (UNCTAD 2000, 3). Transnational corporations are estimated to account for two-thirds of international trade, with roughly half that between parents and affiliates or among affiliates.[6] Transnational corporations are also estimated to undertake some 75 to 80 percent of global R&D.[7]

Greater Investment in Intangibles

Investment in intangibles (education, R&D, and software) has also been increasing dramatically. In OECD countries, public investment in intangibles (8.6 percent of GDP) has nearly reached the same level as investment in machinery and equipment (9.0 percent). Table 1.5 almost certainly understates the level of investment in intangibles, since it does not include private investment in education, public and private investment in skills training, or investment in design, marketing, advertising, brand development, engineering, publishing, and the arts.

With intangibles increasingly important for economic activity and international competitiveness, there has been more trade in intellectual property. Globally, trade in intellectual property, as measured by royalties and license fees (receipts and payments), increased from about $4 billion in 1970 to about $115 billion in 2002 (see Figure 1.7).

Country data on trade in royalties and licensing show the large gap between high-income and developing countries. The high-income countries receive almost

---

[6] UNCTAD (2000, citing *World Investment Report 1996*).
[7] UNCTAD (2000, citing *World Investment Report 1995*).

Figure 1.7 *Worldwide Payments and Receipts of Royalty and License Fees, 1970–2002*

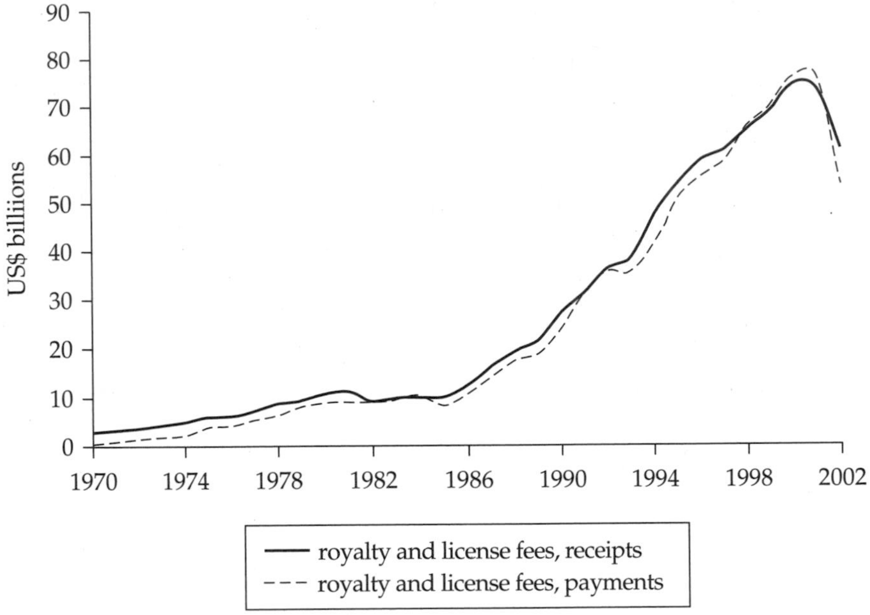

Source: World Bank (2005b).

Table 1.6 *Payments and Receipts of Royalties and License Fees, Selected Regions and Countries, 2001*
($ million)

	Receipts	Percentage of total	Payments	Percentage of total
Low income	**27**	**0.04**	**284**	**0.39**
India	83	0.11	306	0.42
Lower-middle income	**532**	**0.74**	**4,534**	**6.20**
China	110	0.15	1,938	2.65
Upper-middle income	**494**	**0.68**	**4,294**	**5.87**
Brazil	112	0.15	1,245	1.70
Middle income	**1,026**	**1.42**	**8,828**	**12.07**
High income	**71,303**	**98.54**	**64,037**	**87.54**
United States	38,660	53.43	16,360	22.37
Europe EMU	10,381	14.35	24,286	33.20
Japan	10,462	14.46	11,099	15.17
Mexico	40	0.06	419	0.57
World	**72,356**	**100.00**	**73,148**	**100.00**

Source: World Development Indicators 2003, World Bank.

99 percent of all royalty and licensing payments, with low- and medium-income countries paying out an amount disproportionate to what they receive from these sources (see Table 1.6). Three countries—Germany, Japan, and the United States—accounted for as much as 75 to 80 percent of all receipts from royalty and licensing fees in 2001. A big part of the payments for royalties and fees involves intrafirm payments between transnational corporations and their affiliates.

Toward a Knowledge-Based NAFTA Agenda

To take advantage of the knowledge revolution and assure the necessary productivity gains, Mexico needs to move up value chains by developing efficient education, innovation, and ICT systems. This would require creating a stock of efficient knowledge workers and knowledge organizations. This part of the knowledge economy agenda is largely about improving *productive (plant-level)* efficiency.

While the first generation of NAFTA-related reforms was based on low-cost labor, the second knowledge-based generation will be based on lower cost skilled labor. A skilled workforce with high school diplomas and engineers will need to become a major comparative advantage. For instance, average earnings for engineers and researchers in the United States is about $300 per day, while in Mexico it is about $120 per day.[8] Improving R&D links with the United States and Canada—in venture capital and innovation, exchange of researchers and engineers—is at the center of a knowledge-based (NAFTA-plus) agenda. Table 1.7 summarizes the main accomplishments of NAFTA reforms and outlines this emerging knowledge-based agenda.

Worldwide experience shows that such a strategy can be developed in three steps. First, a benchmarking framework is introduced to measure country's initial conditions and progress toward knowledge economy (Chapter 2). Second, core issues of knowledge economy—necessary reforms of innovation, education and ICT systems—are analyzed. This is a question of what **should** be done (Part II of the report). Third, implementation issues of the knowledge strategy are considered. Implementation issues include political economy considerations, investment climate and other issues. Although not analyzed in detail, these issues are touched upon in the analysis of what **could** be done in terms of transition to knowledge-based competitiveness given constraints that Mexico faces (Part III of the report).

---

[8] Data provided by Director General of CONACYT.

Table 1.7 *From First-Generation NAFTA to a Knowledge-Driven, Second-Generation NAFTA*

	Results of NAFTA agenda	*Knowledge-driven (second-generation) NAFTA*
Trade and capital flows: move up value chains	FDI, particularly *maquilas*, as a major source of employment Large stock of accumulated FDI with few links to the domestic economy	FDI and strategic alliances with knowledge organizations abroad as a source of knowledge-based higher-value added jobs: • Attract knowledge-intensive FDI • Promote spillovers from the existing FDI stock: supplier and cluster development • Promote strategic alliances with foreign universities, firms, technology, and research organizations
Labor flows: maximize benefits of migration	Migration and remittances as an escape valve and shock absorber Remittances as a second source of foreign revenues after tourism Large and rapidly growing stock of both low-skilled (largely undocumented) and higher skilled labor from Mexico in the United States	Migration as a source of entrepreneurship, knowledge, and capital for Mexico: • Reach agreement to regularize low-skilled, undocumented flows • Reduce transaction costs of remittances' transfer and create conditions for productive use of remittances • Utilize Mexican professionals abroad: create "brain circulation" and venture capital networks
Services: reposition Mexico's nature and culture	Mexico as a major tourist destination	Knowledge-intensive services as a major source of employment: • Move to higher-brand tourism • Develop engineering and other high value professional services • Develop high-quality health services to attract retirees and health tourists from OECD countries • Capitalize on Mexico's history and culture: promote investment into media, movie industry, etc.

Source: World Bank staff.

2

Benchmarking Mexico's Position in the Knowledge Economy

The globalization of trade, finance, and information has made it easier to narrow knowledge gaps across countries. But the fast pace of change and the difficulty many developing countries have in getting started may widen the so-called "knowledge divide." If the gap widens, capital and other resources might flow to countries with a stronger knowledge base, adding to the inequality.

There is also the danger of widening knowledge gaps within countries. For example, the OECD economies worry that the rapid advances in knowledge may hurt unskilled workers and add to unemployment. There is evidence that technology and technology-related organizational change are widening wage disparities between skilled and unskilled workers, and these impacts are likely to be felt even more in developing countries. Access to education and ICT infrastructure is far more differentiated, and formal safety nets are less prevalent. Left behind, rural areas and the poor run the risk of being excluded from the knowledge-based economy.

This is why Mexico must position itself to take advantage of the knowledge revolution and reduce the risks that it poses. In support of these efforts, the World Bank Institute has developed a framework outlining the main elements that need to be addressed. The World Bank Institute's interactive Web-based tool—the Knowledge Assessment Methodology (KAM)—includes several quantitative and qualitative variables that help to benchmark how an economy compares with its neighbors, competitors, or countries it wishes to emulate on the four pillars of the knowledge economy.[1] The KAM helps identify the problems and opportunities that a country faces in making the transition to the knowledge economy, and where it may need to focus policy attention or future investments.

As a first step to articulate a strategy for moving forward, we disaggregated the knowledge-based economy and competitiveness into four functional areas:

- An economic incentive and institutional regime that provides incentives for the efficient use of existing and new knowledge and the flourishing of entrepreneurship;
- An effective national innovation and enterprise upgrading system: a system of research centers, universities, think tanks, consulting firms, and other organizations that can tap into the growing stock of global knowledge, assimilate and adapt it to local needs, and create new knowledge;
- An educated and skilled population that can create and use knowledge; and

---

[1] The KAM (http://www.worldbank.org/kam) includes 76 quantitative and qualitative variables for assessing a country's position on the four pillars of the knowledge economy framework. The methodology used in the report ranks 121 countries and 9 country groupings with respect to each of these variables. Scores range from 10 for the highest value to 0 for the lowest. The most recent version contains 81 countries and 132 variables.

Figure 2.1 *A Global View of the Knowledge Economy Index*

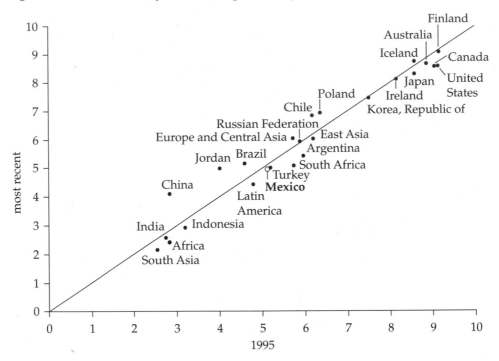

Source: World Bank, "Knowledge Assessment Methodology," http://www.worldbank.org/kam.
Note: The countries or regions plotted below the 45 degree line exhibited a decline in performance during the given time interval, while those plotted above the line showed improvement. There are two possible explanations for a decline: the country may actually have lost ground in absolute terms, or may have improved more slowly than its comparators.

- A dynamic information infrastructure that can facilitate the effective processing, communication, and dissemination of information.

On the basis of the four pillars, we have developed an aggregate knowledge economy index and other scorecard indicators for Mexico (see Figure 2.1). Annexes to this book provide a more detailed description of the methodology. They also compared Mexico to the following set of countries:

- United States, Mexico's main trading partner and a paragon of the knowledge economy.
- The Republic of Korea and Ireland, countries that 20 years ago faced challenges similar to Mexico's and have made meteoric progress toward transformation into a knowledge economy. We also make references to Finnish experience, particularly with regard to the political economy of transition to knowledge-based development.
- China, an economic powerhouse, competitor, and new opportunity.
- Spain and Chile, two dynamic (although obviously very different) Spanish-speaking countries.

Figure 2.2 shows the close correlation between the knowledge economy index and GDP per capita. Clearly, the knowledge economy index is a good predictor of growth performance.

Figure 2.2 *GDP per Capita and Knowledge Economy Index, 2002*

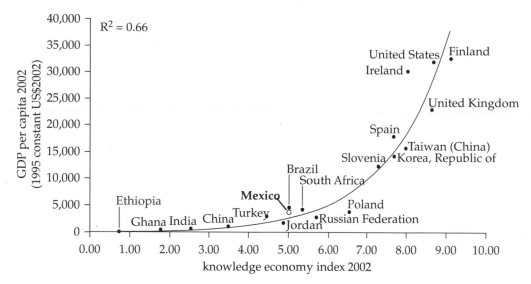

Source: World Bank, "Knowledge Assessment Methodology," http://www.worldbank.org/kam.

On the knowledge economy index as a whole, Mexico does not compare well with its key trading partners or with other Latin American economies. It is behind Chile, Argentina (precrisis), and Uruguay. In terms of the four pillars of the knowledge economy framework presented at the beginning of this chapter, the performance of Mexico is as follows:

- Economic incentive and institutional regime. Strong openness to competition, but weak on regulation; improvement on property rights, but weak on corruption and government effectiveness.
- Education. Weakest pillar from a long-term perspective; poor access and quality.
- Innovation. A very weak pillar, particularly for an economy of its size.
- ICT. Lagging behind leaders in Latin America.

Figure 2.3 shows the performance of Mexico between 1995 and 2003.[2] This basic scorecard is compared with that of the United States, the leading knowledge-based economy in the world.

Figure 2.4 compares Mexico's performance on the four pillars of the knowledge economy framework in 1995 and in 2003. Mexico has shown some improvement on

---

[2] The figure shows the *relative performance* of Mexico as compared to 121 countries included in the KAM. A decline in the most recent period can be attributed to two factors:

- The country may actually have lost ground in absolute terms (which often occurs with education enrollment rates); or
- The country may have made an improvement but the world as a whole made a much more significant improvement (which often happens with information infrastructure penetration ratios).

Figure 2.3 *Knowledge Scorecards for Mexico and the United States*

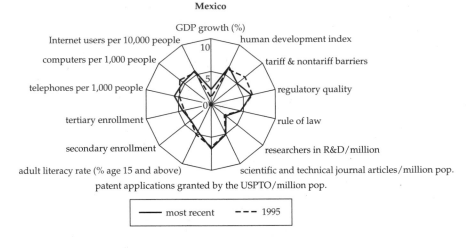

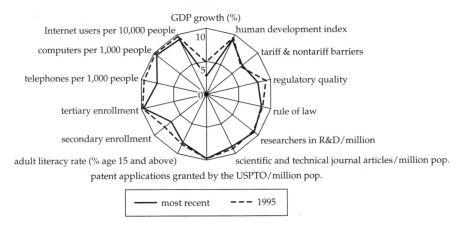

Source: World Bank, "Knowledge Assessment Methodology," http://www.worldbank.org/kam.
Note: Each of the 127 variables in the KAM is normalized on a scale of 0 to 10. The fuller the scorecard, the better poised a country is to embrace the knowledge economy. But an economy should not necessarily aim for a perfect score of 10 on all variables because the scorecards may be shaped by the particular structural characteristics of an economy or by trade-offs that characterize different development strategies.

two pillars (economic incentive regime and education), while on the pillars of innovation and information infrastructure the country lost ground. The changes that occurred over time, however, are quite insignificant.

Note that when a country's performance seems to have declined in the most recent period—that is, the scorecard shows it falling behind, as the scorecard shows for some variables for Mexico—this decline can happen for two reasons:

- A country may have lost ground in absolute terms.
- Even if the country has made a several-fold improvement, it could still fall behind, because the world may on average have improved much more significantly. This often happens with information infrastructure penetration ratios, because of the very fast rate of change globally in this sector.

Figure 2.4 *Mexico's Performance on the Four Pillars of the Knowledge Economy*

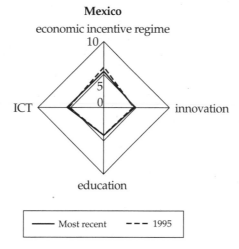

Source: World Bank, "Knowledge Assessment Methodology," http://www.worldbank.org/kam.
Note: The economic incentive and institutional regime: tariff and nontariff barriers, regulatory quality, and rule of law. Education and human resources: adult literacy rate, secondary enrollment, and tertiary enrollment. The innovation system: researchers in R&D, patent applications granted by the U.S. Patent and Trademark Office, scientific and technical journal articles. ICT: telephones per 1,000 people, computers per 1,000 people, Internet users per 10,000 people.

Economic Incentives and Institutions

What does it take for a country to realize the potential of the knowledge revolution? A flexible society and economy with the ability to cope with constant change. This requires economic incentives and institutions that promote the constant redeployment of resources from less efficient to more efficient uses. And this, in turn, requires good macroeconomic, competition, and regulatory policies. The financial system (including venture capital) must allocate resources to promising new opportunities and redeploy assets from failed enterprises to more promising ones. Conditions must be conducive to entrepreneurship, risk taking, and the expansion of small enterprises. Science and industry have to exchange information. Labor markets have to be flexible enough to enable the redeployment of labor. Finally, social safety nets need to facilitate the constant relocation and retraining of people for new jobs, and help those hurt by restructuring.

The ways people receive relevant knowledge—and the incentives for them to use it—are also affected by the institutional structure of a society. These interactions are affected by legal rules and procedures; social conventions; markets; and organizations such as firms and governmental and nongovernmental organizations. Equally important are the institutions that govern the rules and procedures in a society, which in turn determine how decisions are made and actions are taken. A key feature is the quality of government. The integrity and effectiveness of government determine the basic rules of a society. Another important element is the extent to which the legal system supports basic rules and property rights. For example, the creation and dissemination of knowledge are strongly affected by the degree to which intellectual property is valued and property owners' rights protected and enforced.

Strengthening the economic, institutional, and incentive regime, which comprises both macro- and micropolicies, remains a priority for Mexico. Mexico has made improvements in this area since 1995, and continuing progress is important in order to support reform in innovation and education—drivers of the knowledge interface and essential in the creation of a conducive investment climate.

Human Resources

To tap the potential of new knowledge and accelerating technical change, an educated and skilled work force is needed. Ensuring that expenditures on education are allocated efficiently and that the entire population can participate in the knowledge-based economy requires particular attention. Why? Because education is the basis for creating, acquiring, adapting, disseminating, sharing, and using knowledge.

Basic education increases peoples' capacity to learn and to use information. But this is just the beginning. It is also necessary to have technical secondary-level education—as well as higher education in engineering and scientific areas—to monitor technological trends, assess what is relevant for the firm or the economy, and use the new technologies. The production of new knowledge and its adaptation to a particular economic setting are usually associated with higher level teaching and research. In industrial economies, university research accounts for a large share of domestic R&D.

Opportunities for lifelong learning are also essential. Creating a culture of continuous learning and openness to new ideas is critical for a knowledge-based economy. Learning on the job is not sufficient. Learning in multiple environments (at home, at school, and at work) must be fostered through continuing education courses, self-learning on the Internet, and computer-assisted instruction.

On the basic scorecard, Mexico scores fairly well on adult illiteracy in relation to its per capita income. But it scores poorly on secondary enrollment rates and even more poorly on tertiary enrollment rates, which are below the averages for Latin America as a whole and well below some of Mexico's main competitors. This is of real concern. Mexico must expand and modernize its education system by, for example, investing in hiring more teachers. Improved pupil-teacher ratios in schools will increase the standard of education.

Information Infrastructure

The rapid advances in information and communications technologies affect how manufacturers, service providers, and governments are organized—and how they perform. Greater access to ICT is affecting how people work, learn, play, and communicate. As knowledge becomes a more important element of competitiveness, the use of ICT reduces transaction costs and barriers of time and space. It also makes possible the mass production of customized goods and services, substituting for limited factors of production. Indeed, ICT is the backbone of the knowledge-based economy. To support Internet-based economic activities, countries need to ensure competitive pricing of Internet services and provide an appropriate legal infrastructure that covers online transactions.

On the basic scorecard, Mexico still has a long way to go to fully develop and exploit its information infrastructure. This is critical because Mexico can speed up its development by harnessing the new infrastructure. The national information infrastructure consists of telecommunications networks, strategic information systems, the policy and legal frameworks affecting their deployment, as well as the skilled human resources needed to develop and use the infrastructure.

An Effective Innovation System

A country's institutions, rules, and procedures affect how it acquires, creates, disseminates, and uses knowledge. Today the bulk of technical knowledge is produced in developed countries. The disparity in the production of technical knowledge per capita between developed and developing countries is even greater than the disparity of income. Fortunately, developing countries do not have to reinvent the wheel: there are many ways for them to tap into and use the knowledge created in developed countries. So a key element of a developing country's innovation strategy is to find the best ways to tap into the growing global knowledge base. Then it must decide where and how to deploy its domestic R&D capability.

To create and adapt knowledge requires universities, public and private research centers, and policy think tanks. Nongovernmental organizations and the government are also part of the innovation system, to the extent that they produce new knowledge. Institutions central to the dissemination of knowledge include agricultural and industrial extension services, engineering consulting firms, economic and management consulting firms, and government research institutes.

The mere existence of these organizations, however, is not enough. More important is how effective they are in creating, adapting, and disseminating knowledge to those who put this knowledge to use. This is why networking is critical. The effectiveness of networks—and the incentives for acquiring, creating, and sharing knowledge—are also influenced by economic incentives. Relevant in this regard are policies on importing foreign technology through technology licensing, direct foreign investment, foreign collaboration, and intellectual property.

Accelerating the pace of technological progress for economic growth is predicated on a supportive process of helping firms "learn to learn" and on the availability of the requisite human capital (World Bank 2003). The coordination of innovation and education policies is central. While ICT also will play an important role in the longer term by helping to reduce transaction costs and improve the efficiency of government, business, and social services, strengthening the ICT pillar is not a top priority for Mexico under present circumstances. As the knowledge economy pillars are being rebuilt and strengthened, firms are becoming increasingly productive and competitive. In turn, this will translate into higher levels of competitiveness and economic growth, and hence higher standards of living—the ultimate objective of the knowledge economy.

On the innovation benchmark, Mexico fares poorly compared to many of its main competitors. In Latin America, Mexico falls behind Brazil and significantly behind Argentina, Costa Rica, and Chile.

Part II
Major Policy Issues

More than business-as-usual is required to take advantage of new opportunities. Major reforms are needed to create competitive markets and to make major advances in key functional areas.

Toward these ends, we propose the following strategy:

- Upgrade and improve three key functional pillars of the knowledge economy—education, innovation, and enterprise upgrading and ICT systems.
- Finalize broader economic reforms to enhance revenue mobilization and create an even playing field and more contestable markets.

Although this book will not elaborate details of the broader economic reforms in Mexico, a brief summary of key issues in this area is offered below. In the short run, there is significant room for better use of existing public resources through continuous evaluation of programs and policies and a better link between performance of public programs and the amount of resources allocated to them. In the long run, however, the transformation to a knowledge economy, particularly reform of innovation and education systems, will require more public resources; this creates urgency for tax reform.

In order to enhance the framework for transition to a knowledge economy, the following actions are required:

- Create an even and business-friendly playing field by enhancing competition, improving the regulatory framework, and focusing in particular on reduction of costs (including logistical costs) of entry, exit, and doing business.
- Strengthen major factor markets, particularly labor, the financial markets, and the energy market (electricity, gas, petroleum).
- Improve public governance, with a more transparent rule of law, efficient judiciary system, and respect for intellectual property rights.

3

Transforming the Innovation and Enterprise Upgrading System

An innovation system consists of a network of organizations, rules, and procedures that affects how a country acquires, creates, disseminates, and uses knowledge. Key organizations for the creation of knowledge include universities, public and private research centers, and policy think tanks. Private firms are at the center of the innovation system. If the private sector has little demand for knowledge, the innovation system cannot be effective. Effective R&D-industry linkages are vital to transform knowledge into wealth. Therefore, networking and interactions among the different organizations, firms, and individuals are critically important. The intensity of these networks, as well as the incentives for acquiring, creating, and sharing knowledge, are influenced by the economic incentive regime in general.

This chapter begins with an introduction to Mexico's performance in innovation. Drawing on tantalizing parallels between Mexico, Ireland and China, we then outline the main challenges for Mexico's innovation system. The chapter explains the concept of an innovation and enterprise upgrading system and why reform is urgently needed. Important signs of improvement are described. The remainder of the chapter discusses the policy agenda by outlining major recommendations, assessing existing programs, and highlighting implementation issues with regard to business R&D and enterprise upgrading.

Measures of Mexico's Performance in Innovation

In innovation, Mexico falls significantly behind Argentina, Costa Rica, and Chile, and follows Brazil. It is far behind innovation leaders such as the United States, Finland, or Ireland. Innovation remains an area of notable weakness for Mexico relative to comparable countries and its innovation performance is very weak for a country of its size. The number of researchers and scientists in the population is also relatively low; probably underscoring the propensity of the better educated to leave the country.

As Figure 3.1 indicates, Mexico is particularly weak in its ability to turn knowledge into business. Mexico scores very low on the availability of venture capital, the administrative burden for start-ups, the science and engineering enrollment ratio, royalties, license fees received, and private sector spending on R&D. Its low score on the level of entrepreneurship among managers (4.82 compared with 5.02 for China, 6.30 for Ireland, 7.28 for the United States, 6.48 for Chile, and 6.41 for Brazil) coupled with a higher than average burden for start-up businesses suggest significant barriers to enterprise development, and particularly to increasing the business birth rate. This is potentially a very serious hindrance to stimulating a knowledge economy since enterprise development is key to leveraging knowledge for income and job creation.

Figure 3.1 *Innovation Variables: A Comparison of Mexico and China*

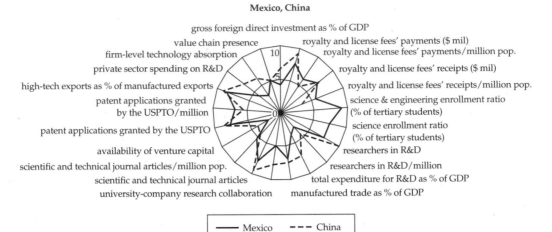

Mexico, China

Source: World Bank, "Knowledge Assessment Methodology," http://www.worldbank.org/kam.
Note: Each of the 127 variables in the KAM is normalized on a scale of 0 to 10. The fuller the scorecard, the better poised a country is to embrace the knowledge economy. But an economy should not necessarily aim for a perfect score of 10 on all variables because the scorecards may be shaped by the particular structural characteristics of an economy or by trade-offs that characterize different development strategies.

Although Mexico starts from a somewhat higher base than some of the other countries to which it is compared, its overall competitiveness has not changed since 1995 (see Figure 3.2). Chile, Argentina, and Costa Rica, however, have maintained their already advanced positions, and Brazil has shown significant improvement.

Evaluating Mexico's Innovation Performance

A comparison of Mexico's innovation performance to Ireland's and China's high-lights the particular challenges in innovation Mexico now faces.

Innovation in Ireland

Ireland has demonstrated that a country traditionally labeled one of the poorest members of the European Union, highly dependent on agriculture and low-end man-ufacturing, can successfully turn its economy into a provider of high-technology services. Ireland's transformation is attributable to sustained and well-targeted investment in education and to a policy framework favorable to foreign direct invest-ment (FDI), notably in the ICT sector. Ireland has one of the world's highest net inflows of FDI (20 percent of GDP), second only to Sweden. It has become one of the most dynamic knowledge-based economies in Europe, and it is the second largest exporter of software. Ireland's GDP grew at an average rate of 8.9 percent from 1995 to 2002.

The "Irish miracle" is not attributable solely to the government's investment in education and its efforts to attract FDI. Substantial European Union (EU) assis-tance has helped Ireland target investments relevant to a knowledge economy.

Figure 3.2 *Global View of Innovation Performance*

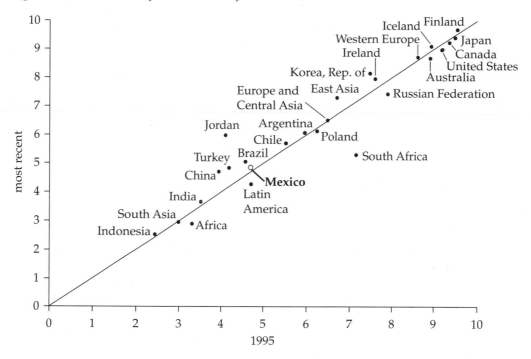

Source: World Bank, "Knowledge Assessment Methodology," http://www.worldbank.org/kam.
Note: The countries or regions plotted below the 45 degree line exhibited a decline in performance during the given time interval, while those plotted above the line showed improvement. There are two possible explanations for a decline: the country may actually have lost ground in absolute terms, or may have improved more slowly than its comparators.

Today Ireland is the headquarters of many European technology giants, and Dublin has taken advantage of its well-developed network infrastructure to become the hub for European telephone call centers. The country has thus come a long way from its traditional low-end manufacturing economy. To become a full-fledged knowledge economy, however, it has to strengthen indigenous innovation. Ireland was extremely successful in attracting major multinationals, yet their linkages to the Irish economy at first remained limited. In response to this challenge, Ireland both increased investments in education and innovation, and responded with a major concerted effort such as the National Linkage Promotion program (see Box 3.5). After an initially slow start, multinationals increased local purchases significantly.

Since 2001, the attractive low wages found in China, India, and Eastern Europe have eclipsed Ireland's competitive advantages, spurring many global companies to scale back or cancel their plans for Irish operations. Ireland had to fight hard to reclaim its status as a major outsourcing destination. By leveraging its work force's brainpower, productivity, and flexibility, Ireland managed to achieve its transformation to a fully fledged knowledge-based economy.

The fruits of this strategy are becoming evident. A number of large multinational corporations (MNCs) have already returned, relocated, or planned to relocate to Ireland in the near future. Dell employs about 4,000 people in Ireland. Dell began outsourcing to India and elsewhere but discovered that product quality was less than expected. Thus, countries like Ireland, which not only ran strong marketing campaigns but strengthened their knowledge base through concerted investments in R&D and education, have seen large multinationals returning. More importantly, the MNCs are returning to turn out products and services higher on the value chain. Today investment is going into higher level jobs in pharmaceuticals, biotechnology, and digital media. On the other hand, countries like Poland, not so long ago an attractive location for foreign investment, are beginning to lose their share of FDI. Because their marketing capacities are weak, they are failing to "sell" their sources of competitive advantage.

This example of Ireland highlights two problems any country must resolve in order to take advantage of new opportunities: the "first mover" problem and the concerted action problem. Change begins with first movers (firms and other actors that are the first to recognize and to capture new opportunities). Initially, these firms (like Dell in our Irish example) tend to be exceptions. The issue is how to make exceptions more mainstream. Scaling up and learning from the experience of first movers and pilot projects require concerted action. A central objective of such action is to build constituencies for reform and change. Raising awareness of what is at stake among key groups creates greater buy-in for the necessary reforms. A related task is *institutionalizing* effective coordination of private and public agents. Top-down vision and leadership, implementation, and follow-up are often indispensable for success.

The objective is to create a virtuous cycle of growth and reform. Success breeds success: first movers become role models, while institutions of collective action make sure that the success is scaled up. These complementarities are mutually reinforcing; stronger performance on one side creates pressures for performance to improve on the other side. To compete in the international marketplace, weaknesses in the domestic business environment must be confronted. (Examples include a judiciary incapable of enforcing contracts and insuperable regulatory obstacles.) As the legal and regulatory environment grows stronger, the private sector "crowds in" firms seeking to profit by creating wealth, and it "crowds out" firms that thrive on opportunistic, rent-seeking activities. This interplay between states and markets helps foster a virtuous cycle—a cumulative, mutually reinforcing process of knowledge-based development.

Innovation in China

Such a virtuous cycle is beginning to emerge in China, a country that is now ubiquitous in Mexico's public debate. As Chapter 2 indicated, China has demonstrated formidable growth in exports. Since 2000, it has significantly outperformed Mexico in growth of exports. Yet China is consistently below Mexico in all four pillars of the knowledge economy. What explains this apparent paradox? Four factors are at work. The first is business orientation. China not only allocates a higher share of gross national product (GNP) to R&D than Mexico (1 percent compared to 0.43 percent), but it outperforms Mexico with respect to these business-related innovation variables: private sector spending on R&D, administrative barriers for start-ups, availability of venture capital, university-company research collaboration, science and engineering enrollment ratio (as percent of tertiary-level students), and articles published in scientific and technical journals. China's superior performance on these indicators suggests that low labor costs are not its sole comparative advantage; China's innovation climate is increasingly becoming a comparative advantage as well.

Business orientation creates a demonstration effect: knowledge-intensive businesses, in particular those located in science parks, are highly visible, and they are important attractions for scientists and students. For these reasons, business orientation matters. The size of the economy matters as well. The size of the Chinese economy is second behind the United States in purchasing power parity. Because of its large and rapidly growing market, China is a magnet for all multinationals, and it has increasingly become a prime location for knowledge-intensive operations as well. Similar to a well-known Indian case, in Mexico a very large number of wage-efficient R&D researchers and engineers are an important factor in this new trend.

Not only is China's performance on business-related innovation variables better than Mexico's; China shows more impressive rates of improvement. Whereas Mexico has made no progress since 1995 in relation to the rest of the world, China's position has improved (see Figure 3.2).

The critical mass of business R&D expertise in China is greatly augmented by 50 million overseas Chinese—the famous Bamboo network. Members of the Chinese diaspora have been instrumental in detecting, adopting, and adapting important technologies at home. This advantage of the diaspora was not automatic: China is a paragon of leveraging its scientific and business talent from abroad.

Taken together these four factors (business orientation, critical mass, rapid progress, and the role of overseas Chinese) suggest that China, unlike Mexico, has crossed a threshold of innovation performance. A virtuous cycle of growth, when improvements accumulate and one good thing leads to another, has become apparent. The bandwagon effect (every multinational wants to be in China for fear of being left behind) is unmistakable.

Key Challenges Facing Mexico

Mexico is familiar with such nonlinear processes. After a slow start in the 1960s, maquiladoras ballooned in the 1980s and 1990s, creating congestion in the border towns. The challenge in the twenty-first century is to go beyond footloose manufacturing and generate a virtuous cycle of growth in knowledge-intensive business. Mexico has excellent innovation organizations (such as the Delphi Engineering Center) and world-class researchers (see Chapter 2), but success has not yet bred success.

Creation of a critical mass of efficient innovation organizations should be one of the country's central objectives. This would allow integration into global knowledge-intensive value chains with significant value added generated in Mexico. To achieve this objective, Mexico will need to transform its innovation and enterprise upgrading system.

Defining an Innovation System

As noted at the beginning of this chapter, an innovation system is a network of organizations, rules, and procedures that affects how a country acquires, creates, disseminates, and uses knowledge. Development of radical or incrementally new knowledge is particularly important in such a system. Traditional measures of innovation include expenditure on R&D, activity in high-technology sectors (biotechnology, ICT), patenting activity (number, intensity), and researchers per 10,000 population. These indicators proxy the ability to generate new knowledge. However, they are not particularly helpful in understanding how a traditional, low-tech manufacturing firm

Figure 3.3 *Learning Capabilities by Type of Firm*

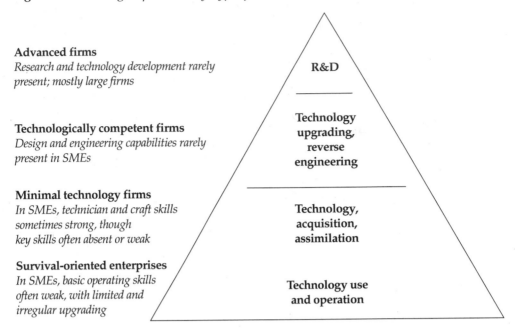

Advanced firms
Research and technology development rarely present; mostly large firms

Technologically competent firms
Design and engineering capabilities rarely present in SMEs

Minimal technology firms
In SMEs, technician and craft skills sometimes strong, though key skills often absent or weak

Survival-oriented enterprises
In SMEs, basic operating skills often weak, with limited and irregular upgrading

Source: Adapted from Intarakumnerd, Chairatana, and Tangchitpiboon (2002, 1445–1457).

can learn to upgrade its capabilities to compete in a more knowledge-based economy. Rather, these indicators are very often just the tip of the iceberg (see Figure 3.3). Concealed below is a layer of firms, mostly small and medium-size enterprises (SMEs). For them the major issue is acquisition of basic skills in marketing, design, engineering, and other operational skills rather than technology upgrading and R&D. For these reasons, the traditional innovation system approach might be applicable to a very limited subset of the economy, such as firms in the export-oriented sectors. It might also be useful for setting long-term goals and objectives.

To be relevant for all firms, this chapter focuses on the innovation and enterprise upgrading system—a network of institutions, private and public, that interact in a concerted manner to enhance firm-level learning and improve productivity. Table 3.1 matches suitable policy interventions with the capabilities of the four types of firms shown in Figure 3.3.

The automotive industry represented 14.6 percent of total manufacturing and 22.1 percent of total manufacturing exports in 2001. Because it is so important for Mexico, this industry serves as a useful example of the significance of gains from enterprise updating (see Box 3.1).

Mexico's Low-Level Equilibrium Trap

Mexico, like most of Latin America, is caught in a low-level equilibrium trap in innovation and learning. Despite very significant changes in the macroenvironment and increased competition within the Latin American economies, economic agents (particularly firms) have not been able to shift toward knowledge activities with higher value added.

Table 3.1 *Instruments to Support Innovation by Type of Firm*

Type of firm	Policy objectives	Instruments and interventions
Survival-oriented enterprises	To build basic competitive capabilities by fostering awareness of scope and benefits of innovation	• Business advisory and support services—SME and microenterprise support agencies • Facilitation of access to finance (including microfinance) • Management and skills development
Minimum technology firms agenda	To foster competitiveness by introducing basic innovation skills and encouraging adoption and application of new ideas	• Support for business development, diversifying customer base • Product diversification and quality improvement • Management and skills development • Internet-based information services • Technology awareness and marketing • Support for technology adoption and adaptation projects • Cluster-based approaches to stimulating innovation
Technologically competent enterprises	To support market development and entry into global value chains by fostering strategic alliances and certain in-house innovation capabilities	• Business development, exports market support • Internet-based information services • Technology transfer support • Incubators and technology parks • Linkages with academic researchers • Laboratory services and metrology services • Consultancy and technical assistance support—e.g., on commercialization, intellectual property rights, licensing, patenting • Supplier development and linkage promotion programs
Advanced firms	To move up global value chains by upgrading in-house innovation capabilities and strategic alliances To diffuse experience of innovation leaders as role models for the rest of the economy	• Support for participation in international R&D networks (e.g., EU 6th Framework Program) • Technology and other innovation-based spin-offs • University-industry collaboration • Support for commercialization • Development of vibrant venture capital industry • To encourage participation of national innovation leaders in national advisory bodies, technology foresight, and cluster processes

Box 3.1 *Discretionary Differences among Firms: The Automotive Industry*

Differentials in firm performance in the automotive industry tend to be very skewed, with few firms having extraordinary performance, several standard deviations above the mean. Figure 3.4 shows a wide variation of value added per worker in the motor vehicles and equipment sector. Even controlling for the size of firms, there is still wide dispersion of productivity. The huge standard deviation shows how much room there is for improvement. In the case of small firms, if the largest observation remained constant and the rest of the firms moved to the upper limit of their range, these changes would increase output by more than 37 percent.

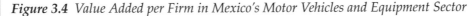

Figure 3.4 *Value Added per Firm in Mexico's Motor Vehicles and Equipment Sector*

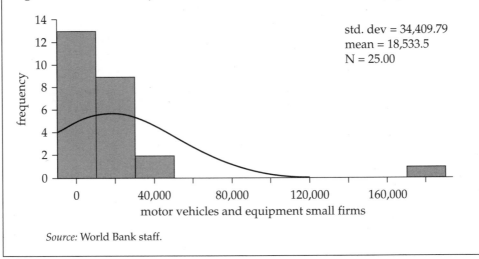

std. dev = 34,409.79
mean = 18,533.5
N = 25.00

Source: World Bank staff.

The low-level trap for Mexico can be defined as a relatively stable equilibrium, characterized by the following features:

- Low level of spending on R&D (0.43 percent of GDP)
- Low share of private sector financing and execution (Figure 3.5)
- Low efficiency of spending on R&D in terms of measurable outcomes (Figure 3.6).

Lederman and Maloney (2002) estimate that the optimal amount of investment is between 4 and 10 times higher than current amounts, and they provide a variety of reasons for this low-level trap. Perhaps the most important reason is the lack of learning capacity to use technology and develop it further in order to converge with innovators. Other reasons include the lack of competitive pressures, the absence of well-functioning capital markets, limited entrepreneurial capital, unstable macro-economic growth, and limited access to intermediate inputs. All of these factors help explain why the technology gap between Mexico and innovators remains significant despite trade, abundant foreign direct investment, significant investment in capital goods, and other existing elements that could spur innovation.

Research increasingly shows the relationship between investment in R&D—particularly within the private sector—and improvements in economic growth and productivity. Constant underinvestment not only results in low levels of innovation output such as patenting, it is also a barrier to increasing growth and competitiveness.

Figure 3.5 *Finance and Execution of R&D in Mexico by Sector, 2000*

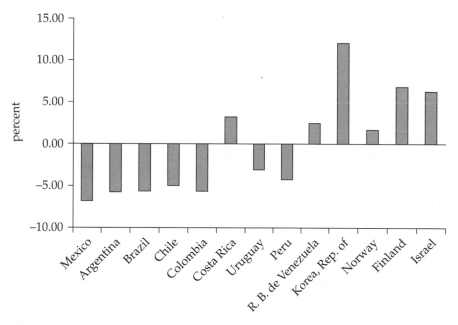

Source: OECD (2001b).

Figure 3.6 *Efficiency of Spending on R&D, Selected OECD Firms, 1985–2000*

Source: Lederman and Maloney (2002).

Why does the low-level trap exist in Mexico, and why is it relatively stable? The majority of R&D spending and execution is in the public sector, yet public sector activity is not particularly relevant for the productive sector, and its efficiency is low. The private sector, perceiving public organizations as not necessarily relevant to its needs, performs innovation activity in isolation or through strategic alliances with foreign knowledge. This relative lack of stake in a public innovation system removes pressure for reform and improvement.

Nevertheless, there are reasons to be hopeful. First, important exceptions (such as the Delphi Technology Center in Ciudad Juarez) signal Mexico's possible future. The policy agenda is diffusion and acceleration of existing positive examples and trends, rather than creation of things from scratch. Second, the stakes are high and worth pursuing, all vested interests notwithstanding. Reform of innovation and the enterprise upgrading system would yield dramatic improvement, not change on the margins. As noted earlier, there is some indication of efficiency gains if most firms reach national best practice. Third, it makes sense to invest in national science and technology capabilities in order to be taken seriously by prospective international partners. Strategic alliances and international networks are the name of the game, not domestic technological capabilities per se. The notion of a national innovation system must be treated with caution.

Three Isolated Cultures of Innovation in Mexico

Whatever perspective one chooses, linkage and interorganizational networks are the center of the agenda. Yet the reality in Mexico is three different innovation cultures, and, accordingly, three isolated innovation systems: universities and research centers (the public innovation system), large export-oriented firms, and survival-oriented SMEs. Box 3.2 describes the role of these three types of institutions in Mexico's automotive sector.

The "Ivory Tower" Science Culture

Mexico's public system for scientific research is sizeable in terms of both basic research produced and resources spent, and it can serve as a significant resource for technology development and application within Mexico. The government of Mexico increased R&D spending from 4 billion pesos to 18.5 billion pesos during the 1990s. In an index created by RAND (Wagner, Popper, and Horling 2003) to rank countries by science and technology capacity, Mexico ranked a respectable number 50 among 150 countries. In an index of technology transfer capabilities, Mexico ranked number 4 in 2001.

Scientific productivity also shows a strong performance. In terms of publications in internationally recognized journals, Mexican scientists were prolific during the 1990s in the fields of physics, clinical medicine, biology, biochemical research, and chemistry. In addition to improving their position in journals, Mexican scientists are collaborating with international colleagues, showing a global awareness of knowledge creation. These indicators provide evidence of world-class-level Mexican research and the potential for knowledge creation within academic institutions.

Export-Oriented Pragmatism: National and Multinational Big Business

The main motor of growth in the last decade, and the key indicator of good economic performance from the domestic economy, is the increase in exports. Table 3.2 shows the revealed comparative advantages (RCA) of Mexico vis-à-vis its NAFTA trading partners. The two largest sectors, in absolute terms for 2000 and in terms of increase from 1973 to 2000, are road vehicles and telecom equipment, products that are knowledge-based industries.

Box 3.2 *Three Types of Players in Mexico's Automotive Sector*

The Mexican automotive sector is composed of automobile assemblers and auto parts firms. It accounts for 16.1 percent of gross manufacturing value added and 2.3 percent of total Mexican GDP—more than any other manufacturing sector. Despite being a mature sector at the global level, sales increased 230 percent between 1995 and 2000, and employment increased 140 percent during the same period, supporting the RCA data shown in Table 3.2.

What makes the industry particularly interesting is the variety of players with different roles. Unlike the electronics sector, which is composed of foreign export-oriented firms, the automotive sector includes both foreign firms, and small, medium, and large domestic firms that sell to the domestic and export markets. These players create a complex system with strategic complementarities that have enabled the industry to grow. Indeed, this particular industry exemplifies the types of innovation culture described above.

Public innovation system. Disciplines related to the automotive sector, such as mechanical engineering, electronics, mechatronics, and material science, are strong in universities and research centers in Mexico. However, no research center or academic institution specializes in research relevant to the automotive sector. The isolation of the system can be seen in the small number of firms that collaborate with universities and technology centers—only 1.5 and 0.7 percent respectively (Constantino and Lara 2000).

Large export-oriented firms. Most large firms, whether foreign (Delphi, Visteon, Federal Mogul) or domestic (Unik, San Luis, Arnecom), seem oriented toward the direct and indirect export markets. With the notable exception of Delphi, which has built a significant capacity for engineering in its Ciudad Juarez facilities, other firms have few research activities. Domestic firms have developed some research capabilities, but they generally still rely on foreign technology licenses that limit, by contract, their opportunity to pursue markets outside of Mexico. Despite this limitation, firms are able to compete at the regional level through a combination of locational advantages, lower labor costs, and incremental process improvements.

Small firms. Before the signing of NAFTA, local content rules fostered the creation and growth of a variety of parts suppliers. Since 1994, most of these firms have disappeared or have been purchased by foreign firms (sometimes their former technology licensors). The few surviving small firms are now second- or third-tier suppliers; they tend to concentrate on small value-added products such as small stamped metal or plastic injection products. These tend to be low-margin commodity products, with high competition. The lack of specific competencies makes these firms easily dispensable. Despite the large purchase volumes, small and medium firms that start selling to the automotive industry often quit after a few months, preferring to sell to less demanding markets such as electric appliances or consumer products.

Source: World Bank staff.

RCA data can, however, create the misleading impression that Mexico has improved its knowledge-generating capability significantly. A closer analysis shows that the vast majority of exporting is done by large multinational companies that use Mexico as a manufacturing base for labor-intensive processes, taking advantage of factor price differentials with the rest of North America, while performing most knowledge-intensive activities in other countries. These firms operate as export enclaves, with minimal links to domestic firms. Similarly, larger firms of Mexican capital have been thriving mostly in sectors where they are exposed to only limited competition (services and resource-based sectors).

Table 3.2 *The Share in Total Exports of Commodity Groups in Which Mexican Strength Is Concentrated, 1993, 2000*
(Percent)

Commodity group	1993	2000
Mexico is strong		
Vegetables and fruit	3.6	2.0
Petroleum	13.7	9.0
Manufactures of metals	2.5	2.4
Telecom equipment	8.9	11.6
Road vehicles	13.6	17.0
Furniture	1.3	2.0
Clothing	2.3	5.2
Both countries are strong		
Power-generating machinery	4.9	3.8
Office machines and automatic data processing equipment	2.9	7.1
Electrical machinery	16.0	15.8

Source: Wagner, Popper, and Horling (2003).

Note: Revealed comparative advantage (RCA) is defined as the share of a product in a country's total exports divided by the share of that product in world exports. A value greater than one indicates that the country has a relative specialization in that particular product. "Both countries are strong" refers to products with RCA greater than one for the United States and Mexico; "Mexico is strong" refers to products for which the RCA for Mexico is greater than one and for the United States is less than one.

Thus, the large domestic firms, which comprise only 1.7 percent of all domestic firms, rely heavily on technology licenses or other types of assistance from foreign companies, rather than developing their own technology, and multinationals rely on their parent companies for most R&D activities.

Survival-Oriented Microfirms and SMEs

The other 98.3 percent of Mexican firms are microfirms and small and medium-size enterprises that are in a weak competitive position. Rather than focusing on innovation, these firms have been surviving and adapting themselves to a variety of ongoing changes, including increased competition as a result of NAFTA; a severe contraction of the economy in 1995; and virtually no financing for investment or working capital. Many thousands of firms have disappeared as a consequence of these changes. The majority of remaining firms are just surviving, using most of their innovation efforts to take reactive measures against changes in the macroeconomic environment, and thereby limiting their growth to retained profits. Constantly adapting in the face of this environmental instability, SMEs have not been able to realize their important innovation potential.

The Problem of Isolation

The first two innovation systems described (science culture and export pragmatism) are relatively strong. They have pockets of world-class, quality institutions, and these institutions are large enough to reap the advantages of scale economies. These institutions could easily be inserted into a global innovation system. However, the existence of institutional sources of innovation is not the only concern; a

Table 3.3 Exceptions and Promising Cases of Innovation at Different Levels

Level	Exception	Promising case	Typical case
Microlevel: individual firms	Delphi Engineering Center	Vitro	Noninnovative firm
Mezzo level: clusters, networks	Monterrey urban cluster	Jalisco electronics and software	Isolated agents
Public sector level: innovation support organizations	CIATEQ	IMP	Science-defined priorities

Source: World Bank staff.

major problem is the isolation of these different elements. This lack of interaction can be seen in a variety of ways: very limited collaboration between industry and academia, the small degree of local content in exporting firms, the limited number of industry consortia, and so forth. Creating these linkages is at least as important as strengthening the individual elements of the innovation system.

Signs of Change and Improvement

Within this context of general lethargy, successful cases of innovation can be found. This heterogeneity within the system shows that, despite the environment, certain agents have had outstanding performance (we will call them exceptions) or have entered a path that might result in innovative activities (promising cases). It is important to identify and understand these cases presented in Table 3.3, both for their relevance and their possible demonstration effects.

Individual Firms

At the microlevel, the firm is the key unit of innovation. Investment is very small, patenting scarce, and individual firms do not interact with other elements of the innovation system, such as research centers and other firms. In terms of patenting, comparative advantage lies in traditional sectors, such as processed foods, soaps, paints, and ferrous metals, rather than in sectors that have experienced rapid growth (Lederman and Maloney 2002). With few exceptions, large firms tend to depend on joint ventures or licensing to obtain their process and product technology. Small firms rarely invest in innovation, as shown by their relatively poor performance. However, some firms have been innovative within this context. The Delphi Engineering Center is an example.

DELPHI ENGINEERING CENTER Delphi Engineering Center is part of Delphi Automotive System, the largest automotive parts firm in the world. Like most other U.S.-based automotive firms, Delphi established several plants in northern Mexico during the mid-1980s, using the country as a base for labor-intensive manufacturing operations.

In 1995 Delphi took a giant step forward by establishing an engineering center in Ciudad Juarez. This center is primarily involved in doing research, design, and development activities for the corporation. The average Delphi engineering center in the

United States employs 500 people; the Juarez facility employed 860 people in 1995 and more than 1,000 in 2004. According to Carrillo and Hualde (1997), the firm cut development costs by 60 percent and delivery time by 20 percent during the first year of operation. This extraordinary performance has continued. During 2002, Mexican engineers at the center were the main contributors to 50 inventions that received intellectual property protection (35 patents, 14 publications, and 3 industrial secrets). While assembly maquilas reacted to the strong peso by decreasing their labor force in 2003 and 2004, Delphi Engineering maintained its employment level. Other automotive firms such as GM and Visteon are creating or expanding their engineering facilities in the country, at least partly following Delphi's success.

VITRO   Vitro is a domestic firm, and Mexico's paragon of innovation. It concentrates in the production and distribution of a variety of glass products, including flat glass, glassware, glass containers, and household products. The firm has been working on innovation for several decades, developing a variety of process technologies that have made it one of the most efficient producers in the world. Since the market has opened, Vitro has been able to better focus its innovative efforts, master faster production engineering techniques, and adapt its production system to changes required by the export market.

According to Dutrenit (2000), Vitro has pursued a dual strategy of being both technologically independent and a fast follower. This shifting between independence and following has diversified risk, but in many ways it has prevented the firm from realizing its full potential. The two competing strategies have created instability in the firm's collaboration with research centers and other institutions. However, the firm has shown great potential in operational innovation, and it could become an excellent example of innovation if its long-term strategy was defined consistently across the organization (Dutrenit 2000, 23).

Clusters and Networks

In successful cases, firms within clusters evoke images of Silicon Valley or of Route 128—pockets of highly innovative firms interacting to create innovation. The clustering of economic activity at this mezzo level shows agglomeration but limited innovation.

MONTERREY URBAN CLUSTER   Perhaps the best example of a cluster in Mexico is the city of Monterrey, located in a barren area with scarce natural resources and an extreme climate. The city is not a cluster in the traditional sense of a number of firms in one industry; rather, it is an agglomeration of a variety of industries with branches of metal working, machinery and equipment, chemicals, and ceramics. The presence of these industries has generated urbanization economies that contribute to the welfare of the region.

In addition to multinational corporations, large multi-industry domestic conglomerates contribute significantly to production. Examples include FEMSA (beverages and retailing), AXA (chemicals, metal, auto parts, food), Proeza (food and automotive), Vitro (glass), Cydsa (chemicals, textiles), Pulsar (biotech, financial), Alfa (chemical, food, auto parts), Imsa (steel, batteries), and CEMEX (cement). Some of these industrial groups acquired two of the largest national banks (Bancomer, Banorte); thus the city is currently increasing its importance as a financial center.

Human resources are developed in 19 universities, the largest of which is the Instituto Tecnológico de Estudios Superiores de Monterrey (Tec). Tec was created in 1943 by Alfa, Vitro, and other leading industrial groups for the purpose of training high-quality engineers for their firms. Tec remains a leading institution in the country, and, following its origins, keeps close contacts with industry. One of its key functions has been to provide a forum at which local firms, government, and researchers can discuss the future of the region. This has resulted in a shared vision, and currently all the economic agents are working toward making Monterrey a center for high-tech manufacturing and services.

JALISCO ELECTRONICS AND SOFTWARE   Central Jalisco has been called the Latin American Silicon Valley. In 2004 international companies with manufacturing facilities there included IBM, Hewlett-Packard, NEC, Motorola, Intel, Siemens, Flextronics, Jabil Circuits, and USI. According to the Secretaria de Economia, Jalisco accounts for 35 percent of production for the largest contract electronic manufacturers, and it creates value added within the region of 27 percent. This would certainly suggest clustering of high value-added activity.

Recently, however, the story has changed dramatically. Firms such as IBM and Motorola, plus many smaller ones, have pulled manufacturing operations out of the region to take them to China and other Asian countries. When asked why they were moving, one of the major firms provided three reasons: China's accessibility to the global market (Mexico deals almost exclusively with the North American market); the presence of most component suppliers in Asia (proximity to suppliers increases the responsiveness of the supply chain); and lower labor costs.

Even though Central Jalisco´s position as a successful electronics cluster is now being questioned, the region still has a significant concentration of talent and knowledge in this industry. The state government and local organizations are making strong efforts to convert the low value-added assembly jobs into higher value-added software development jobs. There is a good possibility that such a transition will succeed. IBM currently runs a Guadalajara Development Lab, which works on developing AS/400 and server applications. This facility is one of the few companies in Mexico to have a CMM 3 certification. A successful conversion into software would not only revitalize the cluster but also provide higher value added and better paying jobs.

Innovation Organizations in the Public Sector

As noted earlier in this chapter, most innovation takes place in public sector institutions. Who are the clients for these innovations? In some cases, the answer is the public sector, but frequently the answer is nobody. Research in Mexico has traditionally been supply driven, with scientists submitting proposals for research grants. Rewards, particularly for researchers in public universities, have been tied primarily to published papers and citations. Joint work with industry has traditionally been penalized by the conservative scientific community. This model has resulted in research that does not necessarily solve any clear short- or long-term needs of society. The exception, as noted above, is the system's relative scientific strength in astrophysics and mathematics.

Table 3.4 shows the largest users of federal R&D resources in the country. Education and energy account for 85 percent of total expenditure. Within this environment a few institutions have seen the advantages of cooperating with production agents.

Table 3.4 *Federal R&D Expenditures in Mexico by Sector and Subsector, 2001*

Main sector (percentage of total)	Main subsectors (percentage of sector)[a]
Education (62.4)	UNAM (27.0)
	CONACYT (23.8)
	SEP-CONACYT (22.0)
	Cinvestav (6.8)
Energy (22.4)	IMP (52.4)
	PEMEX (32.4)
	Instituto de Investigaciones Electricas (8.3)
	Instituto de Investigaciones Nucleares (6.9)
Others (15.2)	Agriculture and rural (49.3)
	Health and social security (19.7)

Source: CONACYT (2002).

a. The subsector percentages do not total 100 percent because only the main subsectors are included.

CIATEQ   The Centro de Información Científica y Tecnológica (CIATEQ) is a notable exception to the usual isolation of public sector innovation support organizations. It is a research center located in Queretaro with the mission of "helping firms increase their productivity and international competitiveness, and providing technological solutions in mechatronics and related disciplines, through highly qualified personnel and cutting edge technology." This mission statement clearly sets CIATEQ apart from other centers, for which research itself is the primary objective. CIATEQ provides specialized services such as special machinery design, fabrication, and automation; metrology services; product prototyping; design and development of casting and metallurgic processes; and design of electronic systems for measurement and control. In order to be close to its customer base, CIATEQ is located within industrial parks rather than near universities, where most other research centers are located. In 2001, CIATEQ generated 47 percent of its total budget through fees from client firms. The CIATEQ model has been so successful that branch centers in the states of Aguascalientes and San Luis Potosí have opened. Most of the expenses for constructing the branch centers were paid by the state governments, which saw great value in having such services in the states.

IMP   In the energy sector, the largest research institution is the Instituto Mexicano del Petróleo (IMP). It is an important generator of academic publications, with 630 papers published between 1981 and 2000. Between 1996 and 2001, the IMP requested 96 patents, the largest number filed by any Mexican institution. However, this number of patents is small compared with the largest foreign requestor for Mexican patents; Proctor and Gamble requested 2,615 patents during the same period. Another weakness is that virtually all of IMP's innovation is done for a single client, PEMEX, the state-owned oil monopoly. The impact of IMP on Mexican society would be greatly enhanced if it were to diversify its clients, including the private sector.

Agenda for Transforming Mexico's Innovation System

Mexico's strategic objective should be a dramatic increase in productivity through knowledge-based integration into global value chains and participation in knowledge networks. A more dynamic and flexible innovation system is needed, one led by private demand and responsive to private sector needs. Strong academic-industry linkages are an important part of international knowledge networks. In the short term, the policy agenda should focus on formulating a cohesive strategy, improving incentives, and increasing the role of the private sector in public programs.

Formulating a Cohesive Strategy

The government has created myriad policies and policy instruments for scientific research, technological development, and innovation. Diffuse mandates, overlapping functions, and bureaucratic considerations have complicated strategy formulation and policy coordination. There is a need to centralize innovation policy and assignment of funding. Currently, CONACYT manages about 36 percent of the funds for public R&D and technology upgrading. Out of these funds, less than a third is for productive innovation. Both figures should be increased significantly, making CONACYT a hub for interorganizational and private-public alliances.

As a first step toward greater cohesion, the government should make a thorough evaluation, preferably using cluster analytical concepts, of its policies, programs, and funding. This audit by domestic as well as international experts should be of high technical caliber, independent in order to avoid capture by vested interests, and representative through collaboration of important Mexican stakeholders. The audit should include the locus for effective decision making and alignment of management responsibilities with accountability for results. The budgeting process should be based on clear priorities.

Improving Incentives

To improve incentives for innovation, linkages between business and R&D can be strengthened in four ways. First, the government should restructure intellectual property rights. Mexico remains the only OECD country where the researcher in a public institution does not have a legal mechanism to claim the upside potential of his or her invention. Second, public institutions should reward staff for success in productive research projects and linkages with the productive sector. Third, rules for the allocation of public funding for R&D should be introduced that favor consortiums between universities and private firms, and between private firms and SMEs. Finally, funding should be targeted to sectors known for excellence and strategic value.

Increasing the Role of the Private Sector

Private sector participation in the design and implementation of public programs must be increased. Although the situation is improving, Mexico's private sector role, both in financing and execution of research and development, is below the standards of comparable countries. The private sector takes a comparatively passive stance on using product and process innovation as a strategic tool for business development. The reasons for this seem to be weaknesses on the supply and demand sides.

Drawing on CONACYT's AVANCE and other programs, the government could enhance its catalytic function by (i) supporting research and training linked to joint ventures between international and domestic technology companies; (ii) prompting international technology companies to create research teams in Mexico through staff exchange schemes; (iii) moving science and technology researchers from government

---

Box 3.3 Innovation through Interorganizational Networks

Two analytical constructs drawn from management science—clusters and supply chains, also known as value-added chains—describe linkages that promote innovation. Economic activity is not coordinated solely through signals generated by an impersonal marketplace; economic activity also involves direct coordination through face-to-face communication.

   Clusters are groups of firms, research centers, and universities that cooperate in a specific area of business in order to achieve economies of scale and scope. Innovation clusters are formed to conduct knowledge-intensive activities. A *value-added chain* is one of the vertical linkages. It describes the full range of activities required to bring a product or service from conception and design, through the different phases of production (involving physical transformation and the input of various producer services), marketing, and delivery to final consumers. A value-added chain is usually defined for particular products (automobiles, electronics, garments, pharmaceuticals), but it typically crosses different industries, and each stage of production is much more closely linked with upstream and downstream industries on the chain than with other producers in the same industry.

   Source: World Bank staff.

---

institutions to companies through specific public-private incentive programs; (iv) leveraging innovation spillovers from FDI through targeted investment promotion; and (v) expanding programs supporting innovation start-ups with matching grants through private venture capital firms and incubation assistance.

   The main thrust of the innovation policy agenda is to promote concerted action in interorganizational networks (see Box 3.3). The private and public sectors will need to work together to overcome what may be low-level technological equilibrium traps in most sectors of the economy. Entrepreneurs have been reluctant to become involved in domestic research and development institutions because of their apparent inadequacies; nonbusiness institutions have been reluctant to develop capabilities because of lack of apparent demand. Catalyzing interventions can be instrumental to overcome this reluctance. The challenge is to make public science and technology endowments more business relevant, and to shift from an emphasis on domestic science and research to closer integration with international research institutions, particularly those of Mexico's NAFTA partners. This requires the cooperation of diverse stakeholders.

   Universities and public research institutes need to overcome narrow academic interests and adopt a more prominent commercial orientation in their efforts to develop cutting-edge service capabilities and generate additional funding. Firms need to seek a more proactive interface with the domestic research establishment. Long-term collaboration will enable firms to improve competitiveness and access domestic R&D. Finally, the government needs to promote alliances and joint ventures by buying down initial launch costs. This will ensure that public-funded research generates economic benefits.

Evaluation of Existing Institutions, Policies, and Initiatives

Mexico's innovation and enterprise upgrading system is composed of private as well as public institutions (see Figure 3.7). Several public institutions participate in R&D-related activities. As shown in Table 3.4, education receives the greatest share

Figure 3.7 *Organizations Involved in Innovation*

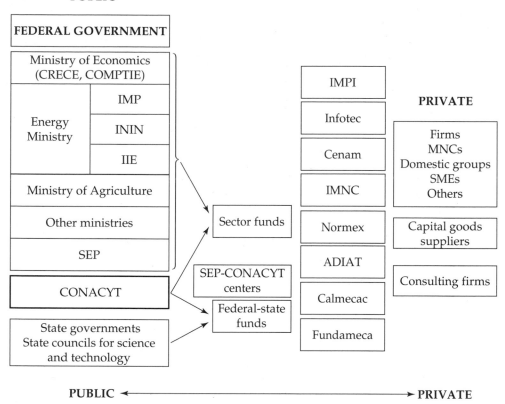

Source: World Bank staff.
Note: Abbreviations in the figure refer to public sector organizations in Mexico, see www.director10.gob.mx.

of resources related to R&D (62.4 percent) followed by energy (22.4 percent). Most of these resources are for basic research, but a wide variety of programs focus on enterprise support. Table 3.5 shows the number of federal enterprise support programs by type and organization.

Enterprise support programs vary widely. There are 98 "legacy" programs from 11 different institutions, plus an additional 31 new programs (not including 20 additional ones on institution attributes and databases). State and local programs also must be taken into account. Aguascalientes is one of the most active states in terms of enterprise support programs; it has 53 support programs dealing with similar issues. In total, there are more than 400 enterprise support programs at the federal and state levels.

The design of each program is the responsibility of the relevant ministry. Even though the budget is centrally approved by the federal congress, which in theory should evaluate trade-offs in the use of total resources, there is virtually no coordination among programs. Each program has its own budget, infrastructure, and human resources; several programs have overlapping objectives.

Few enterprise support programs are directly related to technical innovation per se. Nevertheless, many have an indirect impact on technological capabilities,

Table 3.5 *Number of Federal Enterprise Support Programs, by Type and Organization, 2001*

Federal ministries and agencies	Fiscal	Information	Training, technical assistance, and consulting	Credit[a]	Supply chain	New programs
Bancomext		4	5	11		4
CONACYT			3	3		3[b]
Economía	5	2	6	1	5	21
NAFIN		3	2	14		1
SAGARPA		1	3			
SEDESOL				4		
SEMARNAT	2		2	3		
Other	SHCP 14		STPS 1, SEP 4			SECTUR 2

Source: World Bank staff.

a. Combines the categories of Credits, Risk Capital, and Subsidies with Development Bank Financing.

b. The new CONACYT programs (Fondos Sectoriales, Fondos Mixtos, AVANCE) are included here even though they did not appear in the original source.

since they are geared toward upgrading the quality of inputs for production. For example, all of the programs related to training are important for building human capital, for either general tasks or industry-specific knowledge. Similarly, a number of NAFIN and Bancomext programs help firms to acquire machinery and equipment.

Traditionally, programs directly targeted toward technological improvement have been rare, and they have lacked continuity. For example, the Programa de Modernizacion Tecnológica (PMT) ran only for two years. However, as part of a restructuring effort, PMT was recently replaced by several programs of the Fondo Sectorial of Secretaria de Economía, CONACYT, and AVANCE. The new Economía and CONACYT programs—Economía with the Asesores Tecnológicos Empresariales (ATE) and Consultoria Especializada en Tecnología, and CONACYT with its Fondos and AVANCE—are directly relevant to innovation (see Figure 3.8).

Of particular relevance for firm innovation are the new CONACYT programs of Fondos Sectoriales, Fondos Mixtos, and AVANCE. With these programs, CONACYT is using its experience in evaluating science and technology projects to generate projects that can solve specific problems. These programs are described below:

- *Fondos Sectoriales* are created with matching funds from CONACYT and different ministries, which, in some cases, already have resources for technological development. Each ministry defines priorities that need to be researched and requests proposals from scientific and technology institutions and firms. The funds currently operating are SEMARNAT (environment), SAGARPA (agriculture and rural), SEMAR (marine), SEDESOL (social development), Economia (mostly for private development projects), CONAFOVI (housing), CONAFOR (forestry), Salud (health), SEP (education), SENER (energy), SCT (communications), SEGOB (government), and ASA (Airports). These sets of funds have replaced the traditional Science Support program that once supported research projects. Research for pure science is now supported by the SEP-CONACYT sectoral fund.

Figure 3.8 *Convergence of Enterprise Support and Innovation Programs*

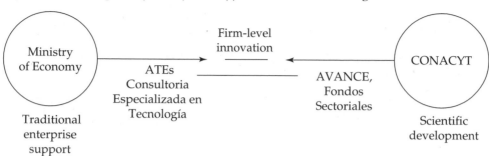

Source: World Bank staff.

- *Fondos Mixtos* are joint funds with a Mexican state, instead of a ministry; each state defines a set of research needs to be addressed. Of the 32 state governments (including Distrito Federal (DF)), 25 have a fund operating; most have already selected their first set of projects. The speed of formation of the 25 fondos shows the growing awareness of the importance of science and technology at the state level. These funds have the additional advantage of promoting decentralization of research. Traditionally, most of CONACYT's resources have stayed in Mexico City, specifically at the Universidad Nacional Autónoma de México (UNAM) and the Instituto Politécnico Nacional (IPN). Indeed, 48.6 percent of the National System of Researchers are going to Mexico City institutions. Fondos Sectoriales, by contrast, has a natural tendency to disperse funds more widely.

- *Programa AVANCE (Alto Valor Agregado en Negocios con Conocimiento y Empresarios)* provides last-mile financing to help translate scientific and technological developments into products, processes, and services with market potential. This fund supports the development of the basic engineering of products and processes; construction and testing of the last round of prototypes; and market testing. The fund also provides financial and technical support for patent registration. Examples in Mexico of innovations going from the lab to the marketplace are very few. This program intends to create a critical mass of successful cases that will spur more firms to follow suit. The "last mile" concept should be viewed as an entry point for facilitating interactions between research organizations and industry. To produce a significant effect, however, a profound reform is needed to enhance research organizations' incentive to cooperate with industry. In the short term, we recommend allocating a larger share of resources to facilitating such interactions. In the long term, AVANCE should be transformed into one key element of the still nascent venture capital industry.

It is clear that CONACYT is attempting to make science more relevant to industry. Some of the funds experienced operational problems at the beginning, but the importance of creating funds that respond to the needs of a specific sector or state is increasingly being recognized. This is a great step forward. Correct evaluation, translated into design and operational improvements, could transform the supply-based science system to one that is based on demand.

Despite the government's efforts to address the private sector's problems with innovation and enterprise upgrading, firms, particularly domestic firms, have not

Table 3.6 Program Evaluations

Program	Results of evaluation
CONOCER *Consejo de Normalización y Certificación de Competencia Laboral*	• Greater labor mobility and promotion under nontraditional criteria. • Greater multifunctionality for the workers. • Increased interest in participating in national certification, including the provision for the worker to pay the cost of certification. • No effect on real remunerations of workers. • Better personal assessments of workers. • No increase in employee-perceived capacity or autonomy of decision making. • Perceived greater support for the training. • No perceived better quality and relevance of the training. • Mixed results for labor relations.
CIMO/ PAC *Programa de Calidad Integral y Modernización/Programa de Apoyo a la Capacitación*	• Period of analysis 1991–1993: 8.5% growth in employment (–1.0% for control group); 10% growth in remuneration (same as control group, though level of payment in CIMO 14% less) • Period of analysis 1993–1995: No positive statistical effect on employment. No positive statistical effect on remunerations. Growth in productivity 7.7% (6.6% in control group). Firms with training plans were 4.4% more competitive than those without.
CRECE *Centro Regional para la Competitividad Empresarial*	Results not statistically robust: 7.1% increase in operating profits; 16.8% increase in employment; 10.7% fiscal and parafiscal impact.
FIDECAP *Fondo para la Integración de Cadenas Productivas*	Qualitative surveys of participating firms in 18 states (2002).
FAMPYME *Fondo de Apoyo para las Micro, Pequeñas y Mediana Empresa*	INP–Economic, Administrative, and Social Research Center, 2002. Qualitative surveys of participating firms in 18 states.
MEX-EX *México Exporta*	No record of evaluation.
PATCI *Programa de Asistencia Técnica y Campaña de Imagen*	No record of evaluation.
PMT *Programa de Modernización Tecnológica*	CONACYT, 25 case studies (2002).
PAIDEC *Programa de Apoyo a Proyectos de Investigación y Desarrollo Conjuntos*	CONACYT, Information on a pilot case (2002).

Source: World Bank staff.

been doing very well. Are the programs, in fact, improving private sector performance? Unfortunately, formal program evaluations are rare and are not always rigorous. The new budget law requires public entities to evaluate all of their public programs yearly, but no standard methodology is applied. Moreover, the institutions themselves pay for the evaluations of their programs, which could bias the results.

Table 3.6 shows SME programs with deficient evaluations. Of 11 programs analyzed, there were no reported evaluations for 3 of them. Of the remaining eight, only one (CIMO) was analyzed using quantitative quasi-experimental methodologies. For this program, Secretaría del Trabajo y Previsión Social (STPS) (the ministry that runs the program) found a significant increase in employed personnel and productivity; the World Bank analysis of the program found no significant effects on productivity. The rest of the programs were evaluated with qualitative surveys, only one of which used a control group. The lack of apparent improvement in the innovation performance of firms suggests that a top-down effort to coordinate legacy programs is of critical importance. A concentration on fewer but more effective and efficient programs is advisable.

Innovation and Business R&D Agenda: Implementation Issues

Concerted action to overcome the widespread organizational isolation of research organizations, education organizations, and the productive sector is essential for transforming the Mexican economy to a knowledge economy. Hence the issue of linkages and networks is a central thrust of the action agenda.

The first priority is to support a number of private-public programs that show tangible results for private sector stakeholders. Such initiatives would build credibility for reform efforts and show both national and global stakeholders that Mexico's innovation organizations do matter.

The following initiatives are recommended:

- Build a shared vision of Mexico as a knowledge economy through a technology foresight process led by the private sector. Certain industries (auto parts and plastics) and regions (Monterrey and Chihuahua) have already demonstrated the importance of long-term objectives and strategic planning. An initiative at the national level would be very useful.
- Improve the design and implementation of decentralized funds. The sectoral and regional funds are an excellent way to help ensure that innovation is relevant to the private and public sectors. Two immediate actions could improve operations: help users identify their research needs and create teams of evaluators who understand the needs of researchers and knowledge users (see Box 3.4).
- Engage successful Mexicans abroad in "brain circulation" networks. Millions of Mexicans live in the United States, and many have become successful entrepreneurs, managers, and politicians. Many of these people still have a strong Mexican identity, which could be used as the basis for an international knowledge network.
- Speed up formation of the venture capital industry on both the supply and demand sides (see Table 3.7) and establish a champion organization to support technology entrepreneurship. Proyecto Innovar could provide early stage funding and networks to companies in Monterrey and eventually

---

Box 3.4 *Improving Decentralized Sectoral and Regional Funds*

Sectoral and regional funds established by federal ministries are increasingly becoming the main channel for allocating public funds. Strategically, this is precisely the way to go: allocate public funds on a demand-driven, decentralized basis while improving the design and implementation of the funds. Stronger incentives are needed to engage international players, bring specialized expertise in project design (the Argentina Technology Fund provides up to $20,000 to SMEs to enhance the quality of their funding applications), and learn from successes and failures, which implies a need for early and continuous evaluation.

Over the medium term, the multitude of funds should be consolidated with clearly specified priorities and operating procedures. Interorganizational and private-public projects are to be particularly encouraged. A good example in this context is Tekes, the National Innovation Agency of Finland. It funds industrial projects as well as projects in research institutes, and it especially promotes innovative, risk-intensive initiatives. More information is available at http://www.tekes.fi/eng/.

A priority for Mexico is to encourage international research and technology upgrading projects, particularly with high performers in the United States and Asia. While assistance from the United States similar to EU structural funds is highly unlikely, NAFTA might consider putting matching funds into jointly funded projects in applied research. One example of such joint collaboration—the United States–Mexico Foundation for Science—recently celebrated its 10-year anniversary and established a good track record of useful initiatives.

Source: World Bank staff.

---

other regions of Mexico with high growth potential (see Figure 3.9). Private investors from Monterrey industrial groups and financial investors, and individuals and funds from the United States, could hold controlling interest, while government donor funds would act as catalysts. Entrepreneurship support could include networking events, training for Mexican fund managers, and policy/advocacy functions. To generate adequate deal flow from local and U.S. sources, hands-on management and high value-added services (such as mentoring and networking) from fund managers, limited partners, and investors will be crucial. Proyecto Innovar could be a powerful entry point for a second-generation (NAFTA-plus) agenda.[1]

Enterprise Upgrading and Linkages Agenda: Implementation Issues

This section is about the mundane but critically important agenda of enterprise upgrading. Whereas the previous section focused on advanced and technologically competent enterprises (the tip of the learning pyramid presented in Figure 3.3), here we focus on "minimal technology" firms and survival-oriented enterprises, largely SMEs, and to some extent on technology-competent firms (the base of the pyramid).

Promotion backward linkages is a main thrust of the enterprise upgrading agenda. To increase local sourcing, there is a need for more active dialogue with

---

[1] Chapter 6 continues the discussion of the NAFTA-plus innovation agenda. We propose a private-public hub for international innovation networks to be broadly similar to Fundacion Chile (see Box 6.2).

Table 3.7 *Venture Capital in Mexico: Supply and Demand*
Supply: The availability of venture funds is limited, and the institutional infrastructure is weak.

Constraints and opportunities	Initiatives under way
Appropriate legal structures for the creation of venture funds are lacking, and the problem of double taxation exists. Investment vehicles are needed to structure tax-transparent venture funds. These funds could be structured in Mexico or offshore in another jurisdiction. The tax transparency of the investment vehicle is particularly important for developing a base of institutional investors in this asset class.	NAFIN is heading a reform effort to streamline the Mexican legal-regulatory framework for establishment of venture funds.
The legal system does not allow flexible and enforceable contracts between venture funds and investors. The lack of protections for minority rights, and their poor enforceability in the Mexican courts, hinder venture investing. Aspects of capital distribution, including redemption rights, warrants, stock options, and dividends, are also prohibited or restricted under Mexican law.	The Mexican Law on Insurance Companies permits the Ministry of Treasury to specify the asset classes in which insurance companies may invest their reserves; Treasury has recently included, for the first time, venture capital as a permitted class.
There are few venture investors and trained fund managers. Mexico's active venture funds manage only a total of $362 million.	
The potential for Mexicans residing abroad to invest and mentor local firms is largely untapped. Few Mexicans return home to invest in or create early-stage companies. In India and China, strong networking groups work to link potential investors and mentors with small companies.	New legislation on corporate governance and institutional investors is being drafted. It will include arrangements for Mexican pension funds.
Institutional investment in venture capital is weak. Institutions such as pension funds, which comprise the bulk of venture investment in markets such as the United States, are virtually absent in Mexico. This is because of legal/regulatory constraints and the lack of perceived investment opportunities. For example, pension funds must obtain legislative approval on a case-by-case basis before they can invest in venture capital funds. Insurance companies have a very low limit on such investments.	
Foreign ownership is restricted in certain industrial and service sectors. Mexico has one of the most stringent foreign ownership regimes in Latin America. There are severe restrictions across a wide range of sectors, in which investment is possible only with the permission of the National Foreign Investment Commission.	
Government support for venture funds has been overly directive. Financial support provided by the government for the creation of venture funds has typically been directed at specific regions and/or sectors, restricting the scope of activity of the funds. Given the general lack of early-stage financing in the country, a broader and less directed approach is advisable. Management of these funds should be selected via a competitive process that encourages international participation in the fund management company.	

(continued on next page)

Table 3.7 *(Continued)*
Demand: The environment for entrepreneurship is weak, resulting in few potential high-growth start-ups suitable for venture capital funding.

Constraints and opportunities	*Initiatives under way*
Enterprises are constrained by traditional business values and an unwillingness to take risks. Despite high levels of entrepreneurial activity (18 percent of the population), investors and entrepreneurs remain focused on traditional business approaches, which are less growth oriented.	A new law—*Ley de Cienda y Tecnologia*—encourages the linking of new technologies with business ventures in order to promote commercialization of scientific research. CONACYT is implementing the law.
Entrepreneurial networking and "angel" investing are weak. Local and national groups that foster networking among entrepreneurs, angel investors, and venture funds are few in number. Networking linkages with Mexicans living abroad (for example in Silicon Valley) are also weak.	
Training for entrepreneurs and SMEs remains weak. Training and education tailored to the needs of entrepreneurs are in an incipient stage in Mexico. Business education is directly primarily toward management of established companies and traditional family businesses.	Endeavor, an entrepreneurship-supporting NGO active in Latin America, has initiated activities in Mexico with the support of leading Mexican industrial groups. Endeavor facilitates mentoring and networking between start-ups and angel investors.
Public research institutes and universities are largely isolated from the private sector. Most research and development in Mexico is undertaken at public sector universities and institutes, which face high barriers to entrepreneurship and linkage with the private sector.	ITESM has launched an entrepreneurship education program.

Source: World Bank staff.

Figure 3.9 *Proyecto Innovar as a Possible Hub of U.S.–Mexico Innovation Networks*

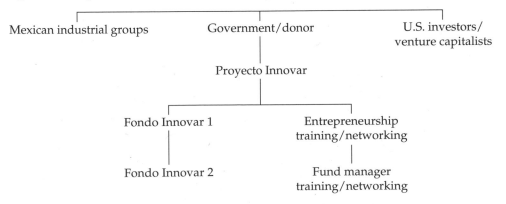

Source: World Bank staff.

Box 3.5 *Ireland's National Linkage Program (1987–1992)*

To deepen FDI involvement in the country and leverage the technology being used to develop an indigenous technological capability, Ireland's Industrial Development Authority (IDA) designed and implemented a National Linkage Program in 1987.

The three main stakeholders in the program were government, industry (primarily multinational corporations), and small and medium-size enterprises. The government provided the political imperative and charged the various state agencies with cooperating with the program. Eight agencies contributed staff and assistance, in part to help SMEs navigate the bureaucracy when seeking the best and most appropriate assistance. The availability of staff members from each agency made it possible to fast track many applications for assistance and to tailor services to the specific needs of both the customers and their suppliers.

The principal sector targeted was electronics, since it was the largest and most dynamic and had the greatest propensity to source locally. Its cooperation was sought, and the MNCs, through the Federation of Electronic Industries, contributed resources to the program costs in the initial two years. Companies were lobbied at high levels by senior agency executives and government ministers to support the objectives of the program. Incoming companies were introduced to Linkage program executives so that local sourcing opportunities could be discussed and developed. MNCs were also asked to provide technical assistance, in association with state technical agencies.

A rigorous assessment procedure was used to select participating SMEs. Existing or potential capabilities were evaluated against perceived supply opportunities. The assessment included a detailed examination of financial management and of the firms' potential.

National Linkage Program executives developed close relationships with key MNCs. Because of the number of agencies involved in the program, a well-balanced and multifaceted team comprising experts in management, business development, technical issues, accounting, and banking was the key to success. This array of skills allowed the team to carry out the initial assessment and selection of suppliers (in close cooperation with MNCs). It also made possible early-stage development workshops with the SMEs.

From 1987 to 1992, locally sourced materials in electronics increased from 9 percent to 19 percent of MNC purchases. While the total population of MNCs in Ireland was about 900 in 1992, approximately 200 proved to be effective participants in the program, with both accessible purchases and a willingness to support. The core group of 83 supply companies participating in the program, on average, outperformed other similar companies dramatically. This can be attributed to the selection process, intensive support, and interaction with demanding customers who forced the supply companies into a competitive mode. Over the period, these companies showed the following performance improvements: average sales growth of 83 percent; average productivity improvement of 36 percent; and average employment growth of 33 percent.

Source: World Bank staff.

---

multinationals to create supplier development programs. Well-designed supplier development programs put the private sector in the driver's seat and serve as a springboard to address numerous constraints faced by private business. Ireland is a paragon of developing national linkage programs that are efficient and driven by the private sector (see Box 3.5).

Mexico has a variety of programs, national and subnational, to develop clusters, value chains, and other networks. The need for concerted action is well recognized, yet the results of these many programs are often disappointing. Why is this so?

Developing a new institution to facilitate linkages and interorganizational networks is an investment characterized by lags and risks. *A learning period* is the lag

---

Box 3.6 *The Switching Period in Supplier Development in the Mexican Garment Industry*

In a series of interviews in 1998 with brand-name American manufacturers, a large clothing retailer described the lag between the time it starts working with a potential Mexican partner and the time its receives the first order. This period is usually at least one year and often one-and-a-half years.

Supplier development is a two-stage process that begins with a half-day visit. This is followed by full-day evaluations, which serve as a diagnostic tool as well as the basis for a business decision. If the parties agree to go forward, the American partner then undertakes to teach the Mexican company how to meet its standards. In a series of exchanges, Mexican personnel are virtually tutored by their American counterparts, sometimes in Mexican plants, sometimes at the American customer's facilities in the United States, and often in both places. One large shoe company, when it began sourcing in Mexico, opened a permanent office in Mexico City; it has two engineers working out of that office who are permanently assigned to each plant.

The switching period for organizational learning can be illustrated by the following graph:

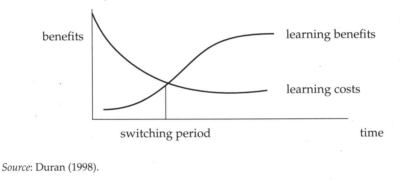

Source: Duran (1998).

---

between investments and outcome. This lag can be quite long and requires patience and follow-up, which many programs are not designed to sustain.

Let us illustrate the concept of a learning period with the example of supplier development and subcontracting. The advantages of subcontracting are well recognized: better suppliers, lower transaction costs, and lower input costs. In supplier development, a buyer (usually a large firm) invests in the organizational and technological development of a supplier (usually an SME), with the expectation that both of them will benefit. The key to supplier development is the switching period, after which the benefits will be higher than the cost of subcontracting. The switching period can be quite long, and the success uncertain (see Box 3.6). Companies are thus reluctant to develop suppliers on their own. However, the uncertainty and the length of the switching period can be reduced through the introduction of *specialized expertise* in supplier development and *effective public programs* of SME support. Both exist in Mexico, but they are in a short supply.

If the switching period is fairly long, the linkage promotion programs should be fairly long to ensure continuous improvements. World experience shows that to be effective in promoting linkages and networks, interventions need to be cumulative, customer oriented, and collective (the Triple-C approach):

- *Cumulative.* One-off improvements are not enough; to remain competitive, firms must be able to change and develop in response to new market conditions and new opportunities. The objective should be to help generate this capacity within groups of firms, so that in the long term public support is no longer needed.
- *Customer-oriented.* Efforts must be driven by the needs and demands of the customer. This forces firms to face up to underlying problems of competitiveness. The most successful interventions are those that help firms to learn about their customers, and then introduce the changes and innovations needed for them to meet market demands.
- *Collective.* Outside assistance should be directed at groups of enterprises rather than individual firms. This means working with business associations, producer groups, and other industry alliances. Where these do not exist, support can be linked to the formation of such groups. Collective assistance has two advantages: it is more cost effective than assisting enterprises individually, and it promotes constructive relationships among firms. This can improve their efficiency and increase the potential for learning from each other.

Other factors in the success and acceleration of linkages and enterprise upgrading include:

- *Reliance on a set of metrics to measure the performance of programs.*
- *Performance-oriented, incentive-driven programs.* Incentives induce self-selection among firms, helping those that help themselves and suggesting exit to those that cannot, because of internal or external factors.
- *Entrepreneurial management.* Successful organizations supporting technology and SMEs are often initiated by social entrepreneurs—individuals with unusual problem-solving and management skills. The success of a support agency is predicated on such an entrepreneurial manager at the top. Successful organizations tend to evolve from a reliance on a key manager to a robust organization with efficient corporate governance.
- *Cost recovery.* A successful support organization should aim for eventual full cost recovery.
- *Follow-up techniques (benchmarking).* Successful programs use benchmarking indicators to diagnose where firms are, what they need to do to improve, and what the alternatives are for those unlikely to survive.
- *Use of ICT.* ICT can leverage the effectiveness of linkage programs. Efforts are needed to develop Internet portals and Internet immersion institutes, improve access to the Internet, and train firms accordingly. A number of these initiatives should be developed at the state level and coordinated at the federal level.
- *Client participation in program design.* Clients not only need to pay for the services of the support organization; they also need to participate in the design and evaluation of programs. To ensure that they do, SME programs should never be run by governments (whether federal or subnational), but rather by an autonomous private management contractor working in cooperation with the government but maintaining its independence.

As noted earlier, successful programs link assistance with performance. For SMEs, in particular, a touch of realism is essential. They need help to identify their possibilities and potential as well as assistance with exit for firms that are not viable. Chapter 6 continues a discussion of the linkages agenda and proposes a National Linkage Promotion program for Mexico, both as a springboard for transition to a knowledge economy and as a "litmus test" of national concerted action.

4

Enhancing Education and Skills

This chapter makes two major claims. First, in the short run, Mexico has a critical mass of educated professionals and "blue collar" workers who can serve as a springboard for the country's transition to a knowledge economy. Yet in the long run (and this is our second claim), human capital may significantly impede that transition. Consequently, a comprehensive reform of Mexico's education system is urgently needed. It will invariably take time to implement such far-reaching changes and for them to start producing results. This is all the more reason to begin now.

The chapter begins with an assessment of Mexico's performance in education and notes its deficiencies in human capital formation. The imperative of lifelong learning is explained and the major challenges currently facing the education system outlined. Detailed recommendations for improving basic, secondary, and higher education and for fostering lifelong learning are then presented. The chapter concludes with a step-by-step education agenda and evaluation of the needed initiatives at the local, state, and national levels.

Benchmarking Mexico's Performance in Education

In efforts to improve its educational system, Mexico has made impressive strides. Average years of schooling increased from 4.77 in 1980 to 7.23 in 2000, about the same level as in Spain and higher than in Italy, Portugal, and Turkey (see Table 4.1). Mexico, however, is at least four years behind Canada, New Zealand, Norway, Sweden, and the United States. In addition, Mexico's illiteracy rate during this 20-year period declined sharply (from 8.5 percent to 2.8 percent) for youths between the ages of 15 and 24. The challenge is to expand educational services to meet Mexico's rapid demographic growth. With a population nearing 100 million, the country is projected to continue growing at 1.5 percent a year (World Bank 2005a). This posits a very significant challenge in the long term.

On such basic indicators as adult literacy rate, pupils per teacher, and secondary enrollment, Mexico scores poorly compared with Ireland and the Republic of Korea (see Figure 4.1). Even less satisfactory is Mexico's performance on more advanced indicators of a knowledge economy such as tertiary enrollment, extent of staff training, availability of management education, and professionals and technicians as a percentage of the labor force.

When compared with the rest of the world, Mexico's position is even more sobering (see Figure 4.2). Mexico is far behind Chile, Argentina, Uruguay, and East European economies. Neither has Mexico kept pace with Brazil and Peru. While Brazil, for example, has shown significant improvement since 1995, Mexico's progress has been quite modest.

Table 4.1 *Average Years of Schooling of Adults in OECD Countries, 1980–2000*

Countries	1980	1985	1990	1995	2000	% change 1980 & 2000
Australia	10.29	10.32	10.38	10.67	10.92	6.1
Austria	7.34	7.49	7.76	8.05	8.35	13.8
Belgium	8.24	8.58	8.87	9.1	9.34	13.3
Canada	10.31	10.76	10.99	11.39	11.62	12.7
Czech Republic	..	..	..	..	..	
Denmark	8.98	9.12	9.58	9.39	9.66	7.6
Finland	7.16	7.8	9.38	9.65	9.99	39.5
France	6.69	6.94	6.95	7.42	7.86	17.5
Germany	8.78	9.64	9.71	10.03	10.2	16.2
Greece	7.01	7.27	8	8.32	8.67	23.7
Hungary	9.06	8.93	8.93	8.83	9.13	0.8
Iceland	7.37	7.77	8.11	8.48	8.83	19.8
Ireland	7.46	7.77	8.78	9.08	9.35	25.3
Italy	5.89	6.16	6.49	6.85	7.18	21.9
Japan	8.51	8.74	8.96	9.23	9.47	11.3
Korea, Rep. of	7.91	8.68	9.94	10.56	10.84	37.0
Luxembourg	..	..	..	..	..	
Mexico	**4.77**	**5.2**	**6.72**	**6.96**	**7.23**	**51.6**
Netherlands	8.23	8.49	8.75	9.12	9.35	13.6
New Zealand	11.47	11.5	11.25	11.49	11.74	2.4
Norway	8.15	9.15	11.56	11.7	11.85	45.4
Poland	8.77	8.81	9.47	9.64	9.84	12.2
Portugal	3.78	3.85	4.91	5.47	5.87	55.3
Slovak Republic	..	..	8.9	9.09	9.27	
Spain	5.98	5.82	6.44	6.83	7.28	21.7
Sweden	9.71	9.46	9.51	11.23	11.41	17.5
Switzerland	10.37	10.15	10.14	10.31	10.48	1.1
Turkey	3.41	3.69	4.14	5.12	5.29	55.1
United Kingdom	8.27	8.52	8.77	9.09	9.42	13.9
United States	11.86	11.57	11.74	11.89	12.05	1.6

Source: World Bank (2004).

Lifelong Learning: A Prerequisite for Participation in the Knowledge Economy

One prerequisite for Mexico to successfully participate in the global knowledge economy is a supply of workers whose training adequately matches the world's shifting demand for certain skills. These "knowledge workers"—encompassing a country's entire labor pool and representing the gamut of professions and skills— possess a level of learning that allows for the rapid adoption and absorption of new technologies. As a result, education in a knowledge economy becomes an unending process that complements and reinforces previous formal academic studies or vocational training to form a cycle of lifelong learning (LLL).

The knowledge economy relies on labor with so-called conceptual skills, skills that go beyond rote memorization and concrete reasoning. Particularly needed is the ability to problem solve in teams and to be creative. Higher order skills related to logic and abstract reasoning are increasingly important as well. Mexico's labor

Figure 4.1 *Mexico's Education Performance*

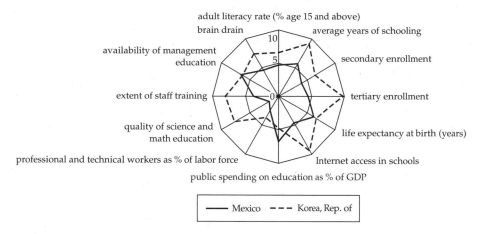

Mexico, Korea, Rep. of

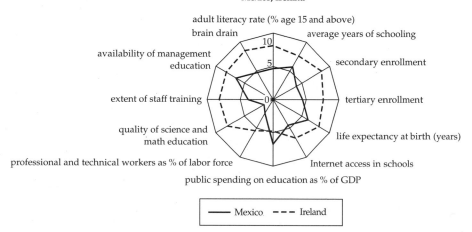

Mexico, Ireland

Source: World Bank, "Knowledge Assessment Methodology," http://www.worldbank.org/kam.
Note: Each of the 127 variables in the KAM is normalized on a scale of 0 to 10. The fuller the scorecard, the better poised a country is to embrace the knowledge economy. But an economy should not necessarily aim for a perfect score of 10 on all variables because the scorecards may be shaped by the particular structural characteristics of an economy or by trade-offs that characterize different development strategies.

force must possess a malleable knowledge base that allows workers to access new learning opportunities throughout their life span. Only then can the country expect to synchronize workers' skills with the rhythms of the global knowledge economy.

An advisable framework for lifelong learning deemphasizes formal education venues—whether in primary schools or tertiary institutions—and focuses on meeting the learners' needs from the cradle to the grave. There must be better integration of formal and informal learning channels and a more cohesive alignment of the different components of a national education system (see Box 4.1). To meet the lifelong learning challenge, Mexico must rethink its education strategy, not simply reform the current education system. The greatest obstacle faced by Mexico and many developing countries is learners' inability to move freely in and out of the

Figure 4.2 *Mexico and the World: Education*

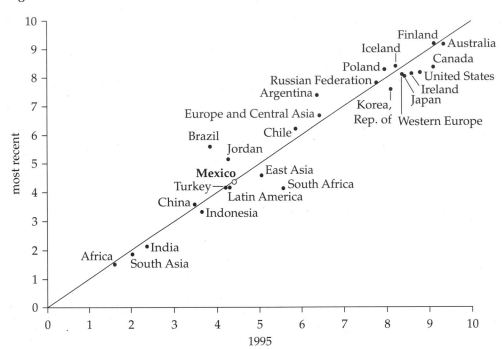

Source: World Bank, "Knowledge Assessment Methodology," http://www.worldbank.org/kam.
Note: The countries or regions plotted below the 45 degree line exhibited a decline in performance during the given time interval, while those plotted above the line showed improvement. There are two possible explanations for a decline: the country may actually have lost ground in absolute terms, or may have improved more slowly than its comparators.

education system at different points. Such movement would foster a more pro-active accumulation of knowledge and help workers meet social, economic, and cultural exigencies without sacrificing learning in the process.

If Mexico fails to devise an educational model that allows for lifelong learning through formal, informal, and nonformal formats, many workers may find themselves with obsolete training given the country's present pace of integration with the global knowledge economy. The case of the robust *maquiladora* manufacturing industry, currently the most dynamic sector in Mexico, illustrates the earnings gap that emerges when workers lack lifelong learning skills in an industry that is highly integrated with the global markets. Since the mid-1980s, the most qualified workers have been acquiring the bulk of average earning increases achieved through improved productivity at the expense of unskilled laborers (see Figure 4.3). For example, white-collar employees in *maquiladoras* (that is, the sector's equivalent to knowledge workers) have been constantly increasing their earnings share relative to blue-collar employees, up from three to one in 1988 to more than four to one in 2000.

Extrapolating this experience of workers within Mexico's *maquiladoras* to other sectors would suggest that as the country increasingly competes in the global knowledge economy, widening wage disparities will further marginalize labor without lifelong learning skills. However, the targeted expansion of Mexico's supply of knowledge workers will enable its economically active population to successfully

Box 4.1 *Structure of Mexico's Education System*

Preschool and Primary Levels
- *Pre-escolar*: Federal programs for children ages four and five. Roughly 15 percent of eligible children are not enrolled.
- *Primaria*: Includes all schools with grades one through six and at least one instructor per grade.
- *Multigrados*: One-room schools with one teacher for all primary grades. Multigrade schools can also have several teachers, but each teacher must teach more than one grade.

Middle School Grades (Grades 7–9)
- *Secundarias*: Schools that enroll nonrural students, many of whom are preparing to enter university upon graduation.
- *Tecnicas*: Vocational training institutes for students who plan to enter the workforce upon graduation.
- *Telesecundarias*: Rural schools that use televised curriculum to achieve distance learning.

High School (Grades 10–12)
- *Preparatorias and bachilleratos*: Upper secondary schools for youth who are going to college. Students must choose one of four academic tracks: physics-mathematics, chemistry-biology, economics-business administration, or the humanities.
- *Tecnnologicas and comercios*: Schools to prepare students for a particular vocational career.

Source: U.S. Department of Education (1999).

Figure 4.3 *Ratio of Yearly Remuneration, White-Collar to Blue-Collar Workers in Mexico's Maquiladora Manufacturing Industry, 1988–2000*

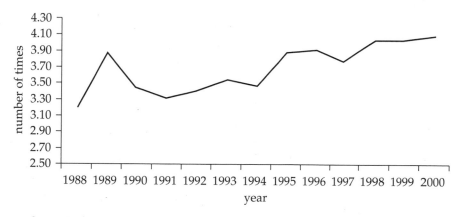

Source: Authors' own calculations based on INEGI (2001).

adopt, adapt, and build upon new technologies as they are developed, consequently upgrading their skills on a continual basis. As a result, the current skills-technology gap between North and South countries could even be narrowed through individuals and firms in the developing world moving from knowledge absorption to knowledge creation—an advancement promoted and furthered by having workers with skills for lifelong learning.

Recommendations for Improving Basic and Secondary Education

Although there is vast room for improvement on numerous indicators of educational quantity (such average years of schooling), Mexico's main priority is to improve educational quality and equity. Following are recommendations that would advance this goal:

- *Encourage continued education.* The continuous cycle of economic slowdowns over the past 30 years has pushed many young adults out of the education system and into the labor market to support their families.
- *Streamline the system of educational facilities and promotion practices.* A rigid organization of basic and secondary schools has not motivated students to advance in their studies
- *Provide accessible schools for small communities in a cost-effective manner.* Although 75 percent of Mexicans live in urban conglomerations, there is a significant dispersion of the population among rural areas. In fact, there are 199,396 towns and villages with fewer than 2,500 inhabitants (INEGI 2001a).
- *Target the needs of minority groups.* The delivery of educational services must be tailored to each of Mexico's multiple and distinct indigenous groups (roughly 14 percent of the population).
- *Promote the enrollment of females.* Local traditions have tended to devalue the education of women in Mexican communities despite the continued rise in the rate of participation by females in the labor force. By 1999 the rate of participation was 33 percent (World Bank 2004).

The suboptimal performance of the Mexican education system at the highest levels of learning will be an impediment for converting large sectors of the labor force into knowledge workers primed for lifelong learning. Instilling logic and reasoning skills among students—a task largely associated with education acquired at least through the secondary level—will be a determining factor in how well Mexico competes in the global knowledge economy.

The country's difficulties in delivering improved outputs to a greater share of Mexicans at the secondary and tertiary levels can be attributed to three principal sources: low attendance levels, high dropout rates, and a low supply of schools at the secondary and tertiary levels. As Table 4.2 illustrates, completion rates for students at higher levels of education decline geometrically, with only 31.5 percent of 18-year-old Mexicans graduating from secondary school; the average for OECD members is 54 percent. In the number of graduates finishing their secondary education, Argentina (40 percent), Brazil (57 percent), and Chile (35 percent) also surpass Mexico (OECD 2003b).

Table 4.2 Schooling Completion Rates in Mexico and Dropouts per Year, by Age Group

	Population size	*Graduates*	*Completion rate*	*Average dropouts per year*
12-year-olds	2,185,691	2,111,820	96.6%	n.a.
15-year-olds	2,090,034	1,327,965	63.5%	230,477
18-year-olds	2,088,225	658,800	31.5%	222,672

Source: Based on data from SEP (2002) and INEGI (2000).

Equity: Making Education Accessible for Everyone

The Mexican government has attempted to address these deficiencies in its education system by changing its approach. Instead of the traditional approach of simply building more schools, it has begun to support various strategies aimed at creating an educational environment that is accessible and equal for all Mexican students. Mexico has launched "Opportunities" (*Oportunidades*), a federally funded initiative to keep youth in the education system. The program, a reworking of the PROGRESA program founded in 1997 under President Ernesto Zedillo, provides cash incentives to low-income families that send their children to school. Each month a transfer payment is made to households from Mexico's lower socioeconomic strata, as long as their school-age children attend school and make periodic visits to community health centers. The program also has a gender component that specifically targets girls. Dropout rates are higher for girls than boys at the secondary level. The low completion rates for women in the secondary education cycle have resulted in higher illiteracy rates and lower average years of schooling for females than males in Mexico. The average length of schooling for Mexican female adults is 6.88 years compared to 7.59 years for males. There is similar inequality in illiteracy rates for women over 15 years of age (10.5 percent) when compared to men (6.5 percent) in Mexico (World Bank World Development Indicators 2005).

Oportunidades has boosted attendance rates among students in the regions where the educational incentive program has been implemented. In addition, the government's program of community-based schools and its network of distance learning centers in isolated rural areas have extended the education system's reach to the country's geographically dispersed population. Another important initiative is *Telesecundarias,* a federal program that provides lower secondary education to over one million Mexican students in scattered communities (including in the United States) through closed-circuit classes. Since the program was created in 1998, enrollment has grown 78 percent to nearly 150,000 students. This increase accounts for 46 percent of the growth in Mexico's overall enrollment figures for secondary education during the same period.

Despite these successful policy interventions, serious deficiencies in Mexico's education system remain. For example, the government's strategy of enlarging Mexico's enrollment must include a consideration of why students are not attending the schools that already exist in their communities. In Puebla, a city in central Mexico with about 1.7 million inhabitants, nearly 12,500 children between 6 and 14 years of age (6 percent of the eligible primary school population) are outside the system, although almost 100 percent of these children live near a school. At present no systematic efforts are being made—either at the federal or local level—to rectify this problem of underutilization of facilities by the communities they are meant to serve. The targeting of the school-age population could be a low-cost complement to the government's expansion of educational services into rural and low-income areas to increase learning opportunities for Mexican students.

Quality: Ways of Assessing Mexican Schools

The most important source of information regarding the quality of education in Mexico is the yearly exam taken by over six million basic education students whose teachers have applied for the *Carrera Magisterial,* a federally funded program that links promotion and salary increases to improved academic performance by their classes. The greatest value of this exam is in comparing the relative quality of education in Mexican schools. International evaluations—such as the OECD's Programme for International Student Assessment (PISA)—tend to be more adequate for comparative assessments of the quality of basic education in Mexico and other countries. Another test, the Trends in International Mathematics and Science Study (TIMSS), can be used for international comparisons of knowledge economy skills.

First administered in 2000 to OECD and nonmember nations, PISA aims to assess how well students have acquired the knowledge and skills required for full participation in society. Participating students are restricted to those finishing their country's compulsory education cycle, and testing is focused on mathematical and scientific literacy (OECD 2001a). As a result, the exam is considered a good benchmark for analyzing whether graduating students have acquired the skills associated with the global knowledge economy (in other words, whether graduating students have the scientific and mathematic acumen needed to analyze, reason, and communicate ideas).

On the whole, Latin American students have tended to perform poorly on such international tests, a trait evidenced by the performance of Mexican students on PISA 2000 (see Table 4.3). Mexico had scores significantly below comparative income countries such as Poland and Latvia. Poland's scores were 479 (reading), 470 (math), and 483 (science). Latvian students performed less well, scoring 458 (reading), 463 (math), and 460 (science). From Latin America, Argentina, Peru, and Chile also participated in PISA (some participated in 2000; others in PISA+, which is considered the same examination but is taken by many more countries). Among Latin American countries, Mexico is one of the best performers.[1] While Mexico's performance relative to other Latin American countries is encouraging, its performance compared to its NAFTA and OECD partners is cause for concern. Mexican students' weak showing on the math component may suggest that they lack the skills needed to compete in a knowledge economy.

When Mexico is compared to other OECD countries using socioeconomic and cultural indicators, Mexico fares poorly. Among Mexican students, 74 percent have mothers who achieved only a lower secondary education or less (the average among other OECD members is 32 percent). When data on Mexico are disaggregated by socioeconomic group, more acute educational inequalities become apparent. For instance, Mexico's score in PISA's reading literacy component improves from 422 to 459—while scores decline in other OECD countries—when compared to member students from a similar socioeconomic and cultural cohort. This result is determined using OECD country averages for test scores as well as for socioeconomic and cultural indicators for the 30-member group. This divergence in the quality of schooling among social classes poses another significant obstacle for preparing Mexico's labor force to participate in the global knowledge economy.

Equally daunting for Mexico to tackle is the regional variation in students' performance. The relative ranking among states for the last six applications of the *Car-*

---

[1] Among 41 countries, Mexico ranked 34th in reading, 35th in mathematics, and 34th in science. Among five Latin American countries, Mexico ranked first in reading (Mexico, Argentina, Chile, Brazil, and Peru), second in mathematics (Argentina, Mexico, Chile, Brazil, and Peru), and first in science (Mexico, Chile, Argentina, Brazil, and Peru).

Table 4.3 *Programme for International Student Assessment, 2000 Results for Selected OECD Countries*

	Reading	Math	Science
Mexico	422	387	422
OECD average	**500**	**500**	**500**
Highest	546 (Finland)	557 (Japan)	552 (Korea, Rep. of)
Lowest	396 (Brazil)	334 (Brazil)	375 (Brazil)

Source: OECD (2001a).

Note: A total of 32 countries were given the exam and ranked within subgroups based on the age-grade level of participating students.

rera Magisterial exam has changed little: Nuevo León, Tamaulipas, and Distrito Federal have been the steady "best performers," with results remaining above 102 points; Coahuila, Tlaxcala, and Colima have been the steady "worst performers," consistently scoring 98 points or lower. Scores are calculated using a median score of 100 and a standard deviation of 10. Exam results also show variations within regions and between types of schools. Urban schools on average score 4.5 points higher than schools in rural areas for the period studied. Qualitative differences between schools are also evident when analyzing states based on socioeconomic indicators. The results of the *Carrera Magisterial* suggest that with the correct allocation of existing government resources and with better delivery of educational services, Mexican public schools could provide the same high-quality learning experience for all of their students, regardless of district. It should be noted that "model" public schools (that is, the best performing) are working with basically the same infrastructure, salary levels, curriculum, textbooks, and training programs that are available for other schools. As a result, institutional practices within schools should be studied so that the day-to-day routines of successful facilities can be identified and their positive experiences disseminated to other schools.

This idea is behind two of Mexico's major initiatives in education—*Escuelas de Calidad* (literally "quality schools") and the *Consejo Nacional de Fomento Educativo* (CONAFE). The first initiative began in 2001 with 2,200 schools. This program supports the adoption of "best practices" by providing up to US$30,000 for schools in urban areas to implement self-designed programs. With the support of school authorities, students, teachers, and parents, the program is designed to improve the physical infrastructure of each school and its pedagogical equipment. The only hindrance for expanding this innovative scheme is the requirement that schools be in states that are willing to cofinance federal support, at a ratio of two to one.

CONAFE, the "National Council for the Promotion of Education," was established in 1971. It provides extra resources to schools that enroll disadvantaged students. CONAFE's compensatory education programs now support more than three million students in preprimary and primary education, and about one million students in *telesecundaria* education, or secondary education delivered via satellite television to remote schools.

Results of recent evaluation (Shapiro and Trevino 2004) show that CONAFE's compensatory programs are effective and well targeted. At the primary and secondary levels, CONAFE significantly improved students' exam performance and decreased inequality between CONAFE and non-CONAFE students. These results were robust even when controlling for relevant background variables. CONAFE appears to be more effective in math instruction at the primary level and in Spanish instruction at the *telesecundaria* level. Through its support of CONAFE's compensatory programs, the World Bank is achieving its goal of improving and expanding educational quality in Mexico.

In 2002 the government began another important initiative to improve the quality of public schools. It created an independent evaluation agency called the *Instituto Nacional de Evaluación Educativa* (INEE). A school's assessment is based on its curriculum, the level of internal and external efficiency, the long-term and positive effects of its learning methods, and equity issues. Through an agreement with state governments, all information is made public about primary, secondary, and upper secondary schools evaluated by INEE. The program, an initiative of President Fox, is aimed at allowing for a transparent review of the quality of the nation's education system, including current programs for community, indigenous, and adult education.

Recommendations for Improving Higher Education

Tertiary education in Mexico historically has been the domain of the middle and upper classes, creating and perpetuating equity asymmetries among the country's different social groups. Students study at public or private institutions, either universities, teachers' colleges, technological institutes, or technological universities. In terms of institutional preference, the majority of Mexican students (64 percent) can be found in government-funded schools that are overseen either by federal, state, or autonomous authorities (see Table 4.4).

Until recently in Mexico, the state was the sole supplier of higher education. This situation created an undersupply of education that is evident in the recent and rapid burst in demand for private universities and technological schools. While enrollment in the federal and state system increased by 32.7 percent between 1990 and 2000, private schools experienced a 165 percent surge in the number of attending students. This booming demand, coupled with lax government regulations, has prompted more private facilities to start operations. Out of the 1,062 new higher education schools created between 1989 and 1999, 74 percent were categorized as private.

As Mexico prepares its students to compete in the global knowledge economy, a set of key issues must be addressed in planning the future growth of higher education and ensuring equal access. The following are points to consider:

- The mismatch between coursework, skills, and labor market conditions.
- The geographic distribution of existing and future facilities.
- The static socioeconomic characteristics of entering students.

Table 4.4 *Higher Education in Mexico: Institutions, Students, and Teachers, 2000–2001*

Controlling entity	Institutions %	Schools %	Students %	Teaching staff %
Federal government	14.4	9.4	17.0	13.6
State government	13.3	6.2	5.6	4.4
Autonomous	3.6	34.8	46.1	45.9
Private	68.8	49.6	31.3	36.1
TOTAL	100.0	100.0	100.0	100.0

Source: Secretaria de Educación Publica (2001a).

- The quality of private higher education.
- Financing options for higher education.
- The ties between universities and industry.

Match Coursework to Labor Market Demands

All students, regardless of their course of study, must learn how to absorb and use knowledge. Rather than mandating specific career paths, the government should put mechanisms in place to ensure students entering a particular field have the skills demanded by a knowledge-economy labor market.

Mexican students, like many of their Latin American counterparts, have selected the humanities as a preferred course of study. Yet Mexico, like most Latin American countries, does *not* have a deficit of individuals enrolled in science and engineering programs in relation to the total number of tertiary students (de Ferranti et al. 2003). Despite its low per capita income, Mexico ranks near the mean for OECD members in the percentage of its graduates coming from engineering and basic science programs (see Figure 4.4). Only Turkey has a lower per capita income, based on purchasing power parity (PPP), than Mexico when considering figures for 1990. Even relative to its NAFTA country partners, Mexico exceeds the share of graduates receiving degrees in scientifically skilled professions in both Canada and the United States (20.4 and 15.8 percent, respectively). Moreover, based on income level, Mexico falls near the median for the number of scientists and engineers it has when compared to Australia, Canada, Norway, and the Republic of Korea, and when compared to other Latin American countries.

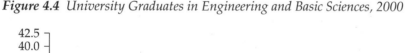

Figure 4.4 *University Graduates in Engineering and Basic Sciences, 2000*

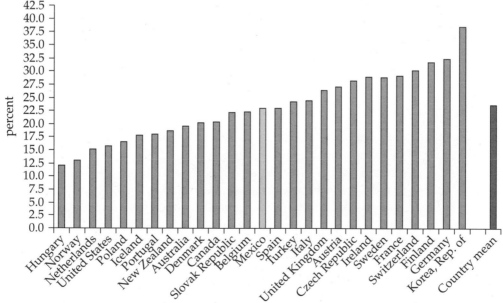

Source: OECD (2002a).

Note: The term "graduates" refers to students completing tertiary level studies in one of the following fields: engineering; manufacturing and construction; life sciences; physical sciences; mathematics and statistics; or computer sciences.

Rather than trying to generate more graduates from a particular field, tertiary education in Mexico should focus on instilling all students with higher order skills, such as problem-solving and reasoning that are prerequisites for successful participation in a knowledge economy. In the United States, heightened demand for laborers with this type of knowledge—regardless of their academic background—has been a product of the increased use of technology in the workplace. As a result, any graduate who is able to adopt and adapt new knowledge is valued rather than only those possessing specialized, "scientific" skills.

According to recent surveys in Thailand and Costa Rica, employers are less concerned with workers' concrete skills than with their general education level and ability to learn on the job. In Thailand 70 percent of employers in manufacturing industries and 100 percent from the services sector rated a worker's "ability to learn" as an important factor in his or her being hired. In Costa Rica, twice as many employers from the technology sector were likely to favor an employee with "learning speed" over one with "specific knowledge."

Not all fields of study in Mexico, however, may be transmitting such skills needed for lifelong learning and working in a knowledge economy. By their nature, Mexican universities tend to prepare ready-to-use professionals rather than multiskilled graduates. Moreover, schools' rigorous coursework and concrete skills-specific curriculum are directed at a population (18 to 24 years of age) that, in many cases, may not have the maturity or the information to make sensible career decisions based on labor market conditions. Upon completing the upper secondary level, graduating students must decide which type of Mexico's four tertiary schools they want to attend. The high degree of specialization of these programs prevents a student from being exposed to other options or freely moving to another course of study.

As a result, such an educational structure may not be the best way for Mexico's youth to develop the skills, knowledge, and attitudes associated with lifelong learning. Instead, one option could be to include a more general, liberal arts component in universities' educational programs for those students who are not certain which profession they want to enter. In this manner, students would be able to advance their learning while at the same time remaining eligible to enter a more career-oriented program within the university at a later time.

Balance the Geographic Distribution of Tertiary Schools

During the past decade, the Mexican government has improved the geographical distribution of university and tertiary schools. Today every state, even the sparsely populated ones, has at least one institution of higher education. As a result, opportunities for tertiary learning are no longer concentrated in the largest urban areas (Mexico City, Guadalajara, Monterrey, and Puebla); rather, they are more equitably distributed across the country. More balanced distribution is desirable because higher education is rooted in local communities, and strong tertiary schools tend to have a positive impact on local economies

However, the heightened profile that Mexico City exerts politically, economically, and culturally in the country has created obstacles for expanding higher education to other regions and to all students in Mexico. With 18 percent of the total population and 23 percent of the country's wealth, Mexico City serves as an attractive location for tertiary schools. As a result, one-third of all graduate school enrollments (32.3 percent) can be found in the capital's universities. Most of the country's higher level research also is conducted in this one city. Almost 50 percent of the more than 8,000 researchers registered with the National System of Researchers (*Sistema Nacional de Investigadores*, SNI) are in Mexico City; slightly more than 29 percent of these researchers are affiliated with the Universidad Nacional Autónoma de México (UNAM). A total of 45 percent of researchers in Mexico City are associated with one of the city's three principal research institutions—UNAM, *Universidad Autónoma Metropolitana* (UAM), and *Instituto Politécnico Nacional* (IPN).

To overcome the prominence that Mexico City plays in higher learning, educational policies should target state universities and efforts to make them stronger. One way to diffuse the spread of knowledge and balance the education provided to all students regardless of their home institution is the *Programa de Mejoramiento del Profesorado* (PROMEP), a government initiative for the professional improvement of teaching staff at public universities. By 2001, this program had granted 3,371 scholarships to full-time professors to attend Mexican universities (71 percent) and international universities (29 percent). As a result, more than 1,000 professors have already received a doctoral or master's degree. Moreover, this increased demand for graduate level courses has helped create 6,231 new full-time teaching positions at universities.

Diversify the Socioeconomic Profile of Students

Currently, Mexico enrolls too few tertiary level students to have a workforce ready to compete in the global knowledge economy. Like most developing countries, Mexico has an education system with spending skewed toward the tertiary level where students from higher income brackets excessively outnumber those from the lowest socioeconomic strata (see Figure 4.5). According to the United Nations Educational, Scientific, and Cultural Organization (UNESCO) and World Bank data for student expenditure as a share of per capita income, Mexico spent 45.2 percent of educational funding at the tertiary level, 13.8 percent at the secondary level, and 11.8 percent at the primary level.

Figure 4.5 *School Enrollment, by Age and Income Group*

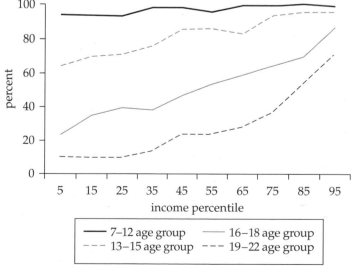

Source: INEGI (2000).

Such regressive spending patterns have led to a de facto educational subsidy for Mexican university students from already economically mobile backgrounds. Among OECD countries, Mexico and the Slovak Republic devote the most to higher levels of education. While the average member spends 2.2 times more per student at the tertiary level than at the primary level, Mexico and the Slovak Republic respectively spend 3.6 and 3.8 times more. As a result of these distributional inequalities, the Mexican government should search for policy interventions that encourage the enrollment of low-income students at the tertiary level. One option is to decrease the opportunity cost associated with higher levels of learning for such students given the trade-off many must make between work and school.

Unlike most OECD countries, the majority of Mexico's public universities do not accredit part-time enrollment programs for college students. This characteristic is in contrast to the increasing number of tertiary institutions abroad that offer part-time course options (evening, weekend, and summer) to encourage working adults to continue their education. In the case of Finland, more individuals are enrolled in nontraditional, continuing education programs at the tertiary level than students who are completing full-time, university coursework. An increased supply of continuing education programs in Mexico would go far toward encouraging more people to enroll and remain in the country's higher education system by decreasing the opportunity cost of learning.

Improve the Quality of Private Higher Education

The country's largely unregulated network of private universities accounts for an important share of Mexico's matriculation growth at the tertiary level. Such facilities have been increasing steadily in number since the 1990s as deregulation encouraged privately run schools to step in and fill the unmet demand for higher education in Mexico. Small in size and offering a relatively low-cost structure, these new institutions have been a welcome innovation, making tertiary level learning more accessible to more Mexicans. However, there are concerns about the rigor and quality of the courses at private universities; few official mechanisms exist to assess them. States should seek out policies that promote private sector participation while permitting government oversight of private schools' efforts to prepare their students for lifelong learning.

Currently, Secretaria de Educación Publica (SEP) is the only agency that confers official recognition on higher education programs by evaluating whether the institution has adequate facilities and faculty (based on size and credentials) and is meeting minimum course-load requirements and sequencing. However, the SEP does not consider the quality of educational outcomes (such as test scores and completion rates). There is also some evidence that small private universities are misleading the SEP to gain accreditation based on inputs rather than outputs. Despite the lax criteria for accreditation, most private universities have not even gone through the process of government review. Only 90 out of approximately 1,200 private higher education institutions in Mexico have been accredited to date. With the rapid rise of private universities in the country, the need for quality control is increasingly acute.

The significant costs—both direct costs (public and private) and indirect costs (personal income forgone)—associated with pursuing higher education require that

---

Box 4.2 *Higher Education and Quality Control Mechanisms in Chile and Brazil*

Two emerging mechanisms for controlling the quality of higher education are government accreditation programs and the required submission of transparent information about the learning outcomes of private school graduates.

Chile has created a successful accreditation system to regulate its heterogeneous offering of private tertiary facilities. While accreditation is voluntary, more than 35 private universities and 106 programs have been or are currently being reviewed. The positive response to the government's policy may be because the evaluation procedure is transparent, nonbureaucratic, and voluntary. Brazil has created a university exit exam; graduates from more than a dozen degree programs must take this exam, regardless of whether they attended private or public schools. This national exam, also called the *Provão*, has grown in reach and respect since it was first made mandatory in 1996. Test results for each institution are made public as a way for incoming students to evaluate a university's educational services, learning environment, and reputation.

Source: World Bank staff.

---

there be industrywide standards and mechanisms for quality control (see Box 4.2). Attempts to improve the monitoring of educational inputs and outputs at private schools in Mexico have been mixed at best. Apart from the SEP's accreditation of private universities, the Federation of Private Higher Education Institutions (FIMPES) does have in place a voluntary quality control procedure for education providers. Yet neither the SEP nor ANUIES (the National Association of Public Higher Education Institutions) has developed a similar accreditation system for a school's faculty and staff.

Expand Financing Options for Higher Education

The expansion of higher education in Mexico has been hampered by the four obstacles described above: the mismatch between coursework, skills, and labor market conditions; imbalance in the geographic distribution of educational facilities; the static socioeconomic characteristics of entering students; and shortcomings in private higher education. Another obstacle is the inability of many students from middle- and low-income households to afford the upfront costs now associated with enrolling at the tertiary level.

The government alone is unable to bear the burden of funding the higher education of more students given the magnitude of resources needed to make tertiary learning accessible to everyone. Already the Mexican state is dedicating nearly 23 percent of all government spending to education, with over one-fifth of this funding earmarked solely for universities.[2] More government expenditures are not the solution to the financing short-fall from increasing university enrollments. Instead we recommend creative partnerships with the private sector to address this problem. Examples from other countries have shown that private funding of student loans for tuition fees and housing costs can lower the economic barriers to expanding higher education. In Chile the government is using various schemes including

---

[2] For more indicators, see http://www1.worldbank.org/education/edstats/.

income-contingent loans (state and bank funded) to give the financial means to students that otherwise would not be able to study at a university. One type of loan is called university credit, an income-contingent loan that is paid back and calculated at a fixed payment or 5 percent of income, whichever is lower. A real interest rate of 2 percent begins accruing as soon as the loan is disbursed. The Corfo credit is a loan made by banks at up to a 9 percent real interest rate for a maximum of 15 years.

Such cost-sharing programs promote efficiency in financing advanced vocational programs and tertiary level studies in developing countries, although they require additional policy interventions to ensure that they do not inhibit low-income students from studying. Dividing the cost burden of higher education between the student, the state, and the private sector creates an efficient and equitable funding scheme because all learners are made at least partially responsible for the cost of their own studies. It is thought that by making marginal cost payments toward their education, students make better learning choices and become more dedicated to completing their studies. In theory, cost-sharing programs also promote equity because those who benefit from an education are the ones directly paying for it. Four financial instruments for implementing cost-sharing schemes are *traditional student loans, human capital contracts* (graduates agree to pay a percentage of their income for a specified amount of time), *the graduate tax* (a set tax applied to income following graduation), and *income-contingent loans* (graduated loan payments based on salary level).

Unfortunately, private financial intermediaries play a very limited role in providing students with funds in Mexico. Costs are shared mainly through a combination of government outlays and self-funding. The government has created a fairly successful student loan program called the *Sociedad de Fomento a la Educación Superior* (SOFES). Funding for SOFES is a tripartite arrangement of the federal government, universities, and the World Bank. The loan program was originally created through FIMPES, the umbrella group that represents private universities in Mexico. Founded in 1998, SOFES now works with 40 universities across the country to provide unsubsidized loans each year to 10,000 Mexican students that are financially unable to continue their higher education. Participating universities act as the conduit for SOFES funds and are responsible for administering the loans. Nonperforming loans cannot exceed more than 10 percent of any university's portfolio; if they do, schools must pay SOFES the difference or leave the program. Some states have launched their own loan programs to help local low-income students continue their education. For example, the *Instituto de Crédito Educativo del Estado de Sonora* has supported needy students in the northwestern state of Sonora since 1981 by relying on the local government's participation for funding.

However, the obvious limitations of such public loan initiatives mean that a larger role of private financial intermediaries in Mexico is needed to give more students financial access to higher education. First, the demand for student borrowing naturally has exceeded the available supply of government spending. Second, international examples from developing countries show that when the public sector has become exceedingly involved in supplying loans, low cost recovery becomes chronic due to student defaults and the government's subsidization of below-market interest rates. Unfortunately, asymmetrical information between the lender and borrower, the lack of collateral, and a still nascent and stable financial system have prevented until now the entrance of private commercial banks into Mexico's student loan business.

Improve Linkages between Universities and Industry

Closer ties between companies and universities could ensure a better match between what students are being taught and what the labor market needs from its workers. There can be improved synergies in tailoring university curricula to needed skills by involving leading firms in course selection and school decision making. In Mexico's system of technical universities (*universidades tecnológicas*), local companies have become actively involved in designing specific programs and in providing apprenticeship-like positions for students. This partnership could be a model for other private sector–school partnerships. Since 1994, technical universities have been growing steadily in number. By 2003, 53 technical universities were in operation. They provide two-year technical programs (the degree is called Técnico Superior Universitario, TSU), and their educational model has been emulated by other tertiary education providers, including private facilities like the Universidad Tecnológica de Celaya and the Universidad Interamericana del Desarrollo.

Government guidelines can go far to foster such linkages. Having teachers and researchers leave the ivory tower and get in touch with industry's everyday realities are a valuable means for encouraging lifelong learning by both professors and their students. Studies have shown that such symbiotic partnerships help to bring fresh, relevant curricula into the classroom. Moreover, the fomenting of ties between universities and the business community is a way to keep schools involved in, and caring about, local affairs. To build these bonds, many publicly funded universities may need to review their current charters and regulations. School administrators and faculty need the right incentives to create the channels for an exchange of ideas and knowledge.

Policies That Foster Lifelong Learning

Promoting policies that allow tertiary schools to better serve their students and expand their academic offering is part of rethinking how a country's education system can best prepare its citizens for lifelong learning. An LLL framework provides individuals throughout their lives—from early childhood to retirement—with a spectrum of formal and informal learning opportunities. The approach is based on the centrality of the learner and involves collective exchanges between the firm, the economy, and society at large. Formal schooling lays the groundwork for a lifetime of learning. The model in this way prepares workers with the skills they need to meet the rapidly changing demands of the global knowledge economy.

Learning institutions and programs in Mexico, to promote lifelong learning, must:

- Shift their emphasis from teaching vocation-specific skills to giving students better-developed capabilities for learning new skills. Vocational education should be increasingly postponed to higher levels of education (for example, from secondary to upper-secondary schools) in countries where such enrollments are high.
- Revise school curricula to teach higher-order cognitive skills that aid learning, problem solving, and analysis, rather than focusing on rote memorization, simple literacy, and specific facts or equations.
- Adopt assessment mechanisms (for example, a school accreditation program, exit exams, and quality assurance systems) to ensure that students make a smooth transition from formal education to the workplace, and vice versa.

Promoting Training for Work

As international experience shows, training is critical for workers if they want to be able to continually compete in the global knowledge economy and not find themselves one day with obsolete skills. Given the education levels of the current supply of labor in Mexico, workers will require scaled-up training at various points throughout their economically productive lives to keep pace with labor market changes. Many countries, both industrial and developing, already have designed new policies to foster in-service training among companies including payroll-levy training funds, tax incentives for employer-sponsored training, and state-funded individual learning accounts (ILAs) for employees seeking additional skills.

Fortunately, Mexico has some of the infrastructure and training networks in place to promote the expansion of on-the-job training. By the 1990s, many Mexican firms were already providing external training—through private companies, industry associations, and government training centers—to their workers. One study showed that the average years of schooling for a Mexican worker in the 1990s raised the likelihood that the worker would receive on-the-job training (Acevedo and Tan 2002). This lends empirical support to the theory that increased education and training are complementary and correlated factors for a cycle of lifelong learning.

In other countries, governments have been able to increase employee-targeted training policies by using the following incentives aimed at the private sector:

- *Levy-grant schemes.* Government administrators use earmarked levies to provide grants to employers for state-approved training programs (as in Singapore and previously in the United Kingdom).
- *Levy-rebate schemes.* Employers are partially reimbursed for approved employee training programs by drawing against their payroll levies (as in Malaysia, Nigeria, and the Netherlands).
- *Levy-exemption schemes.* Employers are made exempt from tax payments if they spend a given percentage of their payroll on training (as in France, the Republic of Korea, and Morocco).
- *Tax incentives.* Tax incentives are given to approved employer training programs that are financed with general government revenues (as in Chile and previously in Malaysia).
- *Entitlement schemes.* Employees are entitled over their lifetime to government funds (usually vouchers or loans) for additional training to be spent as they determine (as in Austria, Kenya, Paraguay, and the United Kingdom).
- *Individual learning accounts.* Individual learning accounts provide individuals with discretionary training funds partially financed by the state, employers, and employees (as in the Netherlands, Spain, and previously in the United Kingdom).

These schemes have been used with success in both industrial and developing countries. For example, Brazil has a system of national training organizations that receive their funding from the general payroll taxes paid by companies. The transfer is equivalent to roughly 2.9 percent of a company's wage bill. In turn, these organizations run training centers that offer specialized courses and sponsor apprentice programs with participating firms using a cost-sharing structure. Since 1970, France has required enterprises with more than 10 employees to earmark 1.5 percent of their payroll and reinvest it in on-the-job training—either by offering internal programs or by contracting out to third-party organizations. The program is considered extremely responsive to the changing needs of the labor market because employers can choose the employees and type of training to be undertaken.

Apart from these incentive programs, some countries use grant-matching schemes to increase the level of training of their workers. Programs in Chile and Mauritius rely on the private sector to administer such initiatives and have reaped positive results. In Mexico, government policies to increase company investments in employee training have been correlated with a reduction in enterprise failures. As a result, grant-matching programs have supported the development of a training culture in Mexico by providing an incentive and a means for enterprises to invest in employee training. A similar phenomenon has been noted in Asia. For example, most Japanese company managers, as part of their responsibilities, must teach training seminars and regularly engage workers in informal training. In the Republic of Korea, the Basic Law for Vocational Training has promoted a strong culture of in-company training. Northern European countries (for example, Germany, the Netherlands, and Scandinavia) as well as countries in Latin America (for example, Brazil and Chile) have also established training programs that rely on private sector participation.

A grant-matching scheme alone will not necessarily lead to an expansion of the market for employee training services. One impediment arises when grants are restricted to state-run training institutions because the private sector will lack the incentives to provide similar services or augment existing services. Particularly important is the way funding for training programs is spent. Funds should support activities that strengthen and diversify the supply of training to stimulate market demand for these services. The Mexican government has managed to promote these goals with its Integral Quality and Modernization Program (*Programa Calidad Integral y Modernización*, CIMO). To improve the productivity of employees at small enterprises, the program hires private training consultants. Funding of the program is split between government and private training institutions (see Box 4.3).

Because of the nature of vocational education in Mexico and other Latin American countries, training programs outside the workplace have been uncommon. Students enter vocational institutes at an early age (secondary school) and begin a course of study that emphasizes specific job skills rather than skills that will develop the faculties for higher order learning. As a result, tertiary level learning and specific skills training rarely have been combined outside the workplace and are still treated as mutually exclusive forces in secondary education. This disconnect partially explains the inadequacy of training in Mexico. Only one-tenth of the economically active population in Mexico receives any kind of regular training. Unless a major shift in education policy occurs, laborers cannot expect to keep up with technological advances and will not be able to succeed against stiff international competition. While basic education marks an important starting point for worker training, the skills and knowledge of Mexico's labor force must move beyond this level if lifelong learning is to occur. Moreover, as examples from Sub-Saharan Africa show, even the learning of basic skills is impeded when the workforce targeted for such training is not literate or lacks a primary school education (Oxenham 2002).

Combating Illiteracy

As it attempts to teach its citizens lifelong learning skills, Mexico must resolve one key issue: the great number illiterate and uneducated adults, or its *rezago educativo*. More than 36 million Mexicans over the age of 15 are illiterate, have dropped out of

---

Box 4.3 *Mexico's Proactive Approach to Supporting Small- and Medium-Size Enterprises*

The Integral Quality and Modernization Program (*Programa Calidad Integral y Modernización*), or CIMO, has proven effective in reaching small and medium-size enterprises (SMEs) in Mexico since it was established in 1988. Under the direction of the secretary of labor, the program helps SMEs upgrade workers' skills, improve the quality of production, and raise overall productivity. The program was set up initially as a pilot project to provide subsidized training to small and medium-size enterprises but quickly expanded in focus when it became apparent that the lack of training was only one of many factors contributing to low productivity. By 2000, CIMO was providing an integrated package of training and industrial extension services to over 80,000 SMEs annually and involving 200,000 employees from different sectors and companies. Since then, private sector interest has grown in the program and now more than 300 business associations participate in CIMO, up from 72 in 1988.

All states and the Federal District have at least one CIMO unit that is staffed by three to four administrators. Most units are housed in the offices of local business associations. This structure promotes fruitful synergies between companies' needs and participating CIMO firms. Staff members organize workshops on training and technical assistance services, identify potential training consultants at the local and regional levels, and actively seek out SMEs for collaborative endeavors. CIMOs work with interested small and medium-size enterprises through a cost-sharing program that provides training assistance and an initial diagnostic evaluation of the participating firm. Currently, CIMO is expanding its support in two directions. First it is assisting groups of SMEs with specific sectoral needs. Second, it is providing an integrated package of services including information on new technologies, production processes, internationally accepted quality control techniques, and marketing strategies.

Evaluation studies in 1995 and 1997 found CIMOs to be a cost-effective method for assisting small and medium-size enterprises. Over a period of three years, the studies tracked two groups of SMEs: one with firms that participated in CIMO in 1991 or 1992, and another with a broadly comparable control group of enterprises that had not participated. CIMO firms tended to have lower performance indicators than nonparticipating firms, but, by 1993, labor productivity had either caught up or exceeded that of the control group. Other performance indicators showed similar improvements. For example, a company's participation in the program increased its profitability, sales, capacity utilization rates, and wage and employment growth; participation reduced the firm's labor turnover, absenteeism, and product rejection rates.

Source: World Bank staff.

---

primary school, or have not completed their secondary education. Of the total adults that fall into the rezago educativo in Mexico, roughly 6.6 million are illiterate, 11 million are literate but have not completed primary school, and another 18 million have not finished their secondary education. Despite Mexico's deepened integration with NAFTA and the global economy during the 1990s, the number of out-of-school adults actually rose, calling into question the ability of the country's economic advances to overcome chronic failings of the education system. With more than 55 percent of Mexicans over the age of 15 falling within the rezago, aggressive policy strategies must be directed at encouraging enrollment in continuing education programs and in skills training programs for adult students who are balancing work and study.

The persistence of the rezago is a reminder that educational reform has yet to fully benefit large swaths of the lowest income quintiles and most marginalized segments of the population. The majority of Mexico's illiterate and poorly educated adults can be found in the states of Chiapas, Oaxaca, Guerrero, Hidalgo, Veracruz, Puebla, and Michoacan. Children in these states leave school out of economic necessity to support their families. In rural areas, most adults classified within the rezago are from economically poor indigenous communities that rarely have benefited from improvements in the education system and continue to face a future of extreme poverty. Most of this subgroup is over 45 years of age and female, creating overlapping problems of gender, age, and ethnicity biases that corrective education policies must address. In urban centers, the socioeconomic profile is slightly different. Adults are literate but have not completed their secondary education. They range between the ages of 15 and 45 and surprisingly maintain jobs in the formal economy.

Reducing the number of adults that find themselves among this rezago will be critical if Mexico aspires to effectively compete in the global knowledge economy. Policy interventions will have to be targeted at dealing with the rezago by focusing upon Mexican workers who are literate but have not yet completed their secondary education. Nevertheless, the financial feasibility of increasing resources dedicated to addressing this problem is doubtful. In spite of the increasing number of Mexicans falling into the rezago, government spending shrunk during the past decade, declining 3.2 percent annually in real terms as a share of total public education expenditure.

Given this budgetary reality, innovative methods will be needed to combat the country's out-of-school population without raising government spending. For example, if the number of yearly certificates granted by the National Institute for Adult Education (*Instituto Nacional para la Educación de los Adultos*) was doubled, the rezago population would arrest its increase. The program, administered by SEP, provides Mexicans over the age of 15 with the chance to learn basic literacy skills and to finish their education (primary or secondary). It also has a component for indigenous students, who are between the ages of 10 and 14 and have left school, to continue their education in their native tongue. The government is currently piloting a promising initiative called Community Plazas (*Plaza Comunitarias),* or PCs. Administered through the National Commission for Lifelong Learning and Training (CONEVYT), the program uses a competency-based curriculum, multimedia equipment (educational satellites, video, and Internet), didactic materials, and tutors to help adults who want to learn how to read and write or would like to complete their education to the primary and secondary levels. President Fox set the ambitious target of establishing 20,000 PCs from the current 600 by the time he left office in December 2006.

Mexico's Policy Agenda in Education

The key for Mexico's education system lies in assisting policy innovations at the local level to expand their reach for a nationwide reform. President Fox and his predecessors have attained quantitative and qualitative advances that can provide the base for building an equitable education system that gives all students the lifelong learning skills essential to compete in the global knowledge economy. But further reforms will require all stakeholders—teacher unions, university faculty, students, and leaders in the private sector—to participate in locally driven strategies to best leverage expenditures for the delivery of quality and accessible educational services in Mexico. In this sense, reforming Mexico's education system is less about increasing government spending than about changing institutional practices.

Given the level of current educational expenditures, Mexico should be achieving better results for its students in both qualitative and quantitative terms. As a share of its gross domestic product, Mexico spends nearly as much on education (4.42 percent) as Australia (4.49 percent), Germany (4.64 percent), Italy (4.55 percent), and the United Kingdom (4.47 percent), but these OECD countries produce students with more average years of schooling, higher literacy, and lower rates of repetition.[3] More strikingly, Mexico dedicates a larger share of national income to educational expenditures than the Republic of Korea (3.75 percent), a country with a highly educated labor force considered able to compete in the global knowledge economy.

Based on principles of lifelong learning, a reformed education system would incorporate successful new approaches and pilots in pedagogy into an integrated system of lifelong learning at the national level. It would also tap private sources to finance the expansion and improvement of educational opportunities. By providing multiple pathways to learning, Mexico will enable its people to learn continuously through life. Its subsystem of tertiary education would have multiple qualified service providers and sources of financing. In the medium term, actions should focus on three major areas: increasing coverage and quality in basic and secondary education; expanding access to higher education; and accelerating the transition to lifelong learning.

Basic and Secondary Education

A minimum standard of achievement in basic and secondary schools must be ensured and access to upper secondary and vocational education expanded. Through promising programs such as the *Escuelas de Calidad* program, Mexico can improve the years in school and skills of its labor force. Strengthening incentives to expand enterprise training and to enrich adult education, particularly at the secondary level, will reduce the undereducated adult population.

The government, schools, and communities should work together to make sure that students have proper facilities (for example, science and computer labs, Internet access, libraries) and good instructional materials. If a rich learning environment is to be constructed for all students in Mexico's primary and secondary schools, teachers must be given reward incentives to improve their teaching methods, their punctuality, and their absentee rates. The quality of the country's education system and access to it also can be improved by instituting:

- School-based and locally devised techniques to assist students at risk, trim dropout rates, and ensure a more fruitful relationship between students and teachers;
- Incentives that can increase the quality of teaching and learning at schools such as linking funding with educational outputs and offering parents vouchers to send their children to the local school they choose;
- Evaluations to assess the quality of learning and use of the results to assist communities, schools, and policy makers in decisions on education;

---

[3] Numbers are calculated according to expenditure levels in 1999, see http://www1.worldbank.org/education/edstats/.

- Adult education programs to diminish the weight on Mexico and the economy from its rezago population by expanding and enriching learning opportunities with content and skills relevant for the knowledge economy.

Higher Education

To expand access to higher education, a dramatic change is required in how the government finances its universities, given the high per student spending at this level and the regressive and distributional effects that this policy has had on the entire education system. Students who can afford to pay higher tuition fees should do so, thus enabling schools to increase their support for those coming from lower socioeconomic levels. Wider and more equal access to higher education in Mexico also could be promoted through the creation of a state-supported market for student loans. Rather than being the sole lender, the government could implement a cost-sharing scheme that provides loan guarantees for students and their families who are unable to borrow under normal market conditions.

As a result, the following actions to reform Mexico's tertiary institutions are recommended:

- Rely much more on private financing of higher education. Scholarship programs, such as the *Programa Nacional de Becas para la Educación Superior* (PRONABES), will never resolve the problem if more attention is not devoted to the creation of a local market for student loans. Income-contingent loan schemes should be emphasized as a way of financing of higher education.
- Strengthen university-industry collaboration. University-industry linkages through competitive funds can ensure that students have a more productive entry into the job market and give universities access to new sources of financing by providing a channel to sell their services and knowledge (that is, administrative and research capabilities) to the private sector.
- Introduce flexible and part-time higher education programs that encourage students to leave or reenter the system as needed. University laws should allow students who have left the system to reinitiate their studies without costly make-up sessions.
- Evaluate and scale up initiatives at the state and national levels that grant greater autonomy to tertiary schools in managerial, financial, and pedagogical matters. Without this change, university structures will not be sufficiently responsive to the ever-evolving needs of industry and the economy.

Lifelong Learning

To accelerate Mexico's transition to lifelong learning, distance education models and pedagogy pilots at the local level should be diversified. Many promising initiatives in this area must be evaluated in order to scale up and spread local innovations. As a next step, we recommend bringing key stakeholders together to design the architecture of an integrated system of lifelong learning. Standards must be developed concerning certification, accreditation, testing, and evaluation, as well as recognition of prior learning.

First, there needs to be standardized mechanisms that accredit prior learning and vocational qualifications that can be applied toward an adult student's educational advancement. Second, vocational counseling and information on career paths and earning streams must be put in place to reduce the opportunity cost and perceived barriers of adult students wanting to advance their learning later in life. In Mexico, CONEVYT can facilitate this process by certifying the quality of different public and private providers and offering funding resources for returning students. Other specific changes should include:

- An overhaul of the curriculum and institutional models that are used in adult education. The design of learning systems must capture the demands of the labor market and students for targeted and relevant educational services.
- Creation of a transparent system that can retrain workers for reentry into a changing marketplace. Various government agencies, the private sector, and workers must come together to design a retraining and certification system that accredits workers based on their skills and competencies.
- Introduction of clear regulations and accreditation procedures for long distance learning programs. To lend value to such services in rural communities, the government must create regulations that accurately evaluate the educational outputs of new learning initiatives involving information and communication technology (ICT).
- Creation of a coherent and nationwide quality assurance system in Mexico. This feedback mechanism will serve as the conduit for providing adequate and timely information to firms, workers, and governments about the quality of educational services and outputs. Such a system is essential if the country hopes to tailor the learning skills of its population to the demands of the global knowledge economy.

Undertaking Reform of Mexico's Education System

Going forward, Mexico's second generation of educational reforms must reallocate current spending to make it more demand driven and results oriented to ensure students gain the skills required for lifelong learning. Yet a reform strategy that promotes a shift in institutional practices inevitably encounters barriers. Mexico's education system, like any bureaucratic structure, has tended to be resistant to dramatic change. This resistance to reform at the national level suggests that it is more advantageous to incorporate stakeholders in bottom-up, incremental policy interventions. By working along the margins of reform with key players, it is possible to sideline vested interests and make them a part of the solution rather than the source of the problem.

International experience shows that the best cases of educational reform have been largely a local affair scaled up to the national level. The school, rather than a government's education ministry or municipal secretariat, has been the center of change and the forum for stakeholders' dialogue. To improve the quality of learning programs, schools must assume a more active role in fomenting bottom-up change and garnering support for their strategies at all political levels. A country's education ministry must avoid the pitfall of blocking reforms and learn how to empower local schools to identify their needs and solidify solutions for them.

Such a decentralized structure of reform cannot be based on a preconceived blueprint. It is a learning process. Competent supervision and monitoring at the national level are needed to foster changes by local schools and their staff. The key for success is to focus on classroom and school dynamics; teachers and students alike must be viewed as learners and community members as strategic partners. As the passage of tuition fees at the University of Sonora showed, parent and community participation can improve outcomes and lead to a commitment to policy reforms long after a political administration leaves power. This civil society involvement is particularly essential in rural areas, given the relatively high opportunity cost associated with a household's schooling of its children. In practice, effective participation means assigning a real and lasting role for parents in education decision making at the local level. It is essential that education inputs meet community interests.

Committed champions in Mexico have initiated local changes by building coalitions with key stakeholders. One example is the decision to impose tuition fees during the 1990s at Mexico's historically free universities. This decision produced uniquely different results based on how the measure was executed at the local level (see Box 4.4). In this sense, the central issue is how to scale up successful local outcomes so they can be replicated at the national level.

Box 4.4 *Achieving Change at the Margin: Charging Tuition Fees at Mexican Universities*

Until the country's educational reforms in the 1990s, the Mexican Constitution provided for free public education at all levels. State-run universities and tertiary institutions were known as bastions of heavy government support, despite the distorted share of funding dedicated to Mexican students at this level compared to funding of students in primary and secondary schools. A large share of university students came from high-income backgrounds; they entered Mexico's low-cost, high-quality public universities after graduating from private secondary schools.

Nevertheless, university students fiercely resisted any form of cost sharing. When the National Autonomous University of Mexico (UNAM) tried to impose a tuition hike in 1999, many of its 270,000 students boycotted classes. The walkout was supported by the faculty. Classes at Mexico's largest university were suspended for nearly a year in response to the rector's call for a US$100 increase in fees from the $8 students were paying annually to study.

The University of Sonora in northern Mexico, however, had a strikingly different experience. It succeeded in passing tuition fees because of the skillful way the administration carried out the policy change. The university introduced a new cost-sharing scheme in 1993 by explaining to staff and students that without supplementary resources the school's reputation for quality teaching and learning would be endangered. Instead of arbitrarily imposing the fees, the school's rector slowly built consensus and heard the community's concerns. After initial resistance, including a widely publicized 2,000-kilometer march by protesters from Hermosillo to Mexico City, students accepted the administration's decision as a way to give the school an injection of fresh funds. The university set up a participatory process to determine how these resources would be allocated and promised that new spending would be directed at initiatives to improve equity and quality at the school. Since 1994, every student has been paying about US$300 in fees to support such programming. A joint student-faculty committee administers the funds, which are used to provide scholarships for low-income students, refurbish classrooms, modernize computer labs, and purchase textbooks and journals. All spending decisions are extremely transparent and posted at the beginning of the academic year so students know exactly how their fees were spent.

Source: World Bank (2002a).

Bottom-up pressures are also important forces for reform, particularly in reforming the dominant position of the national teachers' union in Mexico, the *Sindicato Nacional de Trabajadores de la Educación* (SNTE). A key player in Mexico's education system, the SNTE has almost 1.5 million members and is the largest trade union in Latin America. Since 1992 the SNTE has bilaterally negotiated national issues with the federal government and local matters with each state government. During this period there have been instances of successful collaboration when improving the education system was the common goal for both state authorities and union leaders. As long as the dialogue between the government and SNTE has remained respectful, educational problems usually have been resolved and qualitative reforms reaped locally.

While these local initiatives are an important starting point, they must be supported at the national level. As Mexico evaluates its competitive edge and readiness to enter the global knowledge economy, the retooling of its education system through incremental changes will increasingly become the means to achieving more structural, substantive, and still delayed educational reforms. As Figure 4.6 indicates, the three most important forces of change are market pressures, government regulations and incentives, and partnerships between the public and private sectors to resolve particular problems on a case-by-case basis. Along the margin where all these forces overlap, institutional autonomy is produced and supported by the improved practices, funding, and information that underlie the education system.

Figure 4.6 *Forces for Change in Reforming Education*

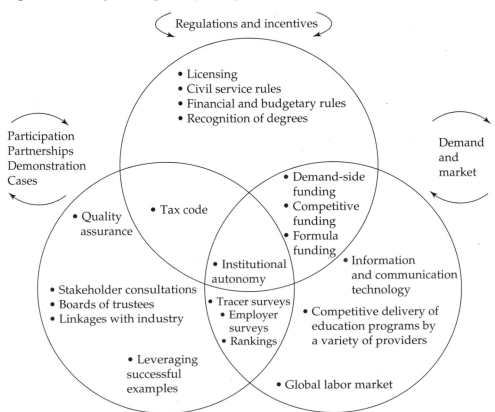

Source: Adapted from the World Bank (2002a).

5

Updating the ICT Infrastructure in Mexico

Mexico's information and communications technologies (ICT) sector has grown substantially during the past decade. The telecommunications component of the sector has grown at a rate that is four times faster than the economy as a whole. In 2004, the GDP indicator for the telecommunications sector grew 22.6 percent, compared to a national GDP growth rate of 4.4 percent. This growth rate can be attributed to a variety of factors, including an ambitious e-development program. Launched by President Vicente Fox on his inauguration day, e-Mexico has won numerous international awards for e-government initiatives. Despite the achievements of e-Mexico and associated programs, many important challenges remain—most notably the unfinished agenda of establishing a better regulatory framework and more effective and up-to-date institutions to address interconnection, pricing, universal access, and the dominance of the telecommunications market by TELMEX. Despite these challenges, a second wave of ICT investors is beginning to make tentative forays into Mexico's ICT sector, attracted by the large unmet domestic demand, strong linkages to the U.S. market, and the opportunity to purchase discounted assets of the financially troubled ICT companies that first challenged TELMEX during the late 1990s.

According to the World Economic Forum, Mexico ranked 44th out of 102 countries in the 2003–2004 Network Readiness Index (NRI), as can be seen in Figure 5.1.[1] This index is a widely recognized measure of a country's performance with regard to ICT readiness and usage. Among Latin American countries, Mexico is ranked third from the top, after Brazil (30th) and Chile (32nd). The NRI is a composite index comprised of several subindices. Mexico's low rankings on the Market Environment Subindex[2] and the Political and Regulatory Subindex[3] highlight the progress the country still needs to make in using ICT to transform itself into a knowledge economy.[4]

On the Market Environment Subindex, Mexico ranked 55th, the second lowest rank (after Turkey with a rank of 57) among OECD countries. The Republic of Korea (19), Japan (7), United States (2), and Singapore (1) had much higher standards. In Latin America, Mexico ranked lower than Chile (31), Brazil (34), and Costa Rica (42).

---

[1] The NRI is defined as "the degree of preparation of a nation or community to participate in and benefit from ICT developments." The NRI not only provides a model for evaluating a country's relative development and use of ICT, but it also allows for a better understanding of a nation's strengths and weaknesses with respect to ICT.

[2] The Market Environment Subindex assesses "the presence of the appropriate human resources and ancillary businesses to support a knowledge-based society. The forces that play an important role in determining the market environment for ICT are varied and include fundamental macroeconomic variables like GDP and import/export, commercial measures like availability of funding and skilled labor, and the level of development of the corporate environment."

[3] The Political and Regulatory Subindex measures "the impact of a nation's polity, laws, and regulations, and their implementation, on the development and use of ICT."

[4] As the source for information in this paragraph, see Dutta, Lanvin, and Paua (2004). The Web site for the World Economic Forum is www.weforum.org.

Figure 5.1 Network Readiness Index, 2003–2004

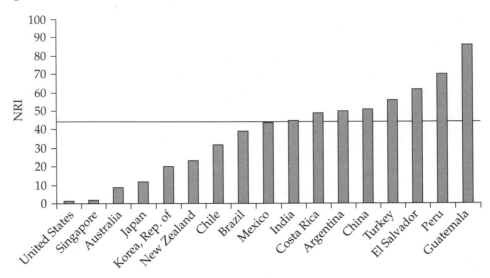

Source: Dutta, Lanvin, and Paua (2004).

Similarly, on the Political and Regulatory Environment Subindex, Mexico ranked low. It was 59th, the second lowest ranking among OECD countries, only ahead of Turkey (73). Among Latin American countries, Mexico ranked lower than Chile (18), El Salvador (40), Brazil (43), Dominican Republic (45), Trinidad and Tobago (47), Jamaica (50), Uruguay (53), and Costa Rica (57) on the Political and Regulatory Subindex. Clearly, Mexico needs to address these political and regulatory environment issues if it hopes to develop an attractive and competitive ICT market.

Three primary variables shape the development of a knowledge economy: access to ICT infrastructure, innovation, and competition. This chapter describes notable trends in Mexico's ICT market with respect to these variables. It then assesses government and private sector initiatives to strengthen the country's information and communication technologies. Recommendations are presented at the conclusion of the chapter.

ICT Performance in Mexico

In this section we examine trends in ICT spending, ICT prices, and in the use of the Internet, fixed line and mobile telephones, fiber optic networks, cable TV, and international long distance service. The dominance of the incumbent TELMEX is also examined.

ICT Expenditure

In the past decade, Mexico's ICT market gradually opened up to competition and foreign investment. According to the telecommunications regulatory agency (Comisión Federal de Telecomunicaciones or COFETEL), from 1999 to 2003, more than US$20 billion were invested in the telecommunications sector alone. In 2003, a time of significant contraction in the global telecommunications industry, investment in the Mexican telecommunications sector represented around US$2.3 billion.

Despite the impressive growth in absolute levels of investment, Mexico's ICT performance, when benchmarked against other countries, leaves considerable room for improvement (see Figure 5.2). Spending on ICT in Mexico as a share of GDP appears much less remarkable when those expenditures are compared to ICT spending in countries with similar GDP. As Figure 5.3 illustrates, Mexico's

Figure 5.2 Benchmarking Mexico's ICT Performance

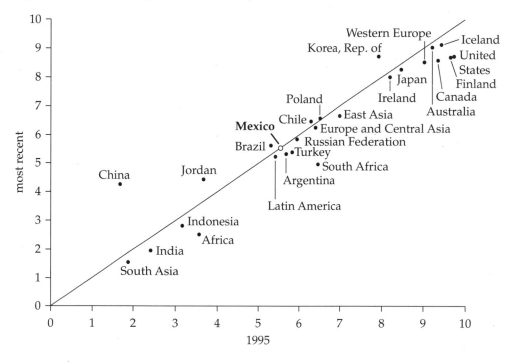

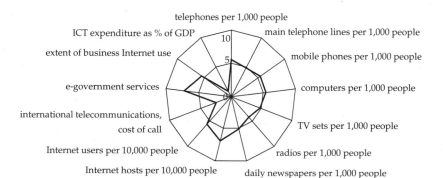

Source: World Bank, "Knowledge Assessment Methodology," http://www.worldbank.org/kam.
Note: The countries or regions plotted below the 45 degree line exhibited a decline in performance during the given time interval, while those plotted above the line showed improvement. There are two possible explanations for a decline: the country may actually have lost ground in absolute terms, or may have improved more slowly than its comparators.

Each of the 127 variables in the KAM is normalized on a scale of 0 to 10. The fuller the scorecard, the better poised a country is to embrace the knowledge economy. But an economy should not necessarily aim for a perfect score of 10 on all variables because the scorecards may be shaped by the particular structural characteristics of an economy or by trade-offs that characterize different development strategies.

Figure 5.3 *ICT Investments as a Share of GDP 2003*

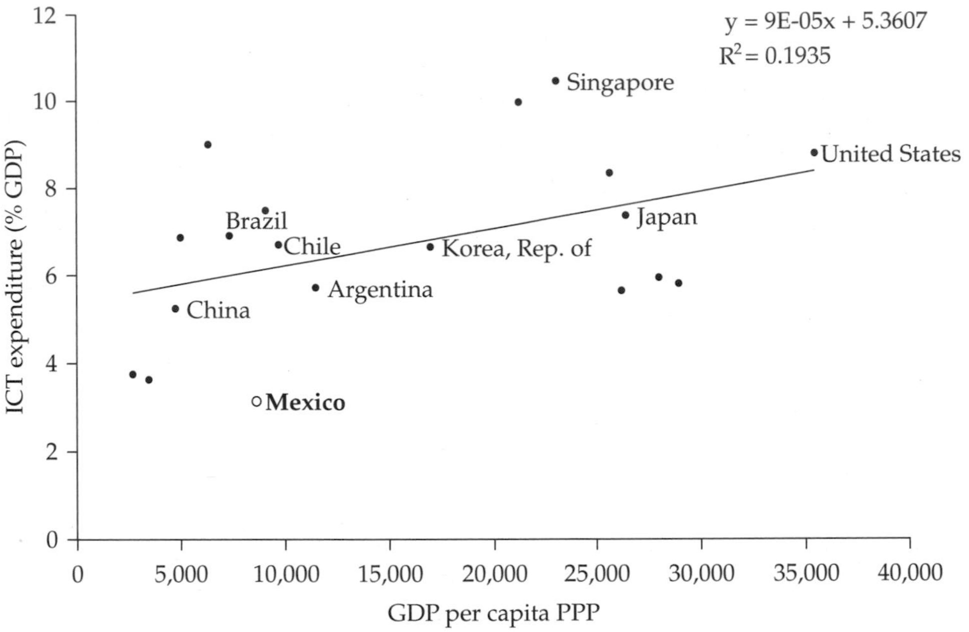

Source: World Bank, SIMA database, 2005.

level of ICT expenditure (3.1 percent) is significantly below OECD countries such as Japan (7.4 percent), the United States (8.8 percent), or New Zealand (10 percent). It is also nearly half that of Chile and Brazil's rates of 6.7 percent and 6.9 percent respectively and lower than the rates of Argentina, Peru, and China at 5.7 percent, 6.9 percent, and 8.4 percent respectively. As a growing number of studies have found, countries with higher levels of investment in ICT experience higher economic and social development growth (OECD 2004). Therefore, it is imperative for Mexico to pursue a more aggressive agenda with respect to investment in this important sector.

Penetration and Digital Divide

Between 1998 and 2004, the number of fixed lines in Mexico almost doubled from 9.9 million lines to more than 18.1 million, with an average annual growth rate of around 10 percent and a fixed line penetration rate of 17.1 telephones per 100 people in 2004. Although this growth has been significant, it is substantially below the rates found in other OECD countries (see Table 5.1). Although in 1991 Mexico, Brazil, and Chile had comparable fixed telephone penetration levels, during the following decade, Mexico's growth levels were significantly lower than those of Brazil, Chile, and other OECD countries.

With respect to ICT use as reflected in the number of Internet users per 100 inhabitants, Mexico's growth rate was lower than that of Chile and the Republic of Korea. From 1998 to 2003, Mexico increased the number of Internet users per 100 inhabitants nearly tenfold (from 1.3 users to 12 users), while Chile's usage grew more than 15 times, from 1.7 to 27.2 Internet users per 100 inhabitants (see Figure

Table 5.1 *ICT Indicators, 2003*

Country	Internet users per 100 inhabitants	PCs per 100 inhabitants	Cellular subscribers per 100 inhabitants	Main lines per 100 inhabitants	Total telephone subscribers per 100 inhabitants
Argentina	11.2	8.2	17.8	21.9	39.6
Brazil	8.2	7.5	26.4	22.3	48.6
Chile	27.2	11.9	51.1	22.1	73.2
China	6.3	2.8	21.5	20.9	42.4
Costa Rica	28.8	19.7	18.1	27.8	45.9
Ecuador	4.6	3.1	18.9	12.2	31.2
India	1.7	0.72	2.4	4.6	7.1
Ireland	31.7	42.1	88.0	49.1	137.1
Israel	30.1	24.3	96.1	45.8	141.9
Japan	48.3	38.2	67.9	47.2	115.1
Korea, Rep. of	61.0	55.8	70.1	53.8	123.9
Malaysia	34.4	16.7	44.2	18.2	62.4
Mexico	12.0	8.2	29.5	16.0	45.4
Peru	10.4	4.3	10.6	6.7	17.3
United States	55.6	65.9	54.6	62.4	116.9

Source: World Bank, SIMA database, International Telecommunications Union (ITU), 2005.

Figure 5.4 *Internet Users per 100 Inhabitants, Mexico, Chile, and the Republic of Korea, 1998–2003*

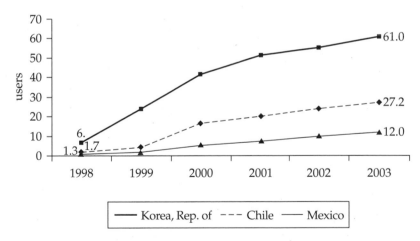

Source: World Bank, SIMA database, International Telecommunications Union (ITU), 2005.

5.4). In Korea, the number of Internet users per 100 inhabitants increased from 6.8 users per 100 people in 1998 to 61 percent of the population by 2003.

Similarly, initiatives aimed at increasing Internet penetration in Mexico must also be linked to efforts to increase Mexico's low level of personal computer (PC) penetration. Mexico has far fewer personal computers per 100 inhabitants than Chile (11.9 PCs per 100 inhabitants) or Costa Rica (almost 20 PCs per 100 inhabitants). The

Figure 5.5 *Regional Distribution of Main Lines per 100 Inhabitants and GDP per Capita, 2004*

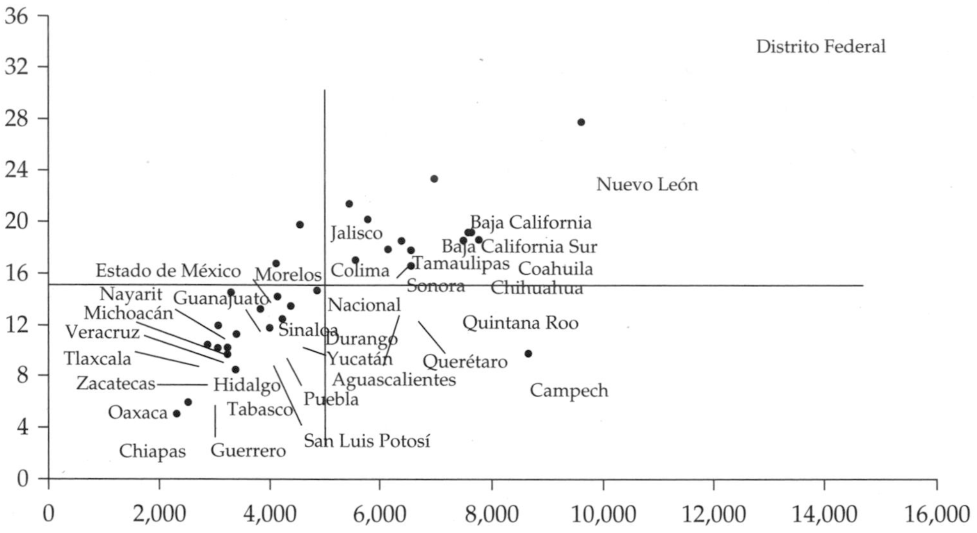

Source: COFETEL. Presentation at Regulatel meeting "Reunión de "Corresponsales" y de coordinadores de AU de cada uno de los 19 miembros de Regulatel," Peru, Januuary 2005.

Republic of Korea, Singapore, and the United States have much higher penetration rates, with more than 50 PCs per 100 inhabitants. Indeed, on a wide range of ICT indicators, Mexico lags behind other OECD countries (see Table 5.1).

The digital divide within Mexico is another major challenge. As Figure 5.5 illustrates, the major cities have much higher penetration levels for main line telephones than the rest of the country. The Federal District has nearly 35.4 main lines per 100 people; southern states have far fewer lines: Chiapas (3.9 main lines per 100 inhabitants), Oaxaca (4.7 main lines per 100 inhabitants), and Guerrero (7.6 main lines per 100 inhabitants). Not only do large numbers of Mexicans lack access to critical ICT infrastructure; the cost of accessing this infrastructure is much higher for inhabitants of the poorer regions.

Mobile, Data, and Cable TV

Mexico's mobile sector has grown at an explosive annual rate of nearly 100 percent since the mid-1990s. Compared to other Latin American and OECD countries, however, cellular penetration levels in Mexico are still low (see Table 5.1). Growth was driven by the speed and efficiency with which the government allocated spectrum from 1996 to 1998; competition; the introduction of calling-party-pays policy by the regulator in 1997 and 1998; and the widespread adoption of prepaid calling cards. Penetration of wireless services was greatest in areas where fixed services had not expanded, including low-income areas. The major challenges facing the sector are the declining average revenue per user (ARPU), which is mainly attributable to the popularity of prepaid calling plans; quality of service and consumer complaints; industry consolidation; creation of incentives to provide Internet services using wireless technologies; and extending service to rural and low-income areas.

Figure 5.6 *Paid TV Subscribers per 1,000 Inhabitants in Mexico, 2004*

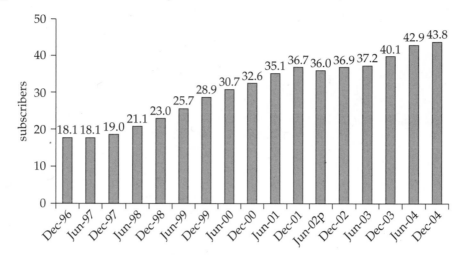

Source: COFETEL Web site, http://www.cft.gob.mx/wb2/COFETEL/COFE_Estadisticas_de_telecomunicaciones_2. Last accessed April, 2005.

Mexico's high-speed fiber optic networks that carry the traffic for telecommunications and ICT service also have grown dramatically since the sector opened to competition in 1996. In 1993, Mexico had about 15,000 kilometers (Km) of fiber optic networks operated by TELMEX; in 2003, it had about 112,000 Km of fiber optic networks operated by at least six different companies.

Another aspect of broadband access infrastructure in many countries is cable and paid television. The number of paid television subscribers in Mexico grew from 18.1 subscribers per 1,000 inhabitants in 1996 to around 43.8 subscribers per 1,000 inhabitants by the end of 2004 (see Figure 5.6).

In 2003, several dozen cable television companies, out of 713 paid television concession holders, applied for a concession to provide data and telephone service over their cable networks. Approximately twenty companies have been granted authority to carry data.[5] However, to date, no cable television company has been granted a concession to provide voice services; neither has TELMEX been granted a license to deliver cable services. The Comisión Federal de Telecomunicaciones (COFETEL) and Secretaría de Comunicaciones y Transportes (SCT) have not granted any such licenses. Allowing entry into voice telephony by cable companies would increase pressure on COFETEL to allow TELMEX to similarly enter the cable TV sector.

As can be seen in Table 5.2, more than 60 percent of Mexican consumers who have high-speed access to the Internet do so through cable networks, and cable television companies have a more than 70 percent share of the total paid television market. TELMEX, which dominated fixed line and mobile networks, does not compete in the paid television market, although it has successfully gained a significant and growing broadband market share through its asymmetric digital subscriber line (ADSL) services.

---

[5] Interview with COFETEL authorities.

Table 5.2 *Technology and Growth for Broadband Internet Access Services (Consumers), 2001–2006*

Access technology	2001	2002	2003	2004	2005	2006	% 2001–2006
ADSL accounts	7,698	44,791	91,201	146,245	206,199	269,061	104
Market share %	12.45	22.54	30.96	37.24	41.41	44.41	–17
ISDN accounts	27,221	24,140	20,278	16,628	13,468	10,775	
Market share %	44.01	12.15	6.88	4.23	2.70	1.78	54
Cable accounts	25,316	122,000	158,600	184,170	206,053	222,537	
Market share %	40.93	61.38	53.84	45.85	41.38	36.73	
Wireless accounts	1,616	7,823	24,510	45,850	72,182	103,455	130
Market share %	2.61	3.94	8.32	11.68	14.50	17.08	
TOTAL	61,851	198,754	294,589	392,699	497,902	605,828	58

Source: Gabriel Moreno Ledezma, Servicios de Banda Ancha en Mexico, 1er Semestre 2002.

Dominance of the Incumbent

TELMEX clearly dominates the long distance, local, and cellular telecommunications markets (see Table 5.3). It provides service to more than half of all dial-up Internet accounts and more than a third of high-speed Internet access accounts. Its share of high-speed Internet accounts increased significantly during 2002.

TELMEX's market share in the international sector in 2003 was about 66.6 percent—often cited as an argument that TELMEX is too dominant. As Mexican authorities have pointed out, TELMEX's market share after five years of competition is comparable to the five-year benchmark of other countries (see Figure 5.7). Indeed, a recent survey of 18 countries found that the average five-year incumbent market share benchmark is 64.5 percent. What is remarkable about TELMEX is not that it is dominant in one market segment, but that it has retained, and in some cases increased, its market power in a number of sectors, causing ripple effects on access, innovation, and prices.

TELMEX's net profit margin and earnings per share from continuing operations are more than twice that of its closest rival (see Table 5.4). TELMEX is also far ahead in operating income as a share of revenues compared to other U.S. and British companies. These data indicate that, if anything, the gap in telecommunications services between Mexico and developed countries is widening.

Table 5.3 *TELMEX Market Shares*

Market sector	Market share	Sector	Market share
International long distance (2003)	61.3%	Internet access: 56-kbps dial-up (2002)	51%
Cellular (2005)	75%	Internet access: 128 kbps and above (ADSL, cable TV, etc.) (2002)	37%

Source: Telegeography (2005). See http://www.telegeography.com/ee/tg2005/chap05-02.php, last accessed April 2005. EMC World Cellular Networks Datapac database 2005. See www.the-infoshop.com, last accessed April 2005. Internet access estimates are based on number of accounts.

Figure 5.7 *Incumbent Market Share after Five Years of Competition*

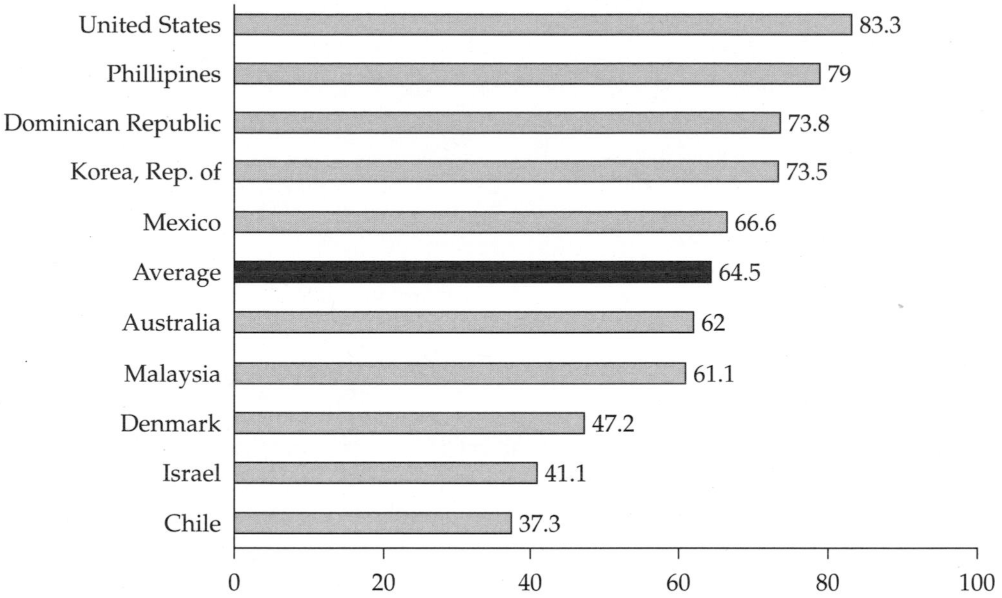

Source: Telegeography (2005).
Note: The average is based on data from 18 countries that report market share information for markets opened for at least five years.

Table 5.4 *Financial Performance of Telecommunications Companies, December 2004*

Company	Annual net income (US$ millions)	No. of employees	Annual sales (US$ millions)	Revenue per employee (US$)	Net profit margin %	Earnings per share from continuing operations (US$)
TELMEX	2,467.8	62,103[a]	12,457.5	201	19.8	3.97
Bellsouth	4,758.0	63,000	20,300	322	23.4	1.85
Verizon	7,831.0	210,000	71,283.0	339	11	2.59
DT	6,277.0	244,645	78,404.0	320	8.0	1.49
France Telecom	3,771.0	218,523	63,879.0	292	5.9	1.52
Telefónica Argentina	(3.0)	9,642	1,033	107	14.8[a]	(0.02)
Tele Norte, Brazil (2003)	73.4	37,690	4,833.8	128	1.5	0.19

Source: Hoovers Inc. Detailed Annual Reports. All based on December 2004 reports. See http:// www.hoovers.com, last accessed April 2005.
   a. 2003.

Prices

Prices are a critical indicator of the success of telecommunications and ICT policies. What follows is an overview of the prices of key telecommunications and ICT infrastructure in Mexico.

Table 5.5 *Telephone Tariffs in Mexico, 1995–2003*

Tariff (US$)	1995	1996	1997	1998	1999	2000	2001	2002	2003
Connection charge									
Business line	480	409	442	383	366	370	375	362	162
Residential line	277	236	123	107	111	119	121	117	105
Monthly subscription fee									
Business line	14	13	19	19.3	19.9	20.9	21.2	20.5	18.3
Residential line	7	9	14	14	14.5	15.5	16.8	16.2	14.5
Local call (3 minutes, US$)	0.07	0.10	0.14	0.13	0.14	0.15	0.16	0.15	0.14

Source: World Bank, SIMA database, International Telecommunications Union (ITU) 2005.

The basic installation fee for residential users has fallen dramatically, as have business installation charges.

In 2003, the basic monthly tariff was about $14.5 for residences and $18.3 for businesses, and the local calling charge was about 14 cents for each call. Prices in Mexico are much higher than in similar countries (see Table 5.5). All calls originating in the public network in Mexico are subject to the basic 14 cents calling fee; in most Latin American countries, however, telephone charges are based on usage, and in the United States local calls are covered by the monthly recurring charge. Businesses in Mexico pay the basic 14 cents calling fee, but residents pay only for calls exceeding 100 per month. TELMEX reports that approximately half of the residential customers make fewer than 100 calls per month. Even so, these charges are much higher than during the period of state-ownership.

Calling charges from a wire-line telephone are 14 cents plus 26 cents per minute, but from mobile to wire-line they are about 23 cents per minute. The difference in these charges arises from access and interconnection charges, as explained below.

Although domestic long-distance and international calling rates have fallen dramatically, they are still high (14 cents plus an additional 20 cents per minute for domestic long distance). Outgoing international calling charges are 14 cents plus an average of 50 cents per minute. Incoming international calls typically are priced at the official settlement rate. The OECD estimates that among its member countries, Mexico has the second highest international calling prices for businesses and the third highest for residential customers, even though Mexico is one of the organization's members with the lowest income.[6]

Calling prices are strongly influenced by access charges that must be paid to TELMEX for the local component of a call. These charges supposedly differentiate between recovering the cost of physically interconnecting separate networks (interconnection) and the "contribution" of various competitive services to recovering the cost of the local network (access). The tariff (at 3 cents per minute in 2000) is still substantially above estimates of the actual costs of interconnection, including the cost of terminating or originating a call (at most 1 cent per minute).

The interconnection charges apply to each end of domestic long-distance calls and to one end of international calls. They also apply to calls between two competing local carriers, except for fixed access carriers, if (i) they offer service in at least 40 percent of the local market, and (ii) the traffic between the two carriers is not

---

[6] OECD (2003b).

Table 5.6 *Local Prices for Telephone Services in Mexico and Other OECD Countries, 2003*

Country	Business telephone monthly subscription (US$)	Residential monthly telephone subscription (US$)	Residential telephone connection charge (US$)	Cost of three minute local call (US$)
Mexico	**18.35**	**14.51**	**104.73**	**0.14**
Argentina	12.94	4.56	51.72	0.02
Chile	9.20	9.20	43.95	0.10
Brazil	13.71	7.72	13.81	0.05
Korea, Rep. of	4.36	4.36	50.35	0.03
United States	42.40	24.75	40.76	0.00
El Salvador	1.62	0.95	6.86	0.01

Source: World Bank SIMA database, International Telecommunications Union (ITU), 2005.

"unbalanced." If both conditions are met, there is no interconnection charge—"bill and keep" then applies to each carrier for all the calls that originate in its network. If the local competitor does not satisfy these conditions, the competitor must pay TELMEX the long-distance interconnection fee of 3 cents per minute for calls that it originates. At the same time, the competitor is paid only 1 cent per minute for calls that originate in TELMEX and terminate in the competitor. Since the local carrier must pay extra to TELMEX for interconnection if a call lasts five minutes for local calling, competitors have a strong incentive not to compete for customers who are likely to have a long connect time with TELMEX customers, such as customers who use the Internet.

For calls from wire-line to mobile telephones, 6.3 cents per minute must be paid to TELMEX for billing and interconnection. The price is 40 cents for the first minute (the 14 cents call charge plus 20 cents per minute to the mobile carrier, plus the 6.3 cents per minute) and 26 cents per minute thereafter. The difference between the interconnection charge for mobile phone service compared to other services is not cost based, and the part that is intended to recover billing costs constitutes double charging. Billing costs are already part of the costs of local service that underpin the prices for installation, monthly access, and the 14 cents usage charge per call. Because this interconnection charge is so high, it strongly discourages the use of mobile telephones.

The price for access to an Internet service provider (ISP) is simply the 14 cents local charge (paid in addition to the monthly fee that the ISP charges for its services). Alternatively, a customer can buy TELMEX's bundled service of a computer, a modem, and its affiliated ISP for a hook-up fee of about $100, a monthly charge of about $40, and the same usage charge of 14 cents per connection.

Businesses that generate large amounts of long-distance and international data traffic typically lease two types of data or circuit services—one to carry the traffic from their offices to the switch of the long-distance carrier (the local loop) and one for the long-distance portion. The long-distance price in Mexico compares favorably with the long-distance price in other countries; the price of a local loop in Mexico, however, is much higher than the price in most comparable countries in Latin America (see Table 5.7). The installation or nonmonthly recurring charge for a local loop with E-1 capacity in Mexico is $19,669, more than twice the price charged by

Table 5.7 *Local Loop Prices for Carriers, 2002: E-1 CAPACITY*

Location (local provider)	non-MRC (US$)	MRC (US$)
Mexico City (TELMEX)	19,669	1,150
Mexico City (new entrant)	8,709	509
Argentina – Buenos Aires	3,000	800
Brazil – Sao Paolo	645	851
Chile – Santiago	1,400	260
Peru – Lima	4,000	1,960
Venezuela, R. B. de – Caracas	1,500	4,000

Source: Company survey by World Bank, Global Information and Communications Technology Department staff. Assumes a one-year lease for an E-1 local access line. Prices are based on those publicly registered.

Note: MRC = monthly recurring charge.

Table 5.8 *Telephone Prices for Rural Telephony*

Type of call	TELMEX rate per minute without VAT (US$)[a]	Telecomm rate per minute without VAT (US$)[b]
National calls	.20	.40
Calls to United States	1.04	1.04
Incoming calls	—	.20

Source: Vidal (2002).

a. Towns with more than 500 people.

b. Towns with 100 to 500 people.

Note: VAT = value-added tax.

TELMEX's competitors, and more than six times the price charged in Buenos Aires. Similarly, the monthly recurring charge for a TELMEX E-1 local loop is more than twice what a new entrant charges in Mexico City; it is more than 40 percent more expensive than the monthly recurring charges in Argentina and Brazil and more than four times as expensive as in Chile.

Consumers in remote rural areas not directly served by TELMEX can make calls through Telecomm, a quasi-private company overseen by the Secretaría de Comunicaciones y Transportes. However, Telecomm is not a carrier, and it must pay TELMEX to transport signals from its hub near Mexico City to the final destination. Telecomm is not considered a public operator and does not have an interconnection contract with TELMEX. TELMEX considers Telecomm a "large user." Telecomm also does not receive the access charges from incoming international calls. As a result, Telecomm's tariffs to users are high for the remote rural consumer (see Table 5.8). TELMEX, in contrast, does not charge for incoming calls. Telecomm has tried without success to establish an agreement with long-distance carriers that would allow it to create a "calling-party-pays" system. Thus, ultimately, people in small (and poor) communities pay more for the same service than people in larger (and richer) communities.

International Long-Distance Service

Over the past 10 years, international long-distance traffic in Mexico has represented a large amount of flows, especially coming from the United States. This has

Figure 5.8 *International Long-Distance Traffic, 1998–2004*

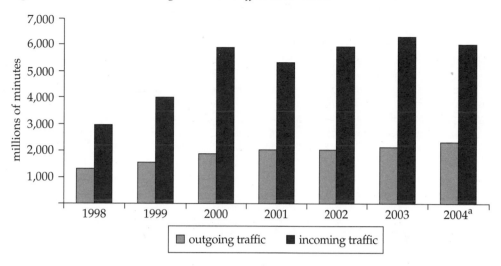

Source: COFETEL Web site. See http://www.cft.gob.mx/wb2/COFETEL/COFE_Estadisticas_de_telecomunicaciones_2, last accessed April, 2005.
a. January to September 2004

translated into enormous income for the Mexican operators, especially for the incumbent, TELMEX.

The government has allowed the Mexican operators to negotiate with U.S. carriers, although they were required until recently to comply with proportional return rules. These rules essentially enabled TELMEX, as the dominant Mexico operator, to set the per minute charge (known as the settlement rate) U.S. or foreign operators had to pay Mexican operators; the amount would then be redistributed to Mexico operators according to each operator's share in the international long-distance market. This permitted a relatively high settlement rate. The heavy incoming traffic (see Figure 5.8) put millions of dollars in the pocket of the Mexican operators.

After years of controversy over this issue, a dispute resolution case was brought before the World Trade Organization (WTO) in 2004 (see Box 5.1). This case was the first telecommunications dispute resolved by the WTO. The WTO decided, in summary, that Mexico's settlement rate and proportional return rules were inconsistent with its WTO commitment and that Mexico needed to put in place new rules for international telecommunications. The WTO agreed, however, that Mexico could continue to prohibit international simple resale. COFETEL is in the process of modifying its rules and regulations to make them consistent with the WTO decision.

Mexico's Regulatory Framework

The government, through the Secretaría de Comunicaciones y Transportes (SCT), is responsible for monitoring the compliance of TELMEX with its concession obligations. It also is responsible for gradually rebalancing TELMEX's highly cross-subsidized telephone tariffs to prepare the company and Mexico's telecommunications markets for competition that was set to begin in mid-1996. TELMEX's tariffs were not fully rebalanced by the end of its monopoly, in part due to the 1994 financial crisis. The failure to rebalance TELMEX's tariffs planted the seeds for subsequent challenges.

Box 5.1 *Telecommunications and the WTO: The Case of Mexico*

The first case of WTO dispute resolution on telecommunications services (and, indeed, on services generally) was initiated in 2000 by the United States. In August 2000 it requested consultations on Mexico's obligations and commitments on basic and value-added services under the General Agreement on Trade and Services (GATS) Annex on Telecommunications and the Reference Paper. Successive rounds of consultations did not resolve the issues raised, and in April 2002 the WTO established a dispute resolution panel to examine the complaint. After meeting several times with U.S. and Mexican government representatives and with 10 third-parties having an interest in the case, the panel issued its final report to the parties in March 2004. The panel's decision was not appealed to the WTO Appellate Body. The WTO's Dispute Settlement Body unanimously approved the panel report in June 2004, and by July 2005 the parties had agreed on a plan to redress the underlying problems.

Mexico had undertaken specific commitments under the GATS Articles XVI (market access), XVII (national treatment), and XVIII (additional commitments, comprising the Reference Paper). With respect to the services at issue, the United States claimed that Mexico had:

- Failed to ensure that TELMEX, the largest operator, interconnects U.S. suppliers on a cross-border basis on cost-oriented, reasonable rates, terms, and conditions.
- Failed to prevent anticompetitive behavior, as regulations empower TELMEX to lead a cartel that fixes rates for international interconnection and restricts supply.
- Failed to ensure access by U.S. suppliers to public telecommunications networks in Mexico, thus preventing them from providing non-facilities-based services within Mexico (through commercial agencies or "comercializadoras") and simple international resale (through cross-border leased circuits).

The dispute was largely driven by economic factors. Although Mexico's international long-distance market had been open to competition since 1997, by 2000 TELMEX's market share still exceeded 60 percent and was rising again. Net international settlements from U.S. operators to foreign correspondents reached a record high of $2.8 billion in 2002, about 20 percent of which was paid to Mexican operators. Although settlements had been declining since 1998, they remained high compared to competitive markets and about double the Federal Communications Commission's benchmark for U.S. operators sending traffic into Mexico. Illegal bypass reportedly resulted in TELMEX losing in 2003 around $230 million or 20 percent of its revenues from incoming U.S. calls.[a]

The agreement reached between Mexico and the United States in April 2004 called for the following actions:

- Within two months of adoption of the panel's report, Mexico will revise its international long-distance rules to allow competitive negotiation of settlement rates by eliminating uniform settlement rates, proportional returns, and the requirement that the operator with most outbound traffic negotiate the settlement rate on behalf of all Mexican operators.
- Within 13 months, Mexico will have in force regulations to license comercializadoras allowed to resell international switched telecommunications services provided by Mexican concessionaires.
- Mexico will continue to have the right to restrict international simple resale (use of leased lines to carry cross-border calls).

The panel report was adopted in June 2004. The agreed implementation plan is well under way.

(continued on next page)

Box 5.1 *(continued)*

Rules for international telecommunications services. New international rules applicable to all telecommunications services were approved by Comisión Federal de Telecomunicaciones (COFETEL, the regulatory authority) in June 2004 and published in August 2004. The old uniform settlements and proportional return rules have been abolished. Now Mexican operators of international long-distance services are free to negotiate individually the terms and conditions of interconnection with foreign operators, including prices for incoming and outgoing traffic. Foreign operators decide to which Mexican operator they wish to deliver their traffic for termination in Mexico. Thus Mexican operators can compete effectively with one another in the large wholesale market of terminating incoming traffic.

International simple resale. Mexico continues to prohibit international simple resale, as agreed. The new rules for international telecommunications services are clear on this, both in the explanatory notes and the rules themselves. International interconnection can only take place at gateways approved by COFETEL. Only Mexican companies that have concessions to install, operate, and exploit public telecommunications networks authorized to provide international services can receive authorization to set up international gateways.

a. TELMEX Annual Report 2004.

Ever since Congress began debating the new telecommunications law in late 2001, the SCT and the regulator, COFETEL, have been reluctant to take action on controversial issues such as unbundling, collocation, and resale regulation. COFETEL, however, has acted on a number of low-key, though important, issues such as numbering, dominance rules (now frozen due to legal challenges), tariffs, and local loop competition. Because of political opposition, the new telecommunications law was never passed. Thus, COFETEL was left without a strengthened regulatory framework fostering independence and institutional credibility.

The 1995 Federal Telecommunication Law called for the creation of a regulatory body as part of the SCT, but the law did not specify the powers and authority of the regulator. As a result, SCT drafted a presidential decree that created COFETEL on August 9, 1996, as a regulatory body. It has a chairman and three commissioners without set terms who are nominated by, and can be removed at the will of, the SCT Secretary. Between 1996 and 2004, COFETEL was led by four chairmen, and it has not had the stability needed to create a strong new institution capable of regulating a complex and powerful industry.

COFETEL lacks adequate enforcement powers and independence. One of the main reasons for its lack of independence is that it does not have powerful leadership that can make independent decisions without political pressures. The head of the COFETEL is nominated without a fixed term of office. A recent institutional analysis of the water, energy, financial services, and telecommunications agencies concluded that a regulatory leader is urgently needed to legitimize these regulatory entities (OECD 2004).

Mexico has several fairly effective quasi-independent regulatory bodies that can be used as models for the establishment of a more independent and effective COFETEL. One of them is the Comisión Federal de Competencia (COFECO). This Competition Agency, created through the Federal Competition Law, has legal powers that give independence and autonomy to the regulatory agency. It is headed by a board whose members enjoy 10-year staggered terms.

Interventions and Programs Supporting ICT Infrastructure

Despite the ongoing debate on whether or not to modify Mexico's telecommunications law, the government and the private sector have taken a number of notable steps to foster innovation and growth in the ICT sector. The following is a brief overview of some of these initiatives.

e-Mexico

In his address to the nation on December 1, 2000, President Fox stated the objective of e-Mexico: "to use the revolution of information and communications to project a national character and reduce the digital gap between Governments, companies, homes and individuals, with a reach to the last corner of our country." The e-Mexico Project has three major initiatives: (i) the connectivity initiative to extend broadband Internet access to 10,000 locations throughout the country; (ii) the applications initiative to develop applications in education, health, small and medium-size enterprises (SMEs), and e-Government; and (iii) the implementation initiative to build telecenters, access points, and local area networks in schools, health centers, community centers, municipalities, and associations of producers. The e-Mexico program hopes to build on the existing capacity of the telecommunications infrastructure (100 percent digital), to use this infrastructure to deliver applications, and to provide government services in ICT directly to citizens.

The e-Mexico coordinator reports directly to the SCT Secretary. A high-level official in the Office of the Presidency is also partly responsible for monitoring implementation. e-Mexico has a small staff to coordinate the activities of other secretaries and ministries responsible for e-education program, e-commerce, and e-Government.

One of the e-Mexico coordinator's tasks is to act as a catalyst for the line ministries in their efforts to develop specific projects. These projects range widely from developing Web pages to implementing programs to deliver and procure education and government services through the Internet. Mexico's information technology industry has been very supportive of the e-Mexico initiatives developed by the Secretary of the Economy to support the Mexican software industry. The Secretary of the Economy has developed similar programs aimed at using ICT to increase the competitiveness of Mexican companies in more than six key industries.

After nearly two years of preparatory work, e-Mexico initiatives started operating in 2002. That year the government allocated nearly $75 million for the first of three stages of the e-Mexico connectivity program. A partial subsidy was given to a private sector company to provide broadband connectivity to 3,200 Centros Comunitarios Digitales (CCDs), or digital community centers, connected via a VSAT satellite network. After extensive studies, the e-Mexico program on September 3, 2002, issued a request for proposals to establish 2,443 CCDs nationwide, especially in Mexico's poorest rural areas. Each CCD would have at least three computers with high speed connectivity. The service provider had to promise to manage and run these systems as well as provide a range of services. The government subsidizes these CCDs in two ways. First, it provides free high-speed connectivity via satellite transponder capacity "reserved" by the SCT for five years for "social purposes" from Satmex when it was privatized, and from the concessions of the satellite service providers. The winning bid must pay for the cost of installing the VSAT antennas and the equipment to run the CCDs. Second, the government provides a one-time payment to the CCD service provider to help offset the capital costs of building the VSAT antennas and CCD equipment. The service provider was also guaranteed that each CCD would be paid $30 a month by the school or municipality where the CCD was based.

On December 3, 2002, Interdirec was selected as the winner of the first CCD program. It outbid proposals from TELMEX and Avantel. Interdirec is a relatively small company that has been using innovative wireless technology to provide distance education and Internet access in several Mexican communities. By 2003, the first 3,200 CCDs were installed in all the municipalities of the country. In 2004, two more biddings of 2,000 CCDs each were launched by the SCT. The winner of both biddings was TELMEX. By the beginning of 2005, 7,200 CCDs had been installed around the country. For 2006, the SCT expected to have more than 10,000 CCDs installed in the municipalities.

Fondo de Cobertura Social de las Telecomunicaciones

In 2002, the congress authorized a US$70 million budget to develop a fund to foster access to telephones in rural and low-income areas—the Fondo de Cobertura Social de las Telecomunicaciones (FCST). A committee with representatives of the public and private sectors was established to oversee the FCST. COFETEL developed both a study to determine which localities would benefit from the fund as well as a feasibility study. The uniqueness of this fund is that its objective is not only to install public telephone lines; its primary purpose is to increase telephone penetration through residential lines in rural localities with more than 500 inhabitants. Specifically, the objective is to reduce the access gap of localities with the least telecommunication coverage around the country. The FCST was designed to use at least 70 percent in residential fixed lines (with any technology) and up to 30 percent in public telephone lines.

The establishment of the FCST as Mexico's first universal access fund is an important development. However, the FCST depends entirely on arbitrary budgetary allocations instead of on an annual assessment on the revenues of telephone companies of 1 percent to 2 percent as is the case with similar funds in Brazil, Colombia, and Peru. In the United States, telephone companies are collectively assessed by several universal access funds an average of 2 percent to 5 percent of revenues. In 2002, the FCST was allocated $70 million, and in 2003 it was allocated less than half the 2003 amount. The ITU estimates that in 2003 Mexico's telecommunications sector had revenues of around $17 billion, which means that a 1 percent tax on Mexican telecommunications companies would raise about $170 million for universal access programs on a sustainable basis. Such an assessment would provide sufficient funds to put in place a more effective, comprehensive, and sustainable universal access program.

In 2004, a first bidding of approximately US$30 million was made, and use of radiofrequency spectrum (1.5 Ghz) was launched. This bidding included around

3,930 localities that will benefit around 3.2 million inhabitants. This first bidding is expected to provide around 125 thousand lines; 30 percent of the cost of each line will be covered by the fund (capital investment) and the rest by the winning operator (operating costs). The operators will charge only the outgoing calls through a prepaid calling card scheme; the installation fee and the telephone device will be covered by the fund. The fund will cover the first 30 percent of the lines demanded in each locality; the rest will be covered by the operator entirely or by incoming competitors.

The bidding was allocated in March 2005 to the lowest cost offered by the incumbent TELMEX, which is expected to start expanding the service in these localities.

e-Government

The Mexican government has implemented the following initiatives to provide different types of online services to its citizens.

System for government procurement (www.compranet.gob.mx). This system enables government purchasing departments to publish all their procurement needs, including products, services, leasing, and public works. Potential suppliers may access this information and bid for specific contracts using the same portal. There were almost 28,000 public bids conducted using Compranet in 2003. Today, 100 percent of all public bids are registered on Compranet, and 40 percent of them were totally conducted via Internet (64 percent of value). During the first half of 2004, another 80 government agencies joined the Compranet system.

Univocal Registry of Authorized Persons (Registro Unico de Personas Autorizadas, RUPA). This registry has the purpose of enrolling citizens who often work with many government agencies and will issue them a univocal identification number that will be used as the only identification required to work with government agencies. The decree mandating the creation of this registry was published in May 2004. The Ministry of Finance worked with the Ministry of Public Function (SFP) to define the rules and standards for the advanced electronic signature to be used across all government agencies (and the related procedures and technology). RUPA will be consistent with these regulations.

CitizenPortal of the federal government. The portal www.gob.mx is part of the e-Mexico system and the "Presidential Agenda to promote better government." It is one of the most noticeable achievements of the government's digital strategy. Daily, www.gob.mx receives 12,000 visitors. It is a "world-class'" e-government portal at the national level. The portal has been acknowledged internationally and was awarded first place for the *2004 Stockholm Challenge Award* for the e-government category. www.gob.mx represents a single access point to all levels of government services and provides answers to the informational needs of the community.

Tramitanet. This subportal (www.tramitanet.gob.mx) consists of an online catalog of federal and some state transactions ("*tramites*") made available on the Internet. For each *tramite*, information is provided about procedural steps, required documentation, location and working hours of the government office, and the cost of filing and/or complying with the proceedings. The new regulatory framework mandates that electronically generated and submitted federal *tramites* be accorded the same legal value as *tramites* conducted by traditional methods. Federal *tramites* can be "signed" with a basic certificate for high security certification procedure administered by a government entity or notary public. To obtain a certificate, an individual or corporate representative must first appear physically before the certifying authority for the purpose of "binding" the user's identity. Unfortunately, this legal certainty is not available for all state level *tramites* because some of them do not have the legal frameworks in place to support electronic forms and proceedings (digital signature, data messages, and so forth).

e-Government at the state and municipal levels. The states of Puebla, Sinaloa, Aguascalientes, Baja California, and Coloma are the leaders in e-government. Coloma has leveraged scarce resources to offer digital services, deploying interactive kiosks developed locally. Puebla has partnered with a private company to issue driver licenses. In most of the states participating in e-government, the person in charge of information technology (IT) reports directly to the governor. Most states, however, have not made the most of the federal government's infrastructure to offer better services to their constituents through the use of technology. To assist them, the federal government has provided a portal (www.e-local.gob.mx) to enable municipios and states to strengthen their institutions and share good practices.

Concession Requirements

Before 2002, the year the FCST was created, Mexico did not have an explicit universal access program for increasing access to telecommunication services. It only had the programs contained in TELMEX's concession requirements, the Telecomm payphone program, and concession build-out requirements in other carrier concessions. The FCST has been an important first step to implement universal access.

When TELMEX was privatized in 1990, it was given a six-year exclusivity period. As part of its concession requirements, TELMEX was required to comply with certain network expansion needs by 1995. It had to expand the number of telephone lines nationwide by 12 percent each year; provide telephone service in population centers greater than 5,000; and offer rural telephony via payphones in population centers greater than 500. The TELMEX concession required the company after 1995 to comply with four expansion programs negotiated with the SCT. TELMEX complied with its concession requirements. Since 1999, the SCT has not imposed new build-out requirements on TELMEX, although TELMEX must continue to provide services to all areas where it currently provides services as a result of its concession requirements. The SCT has not imposed new universal access requirements on TELMEX as part of an effort to undercut TELMEX's opposition to SCT and COFETEL initiatives to increase competition.

Policy Agenda for ICT Infrastructure

Although they contribute to the development of a knowledge economy, e-Mexico, FCST, and related connectivity programs do not address the most important challenge: dramatically increasing and expanding private sector provision of ICT infrastructure in Mexico. Meeting this challenge would require a level playing field, elimination of entry barriers, healthy competition, and increased access to ICT services. Following are nine recommendations to facilitate the achievement of these goals.

1. Rebuild the credibility, effectiveness, independence, and transparency of COFETEL.

In order to create a level playing field, the Mexican government must make institutional changes in COFETEL. Despite a promising beginning, the commission is a weak regulator that does not inspire the confidence new entrants need to invest in this sector. This has become the single most important barrier to ICT growth in Mexico. Congress should adopt amendments to the Federal Telecommunications Law that would make COFETEL as independent and transparent as the Comisión Federal de Competencia. Congress, however, should set aside amendments concerning more technical issues—such as interconnection, tariff, and unbundling—which could be better addressed by a more effective COFETEL. As amended, the law should remove the ability of the SCT to oversee COFETEL and, equally important, mandate that COFETEL immediately adopt and follow transparent decision-making procedures. COFETEL should have the power to develop and implement its own regulations and not simply be responsible for implementing those developed and approved by the SCT. Its chairmen and commissioners, nominated by Congress, should be appointed for fixed terms, and should be removed only for gross ethical violations.

To send a dramatic and clear signal that there is an institutional break with the past, congress should direct COFETEL to report to the Secretariat of Economy. This proposed change could have the added benefit of increasing coordination between COFETEL and COFECO—the telecommunications and competition regulators. COFETEL must have adequate financial resources. Congress should make sure it can finance itself through fines and license fees. The commission also should be held accountable to congress for its annual budget. Making COFETEL a more effective regulatory agency with increased autonomy and transparency will not only strengthen COFETEL. It also will reduce the ability of disaffected parties to misuse the judicial system to reverse or delay regulatory decisions through the use of amparos (court-ordered releases of deposits).

2. Simplify and streamline the licensing regime for new entrants.

This recommendation, and recommendations 3 and 4, will help eliminate entry barriers and foster competition. Mexico's current concessions, permits, and licensing regime is complex and imposes burdensome information requirements that cause unnecessary delays, not only for new entrants, but also for current concession holders who simply wish to amend their existing concessions. Mexico would be better served by adopting a simplified licensing regime, along the lines adopted by the European Union, Argentina, Chile, or Peru. A company wishing to provide domestic voice service, or a concession holder seeking to add services to its concession, needs to provide extensive financial, business, network, and technical information to SCT and COFETEL. The entire process takes at least nine to twelve months, and the legal fees are considerable. In sharp contrast, class licenses in Europe in most cases are granted automatically or within a period of weeks. Simplified licensing regimes for value-added services are needed to foster the development of ICT service providers and applications. In Europe the licensing process is usually a simple process of self-certification. In Peru, the value-added service application is a simple two-page document, and registration is typically granted within a couple of weeks.

Although some of these barriers may have served a purpose before Mexico's transition to a more competitive telecommunications market, it is time Mexico followed international best practice with a more streamlined and simplified licensing regime that operates within a stipulated period of time. Such an approach would enable COFETEL to devote more staff and resources to revising and updating regulations and taking action against monopolistic behavior.

3. Eliminate requirements to register contracts with COFETEL for all but the incumbent.

Currently, concession holders must submit all of their draft contracts to COFETEL for its approval before they present them to new clients. The approval process for the generic contracts can take months, and COFETEL sometimes uses this time to impose additional regulatory requirements on certain services. These requirements hinder the ability of companies to rapidly introduce and tailor new services and contracts for clients. If the contract that is signed deviates significantly from the generic contract approved by COFETEL, the company can incur legal problems. All interconnection agreements between concession holders must also be approved by COFETEL before they can go into effect. While imposing such requirements on an incumbent carrier may prevent monopoly activities, their imposition on new entrants contributes to delays and uncertainty regarding new ICT services that may not neatly fit into the regulatory classifications of COFETEL. International best practice allows nondominant companies to freely enter into and modify contracts with their clients.

4. Eliminate legacy voice-centric regulations.

A significant number of COFETEL regulations, concerning international long-distance and interconnection rules, for example, focus on the provision of voice services and leave much ambiguity with regard to the rights of companies that provide data and corporate services. COFETEL should issue resale regulations to enable any service provider, not just companies with voice concessions, to lease and resell capacity from other companies. Such regulations are permitted under the 1995 Federal Telecommunications Law. In the past the commission's refusal to issue resale regulations may have encouraged companies to invest in infrastructure earlier. Today such regulations mainly act as an entry barrier to new operators that can package services to serve small businesses and other niche markets. While voice-centric regulations need to be eliminated or revised, new regulations are needed to foster and ease the interconnection of data networks.

Other voice-centric regulations are requirements imposed on the concessions granted to backbone operators. They are required to certify that none of their customers is carrying voice traffic that terminates or originates on the network of a Mexican operator that has a long-distance license. Such a requirement is an attempt to force backbone companies to police their customers in order to reduce voice-over-the-Internet (VoIP) traffic. In most OECD countries, VoIP traffic is classified as a data service and is unregulated. As a result, VoIP in OECD countries has grown dramatically. More recently, COFETEL has proactively enforced its regulations by shutting down companies that carry VoIP traffic but that only have value-added licenses.

5. Require automatic review of regulations.

Every two to three years COFETEL should review its regulations. Those that hinder competition, market entry, price reduction, and network expansion in response to changes in technology and market conditions should be amended or eliminated.

We have recommended actions to eliminate entry barriers and foster competition (recommendations 2–5). Our final recommendations are intended to promote equity and increase access.

6. Foster broadband deployment and reduce local loop costs through competition.

In markets with more than one provider of local loops, the price and quality of service improve dramatically. The government should foster increased local loop competition by promoting the provision of service to business and residential consumers by cable television service providers, by wireless local loop providers, and by data service providers.

7. Build consensus for universal access, establish a universal access tax, and rebalance tariffs.

The government should undertake a consensus-building campaign on the priorities for universal access. It should consult with state and municipal authorities, identify and remove legal, licensing, and regulatory barriers to private sector participation, and ensure provision of service to underserved communities and to small businesses. The e-Mexico initiative is a unique approach to provide broadband infrastructure and services in rural areas. It can lead to innovative ICT programs that promote economic development and improve education.

As noted earlier, the e-Mexico connectivity and FCST programs do not constitute a comprehensive and sustainable universal access program. In order to reduce the digital divide within Mexico, congress should establish a neutral universal access tax (capped at 1.5 percent), finish rebalancing tariffs, and transform the FCST into a sustainable universal access agency housed within COFETEL. The FCST should be given the mandate to develop an effective and comprehensive universal access program using the FCST funds. As previously noted, a 1 percent tax on the revenue of Mexican telecommunications operators could raise approximately $170 million for universal access, more than twice the 2002 congressional appropriation for the FCST, and nearly six times the congressional appropriation for FCST in 2003. All government programs to increase access to ICT infrastructure—including the e-Mexico connectivity initiative, Telecomm's rural telephony program, and Sepomex's ICT program—should be reviewed and modified by FCST as appropriate. Ideally, all three programs would be part of the fund since this would allow better coordination between them and avoid duplication of efforts. FCST could be made a part of the new COFETEL, or it could be a part of the new ICT secretariat. If the latter is the case, the FCST agency and COFETEL need to be given explicit mandates. FCST could be responsible for developing and implementing policies dealing with the allocation and administration FCST resources, while COFETEL could be responsible for developing regulations and enforcing them.

8. Eliminate cross-subsidies.

COFETEL should undertake a transparent and public initiative to determine whether Mexico's current interconnection and tariff regime contains cross-subsidies between services and companies. Where cross-subsidies exist, COFETEL should decide whether they should be phased out, as well as how to replace them with more transparent programs that will foster competition. This initiative should examine the TELMEX public payphone program in towns with populations between 500 and 2,500, and the Telecomm rural telephony program, to determine whether the programs are financially self-sustaining, whether there are tariff or regulatory barriers to the independent functioning of the programs, and whether a review of their cost structure is needed to distribute the costs equitably. Reaching the underserved with low-priced efficient service is the goal.

Conclusion

In conclusion, Mexico's telecommunications sector grew considerably as a result of the privatization of TELMEX in the early 1990s and of the gradual sector liberalization that began in 1995. The Fox administration efforts to transform Mexico into a knowledge economy, mainly through its e-Mexico initiative, have also resulted in notable improvements in e-government. However, Mexico lags behind all OECD countries and many Latin American countries in terms of widespread access to telephone and broadband Internet infrastructure. Though Mexico has introduced limited regulatory changes to make its regulations consistent with the WTO ruling, it has failed to introduce broader changes that are required in order to enable Mexico to use ICTs as a tool to transform its economy. Furthermore, this report finds that Mexico's regulatory framework and institutions are quite weak and have not only failed to foster competition, but that they put in place regulations that foster anti-competitive behavior and protect the dominant operator.

   Although they provide important contributions toward the development of a knowledge economy, e-Mexico, FCST, and related connectivity programs do not adequately address the most important challenge—that of dramatically increasing and expanding private sector provision of ICT infrastructure in Mexico. To do so requires more effective regulatory frameworks and institutions that will establish and safeguard a level playing field, eliminate entry barriers, foster healthy competition, and increase access to ICT services.

Part III
Implementation Options

Recall from Chapter 1 the parable of two family-owned firms that were once identical. Then one began growing rapidly, while the other could barely survive. All of a sudden, the story—set in Latin America—takes a magically realistic turn: a high and benevolent government official sees (at a glance) what the government ought to do: help the struggling firm escape its vicious circle and participate in learning networks. Given the similarities of the firms, and the demonstrated success of one, the failure of the other looks more like an accident than like destiny. Surely the role of government, in parables and reality, is to protect citizens and their crucial projects from avoidable accidents?

The government may have good intentions, but getting from the general idea of what to do to the specifics of how to do it is another matter. A young official, clear-minded and innocent of all of the past missteps of economic development policy, is charged with figuring out "the how." She quickly notices subtle but relevant differences between the two neighboring firms. The successful firm had access to capital at a crucial moment through the owner's rich uncle; the owner of the failing firm was not favored by rich relatives. Regional banks and government lending programs had so much trouble assessing the prospects of turning the struggling firm around that they hesitated to make a loan. With regard to the skills of the owners of the firms, the story is similar. When it comes to hands-on experience with garment making, both owners are alike. But the successful one has five more years of formal schooling (the rich uncle again) and so can read—with a facility that the other owner lacks—manuals on factory layout, plant organization, the correct way to sew a new kind of fabric, and accounting.

The official is bewildered. The list of remedial measures the struggling firm should take in order to succeed is the result of cursory inspection. Is it sufficiently complete? How would one know? Suppose that the official, pressed for time, decides that the cursory list is complete enough for starters. What should the sequence of measures be? Plainly, it is impossible to change everything at once. Change must be incremental. Some steps may be preconditions for the success of others, so the steps toward change cannot be ordered haphazardly. It makes sense to offer literacy training before providing finance, so current reading could inform the use of the fresh money. On the other hand, wouldn't the credit, and the restructuring it enables, create a sense of urgency and opportunity that would motivate attention to remedial reading classes? What about doing both steps simultaneously? And what about reform of the domestic thread cartel, if the domestic producers really are engaged in unlawful collusion (and if the government can do something about such things)? As soon as these questions are formulated, they tangle into a Gordian knot that we will attempt to disentangle in this part.

6

Toward National Vision and Leadership

Examples of Best Practices: Finland, Ireland, and the Republic of Korea

Finland, Ireland, and the Republic of Korea have engineered successful transitions to knowledge-based economies. In all these cases, national economic crises compelled diverse actors to implement a new agenda through national agreements on goals and mechanisms to move forward. The crises also prompted policy makers and private sector leaders to lengthen the time horizon of the policies adopted. Thus, Nokia—Finland's first mover toward an innovation-based economy—dramatically increased R&D investments. Finland responded by increasing public R&D and transforming the innovation system to fit business needs. Members of parliament took courses and went on study tours demonstrating the need for the new agenda. National public innovation organizations played a crucial role by transforming technology into businesses and ensuring a critical mass of demonstration cases.

Ireland also exemplifies a successful combination of top-down and bottom-up policies. It invested in education and R&D infrastructure in the 1980s and then undertook drastic policy changes beginning in 1987. To complement its top-down policies, Ireland instituted pragmatic bottom-up programs—regional partnerships to mitigate high unemployment and a program to expand national-supplier linkages from foreign direct investment (FDI). The Republic of Korea's powerful national vision, initiated by a private sector champion, was advanced through effective government coordination (see Box 6.1).

Lessons for Mexico

Three lessons from Finland, Ireland, and the Republic of Korea are relevant for Mexico. First, simple institutional recipes do not exist for concerted action. Mexico will need to devise its own recipe for a knowledge economy. Given its great regional diversity, Mexico's regional and state-level policy initiatives can be a key entry point for a knowledge-based economy. Mexico has already advanced quite significantly in that direction. Subnational initiatives (for example, the Monterrey Knowledge Technopolis) are important springboards for more systemic reform agendas.

Second, even when major crises call for urgent economic transitions, countries must "prepare the bases." This essential preparatory stage can be seen in the initial *Vision Korea Report* and in Finland's major effort to facilitate and accelerate business R&D.

Third, although major reform efforts from the top are vital, they may not provide the all-important impetus for transformation. Concerted effort must evolve. Bottom-up experiments in Mexico, already well under way, must mature. These transitional stages then must proceed to concerted efforts. (The knowledge strategy in Korea is one example.)

111

Box 6.1 *The Republic of Korea's Transition to a Knowledge Economy: From Vision to Implementation*

In 1998, in the wake of a financial crisis, the Republic of Korea officially launched a national strategy to become a knowledge-based economy. The initial impetus came from the private sector—the Maeil Business Newspaper—which concluded in 1996, even before the crisis, that there was an urgent need for a more coherent vision of the future of the Korean economy. This newspaper launched the "Vision Korea Project" as a national campaign in February of 1997, and it developed the first *Vision Korea Report*.

Eventually, the government—the Ministry of Finance and Economy—became the main champion of the policy agenda for the knowledge economy. The Korean Development Institute, a so-called system integrator, coordinated the work of a dozen think tanks. A joint report by the World Bank and the Organisation for Economic Co-operation and Development (OECD) outlined concrete steps for reforms in the various policy domains. Progress was monitored closely. As a result, inertia or resistance was identified and addressed. Korea's knowledge strategy of April 2000 evolved into a three-year action plan for five main areas: information infrastructure, human resources, knowledge-based industry, science and technology, and elimination of the digital divide. To implement the action plan, Korea established five working groups involving nineteen ministries and seventeen research institutes, with the Ministry of Finance and Economy coordinating the implementation.

Every quarter, each ministry submits a self-monitoring report to the Ministry of Finance and Economy, which puts out an integrated report detailing progress. The midterm results and adjustments to the plan are sent to the executive director of the National Economic Advisory Council, which reports on the progress of implementation and gives an appraisal of the three-year action plan to its advisory members.

Source: World Bank staff.

Toward Concerted Action

To move forward, Mexico needs to implement major reforms. The reform agenda is as challenging as the institutional impediments to reforms. The economic agreements (*Los Pactos*)[1] of the 1980s were good examples of pragmatic institutions to carry out economic liberalization and contain inflation. The new agenda built around a concept of knowledge may need a similarly far-reaching mechanism. For lack of a better title, we can call this a Knowledge Economy Pact. Such an agreement would entail a combination of top-down and bottom-up policies, and, unless there is a wake-up call of a crisis, it is likely to evolve gradually and over time.

Drawing on a diversity of best practices, we suggest that Mexico construct its Knowledge Economy Pact in three stages: the immediate agenda, the medium-term agenda, and the long-term agenda. Table 6.1 presents in detail these agendas with regard to innovation and enterprise upgrading, education, and ICT infrastructure.

The art and craft of policy making is about sequencing the various horizons of a policy agenda in a virtuous circle of growth and reforms (see Figure 6.1). To get around the many institutional rigidities impeding progress, Mexico must create momentum for change by fostering stakeholders' awareness; reach consensus on

---

[1] The first Pacto was "Pacto de Solidaridad Economica" (December 1987–December 1988); it was replaced by "Pacto para la Estabilidad y el Crecimiento Economico" (PECE) from January 1989 to 1992.

Table 6.1 *Implementing the Transition: Sequencing Policy Agenda in Innovation, Education, and ICT*

Stage of the policy agenda	Benchmarks for innovation and enterprise upgrading	Benchmarks for education	Benchmarks for ICT
Immediate agenda *Top-down:* Build awareness; promote a sense of urgency; develop a national system of monitoring; evaluate ongoing pilot projects. *Bottom-up:* Undertake new pilot projects.	Develop and implement private sector–led technology projects (Programa Avance); introduce sectoral and regional technology and innovation funds.	Develop new innovative projects of lifelong learning, relying on ICT; introduce new pedagogical methods; improve involvement of stakeholders in learning and teaching.	Reduce perception of regulatory paralysis; increase regulatory transparency and strengthen sector regulator; identify and assess the supply and demand barriers to increased access and use of ICTs; share results with key stakeholders to generate dialogue on overcoming the barriers.
Medium-term agenda *Top-down:* Put in place the system for monitoring progress toward a knowledge economy; link projects to budgetary priorities; institute a shared vision of Mexico as a knowledge-based economy ("Mexico 2025"); scale up and consolidate national programs that received positive evaluation. *Bottom-up:* Implement state-level knowledge economy initiatives.	Strengthen innovation linkages with the United States and Canada; implement technology foresight processes with regional and private sector leaders; establish a new demand-driven and private sector–led mechanism to allocate public funds for innovation and upgrading; establish Fundación Mexico, adapted from the model of Fundación Chile.	Bring key stakeholders together and design the architecture of an integrated system of lifelong learning; scale up promising programs such as Escuelas de Calidad, Consejo Nacional de Fomento Educativo (CONAFE); introduce income-contingent loans to facilitate private financing of higher education and initiatives in lifelong learning.	Implement second-generation ICT access programs (scale up with a focus on poor states); develop and implement programs to foster greater demand for ICT by business, government, and the education sector; establish a universal access fund.
Long-term agenda Reduce the power of dominant players; introduce a new incentive structure.	Engage in major reforms; change incentive structure for innovation so that business R&D reaches at least 50 percent of total budget and the structure of R&D spending becomes less concentrated (e.g., UNAM becomes less dominant).	Engage in major reforms; change incentive structure for education providers (e.g., curbing the power of unions); create a national lifelong learning system with a multiplicity of qualified service providers and sources of financing.	Create a more even and contestable playing field, with strong regulatory capabilities (e.g., TELMEX becomes less dominant). Establish a strong and independent sector regulator.

Source: World Bank staff.

Figure 6.1 *Virtuous Circle of Growth and Reforms*

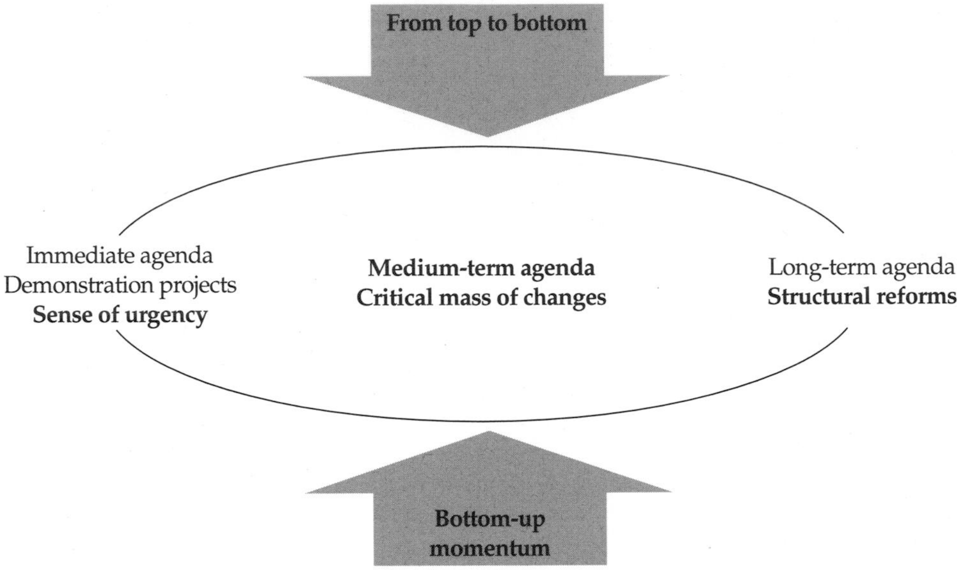

From top to bottom

Immediate agenda
Demonstration projects
Sense of urgency

**Medium-term agenda
Critical mass of changes**

Long-term agenda
Structural reforms

**Bottom-up
momentum**

Source: World Bank staff.

how to tackle key obstacles at the national level (to enhance demand for an institutional change); and then move ahead with concrete, manageable, bottom-up approaches that can serve as demonstration projects to move the larger agenda.

Sequencing the Policy Agenda

When viewed together, the immediate, medium-term, and long-term dimensions of a policy agenda for the knowledge economy present a comprehensive strategy for reform over time.

Immediate Agenda

Building awareness of the need for innovation, developing a system to monitor progress, and implementing new pilot projects are the main tenets of the immediate agenda. Mexico is already engaged in significant new initiatives on innovation, education, and ICT. Because of the sheer diversity of new programs, priority should be given to monitoring and evaluation. Evaluation should be viewed as a valuable management tool to help improve performance, not a way to assign blame for failures and problems. Such forward-looking evaluations are crucial to proceed to the next stage of consolidation when diverse pilot projects are aggregated at the regional and sectoral levels.

Bottom-up initiatives must be complemented with top-down efforts. A massive campaign should be launched to raise awareness of the urgent need for reforms and the high payoffs that can follow. The government can champion a search for pragmatic, step-by-step reform strategies and ways to monitor progress and set priorities. Global strategic consultancies could be contracted to lend additional credibility to these efforts. They can help adapt global best practices to Mexican reality.

Medium-Term Agenda

The agenda at this stage focuses first on pragmatic actions not requiring parliamentary approval that can yield results in the medium term. Mexico's Competitiveness Agenda, elaborated by the government in 2004, is comprehensive and well thought out. It addresses the knowledge economy from this medium-term perspective. Particularly in the areas of education and innovation, government programs that have received positive evaluation, yet have remained relatively small, could be scaled up and consolidated. As discussed in chapter 3, in collaboration with federal ministries and state governments, CONACYT has established a diversity of sectoral and regional funds. These funds could be consolidated with clearly specified priorities and operating procedures. Interorganizational and private-public projects are to be particularly encouraged. A good example in this context is Tekes, the National Innovation Agency of Finland. It funds industrial projects, as well as projects in research institutes, and especially promotes innovative, risk-intensive projects.

In education, promising programs include *Escuelas de Calidad, Consejo Nacional de Fomento Educativo* (CONAFE). Income-contingent loans can facilitate private financing of higher education and lifelong learning initiatives. The government also should bring key stakeholders together to design the architecture of an integrated national system of lifelong learning. Issues to be addressed include the following: accreditation of multiple providers, certification of prior learning, vocational qualifications, vocational counseling and information on career paths and earning streams, quality of different public and private providers, and financing mechanisms.

The successful transitions in Ireland, the Republic of Korea, and Finland (see Chapter 3) indicate that actions designed to yield immediate results should be complemented by longer term efforts, with results bearing fruit after 2007. These actions prepare the bases for a major concerted effort—an effort that articulates a shared vision of Mexico as a knowledge-based economy, an effort that has a visible and tangible demonstration effect by consolidating existing initiatives. "Preparing the bases" recalls the Japanese proverb: "A vision without an action is a dream. An action without a vision is a nightmare."

Collaborating with private sector champions and civil society, the federal government can begin to formulate a compelling yet realistic vision of Mexico as a knowledge-based economy. Its objective is to shift gears from business as usual to a more urgent concerted action. Building awareness would create a vivid image of what is at stake for every Mexican—the poor, the middle-class, and members of national industrial groups and multinational corporations. The experience of Korea (which has a centralized economy) exemplifies how a shared vision can emerge from outside the government as the result of private sector champions and the media (see Box 6.1).

The central objective of the "preparing the bases" stage is to package isolated efforts to achieve a tangible and visible demonstration effect.

For instance, a private-public bridge organization, Foundation Mexico, could scan new opportunities and put them into practice. One model for such an organization is Fundación Chile (Box 6.2). Two adaptations of this model, however, would be needed. First, the hypothetical Foundation Mexico must have a much more decentralized structure (the hub of a network of innovation organizations rather than a mini-innovation system under one roof). Second, Foundation Mexico would need a closer link with the United States, with U.S. technology leaders playing an

Box 6.2 *The Fundación Chile Model and Its Relevance for Mexico*

One of the most successful attempts in the Latin American region to establish national "antennae" for new technologies is Fundación Chile, originally a joint effort between the Chilean government and the U.S. firm ITT, but now largely autonomous. Fundación Chile uses four main techniques in its technology transfer and dissemination work: (i) it captures and disseminates technologies to multiple users though seminars, specialized magazines, and project assistance; (ii) it develops, adapts, and sells technologies to clients in the productive and public sectors, both in the country and abroad; (iii) it fosters institutional innovations and incorporates new transfer mechanisms; and (iv) it creates innovative enterprises, almost always in association with companies or individuals.

The creation of demonstration companies by Fundación Chile has had a mixed record with some successes and some failures, but overall the companies have been effective in disseminating new technologies. The companies are transferred to the private sector once the technologies have been tested in practice, and their economic profitability has been established. One of the most successful cases exemplifies the successful development of a knowledge cluster. The salmon industry, in a period of 10 years, grew to become a dynamic export sector. By 2004, Fundación Chile had launched 61 such ventures, three-quarters of which have been sold to private investors. The six leading companies have generated more revenues than the total cost of investment into companies by Fundación Chile to date.

The systemic technology focus of Fundación Chile includes biotechnology, management, environment, financial engineering, and information. Recent focus areas include forestry genetics and DNA vaccines for aquaculture. Fundación Chile has also identified the links needed to transform developing clusters with comparative advantage into a business practice. The clusters include the agribusiness, marine, tourism (agro/eco), forestry, and wood processing sectors.

Fundación Chile is a powerful private organization that performs all of the functions of the project cycle, from identification of market niches to creation of firms that can take advantage of opportunities. It is an innovation system as it should be, all under one roof. Foundation Mexico, described earlier, can be thought of as a reinvention of Fundación Chile in the Mexican context. Key features of Fundación Chile's success and their relevance in Mexico are presented in Table 6.2.

Table 6.2 *Fundación Chile as a Model for Foundation Mexico*

Factors contributing to the success of Fundación Chile	Relevance for Mexico
An entrepreneurial, highly paid, and highly professional management team established over the course of many years.	A shortage of top-notch managerial teams; achieving this feature of Fundación Chile would be a challenge but a challenge that could be met.
Arms-lengths relationships with the government; operates as a business, not as a public sector organization.	Critical for second-generation NAFTA; will establish an important precedent in governance.
Private shareholders that do not expect an immediate return and tolerate risks (oligarchs with a strategic agenda).	A litmus test for the new generation of private-sector champions.

Source: World Bank staff.

active role in terms of management, generation of deal flow, and contribution to the capital endowment. Provided efficient leadership and management from the private sector, such a foundation could become a symbol of success in technology and innovation alliances with the United States and Canada. For Monterrey's leading industrial groups, a vibrant and commercially successful Foundation Mexico could become a flagship organization of the knowledge economy, just as the Monterrey Institute of Technology, created in 1943 by Monterrey's industrialists, was at that time a symbol of Mexico's industrialization.

Another example is Monterrey Knowledge Technopolis—an initiative championed by the state government and private sector leaders to transform Monterrey into a knowledge-based economy. The Monterrey Knowledge Technopolis already meets three important prerequisites as a crucial pilot of the knowledge-economy agenda: highly promising institutional experiments in many areas (see Box 6.3), a sense of urgency for change, and private sector and public sector leadership. The current focus of the Monterrey Knowledge Technopolis is on infrastructure; there are plans, for instance, to create technology parks for companies. While infrastructure is important, so is building an environment for knowledge-based entrepreneurship by improving the quality and private sector orientation of education systems and facilitating innovation networks between Mexico and the United States. Cross-border ties can be strengthened through research, technology, and education

---

Box 6.3 *Monterrey Institute of Technology and TecMilenio: Educational Spin-off as a Model of Lifelong Learning*

The Monterrey Institute of Technology in Mexico is a premier private education organization with 33 campuses across the country. It is a franchise system of local campuses, each financed and governed by local leaders in the private sector. The Virtual University, a worldwide leader in distance learning, has championed a continuing education agenda throughout the Spanish-speaking world, making inroads into such giant markets as China. To reach poor students, the Institute launched a spin-off—TecMileno (Millennium University). It offers the high quality of education associated with the Tec de Monterrey brand yet at dramatically lower costs. By May of 2004, approximately 10,000 students had enrolled; per student costs were approximately three times lower than in the parent organization.

Several factors make it possible to dramatically reduce costs without compromising quality. The curriculum is designed and often delivered by managers of private sector firms. With some of these firms, TecMilenio shares offices, so students and teachers can work, learn, and teach in the same location. To have the best professors and best courses available for students, distance education is highly utilized. Pedagogy is based on problem solving and conceptual tests. Yet testing is standardized and centralized. Remuneration of the teachers depends on the testing results of the students. A small management structure draws on carefully selected professors from Tec de Monterrey staff and translates industry needs into pragmatic curriculum. This curbs professors' vested interest in using the same teaching materials they have for decades. Content is determined by industry needs. By year 2010, TecMilenio plans to have reached an enrollment of 100,000 students.

TecMilenio draws on the strengths of its parent organization, Tec de Monterrey, while avoiding many of the rigidities of established organizations. Indeed, TecMilenio is evolving into a model of "lean and mean" low-cost learning.

Source: World Bank staff.

consortia. Promotion of diaspora networks can encourage successful Mexicans living abroad to invest and/or set up shop at home.

Both Proyecto Innovar (see Chapter 3) and Foundation Mexico could become hubs of innovation, bringing together Mexico and its NAFTA partners to put technology into business. The start-up costs of technology development would be higher for Foundation Mexico; it could invest its own resources in identification of new market niches and invest in applied R&D to transform opportunities into commercial projects. In both cases, the government of Nuevo Leon in collaboration with federal agencies, such as CONACYT and the Ministry of Economy, would facilitate private sector leadership in building an environment for entrepreneurs. Leading Mexican organizations and U.S. partners, working together, can stimulate cross-border innovation. Private sector champions willing to contribute their time and financial resources will be crucial. Private-public consultations can help transform the personal visions of the private sector champions into specific projects.

Long-Term Agenda

Economywide changes at this stage lead to a national accord on the knowledge economy. As we discussed earlier, Mexico requires major reforms in education, innovation, ICT infrastructure, energy, labor, and the financial markets. The reforms will need to create an even playing field to ensure efficient entry and exit of diverse service providers. Strong regulations are needed to maintain service and guarantee conformity with minimum standards. The agenda includes curbing the power of the teachers' unions; creating greater incentives to reward educational quality; improving standards on certification, accreditation, testing, and evaluation, as well as recognizing students' prior learning. ICT infrastructure reforms would create a more open marketplace and develop incentives for new entrants, reducing the dominance of TELMEX. Labor market reforms would ease employment protection provisions, establish revenue support systems in the case of job loss, and modernize the collective bargaining framework.

Implementation of this agenda requires a major concerted effort. The challenge here is to proceed with major reforms and create a new governance structure for private-public collaboration. A knowledge economy accord (*Pacto*) can be seen as a postcorporatist agreement facilitating cooperation between the national government, the private sector, and subnational entities.

Strong, high-powered incentives are often required to motivate private actors to engage in concerted action and create organizations that serve public or club goods rather than private interests. Quasi-rents—rents contingent on performance and private-to-private collaboration—provide such an incentive (see Box 6.4). Public subsidy in a well-designed supplier development program is an example of such quasirent. Private companies take the lead and share the major risk by jointly developing their SME suppliers. Yet the state might be willing to raise returns on its investment in supplier development by subsidizing, for instance, continuous retraining of workers, but only under certain conditions. The supplier program must actually deliver results in terms of new SME suppliers developed, and their level of employment and productivity. Thus, there is a subsidy, but it is contingent on the willingness of large firms to organize a group of potential suppliers, invest managerial time, and reform procurement procedures to open them up to new entrants.

Box 6.4 *Quasi-Rents as a Motivation for Concerted Action*

The success of Japan, the Republic of Korea, and other Asian high performers is well known. While state activism has undoubtedly played a role, the particular aspects of state intervention that were useful rather than counterproductive are debatable. An increasingly influential market-enhancing view pioneered by M. Aoki singles out government as a facilitator of market institutions and of concerted action to create such institutions.

Patents—temporary protection granted in exchange for successful commercialization of R&D—is an example of quasi-rents; that is, rents contingent on performance. Quasi-rents seem to be important when private risks are high, concerted action is difficult, and high-powered incentives are required to elicit action. The major issue is whether the government is capable of enforcing its own rules to make sure that additional incentives are actually contingent on performance rather than on traditional lobbying. To prevent self-dealing, it may be necessary to require substantial private effort before any government involvement becomes a possibility.

Perhaps the best-known example of quasi-rents is export promotion in Korea. The government subsidized export credit to firms, but only on the condition of strong export performance. This system is difficult to replicate. It requires unusually strong monitoring and implementation capabilities on the part of government. In the age of the knowledge economy, products and processes change so quickly and continuously that picking winners becomes more and more difficult.

The challenge now is to pilot decentralized mechanisms based on quasi-rents, as a motivation for private actors to innovate and engage in the creation of new institutions that deliver public goods.

Source: Aoki et al. (1997).

Rent opportunities, to be captured, require a lot of the firm in terms of thinking, doing, and risk taking. Consequently, there are not many takers: rent opportunity is not necessarily a strong enough motivation to induce firms to do new things. Allocation of quasi-rents is therefore by self-enforcement and self-selection. Rather than the government picking winners, private agents choose to participate on the bases of their capability and propensity to innovate.

One example of such new generation of programs is a pilot supplier development program into a national supplier development program that is broadly similar to the Irish linkage program discussed in Chapter 3. The outcome of such a program is improved quality, technology, and marketing and design capabilities of suppliers, and a better quality of inputs for buyers. For instance, a pilot application of supplier development methodology prepared by Nacional Financiera (NAFIN) and United Nations Development Programme (UNDP), which involved 5 large Mexican buying firms and 24 SMEs as their strategic suppliers, resulted in the course of a year in significant gains for small suppliers and large buying companies. The thrust of the methodology is a coordinated private sector–driven provision of technical assistance (ranging from simple auto-diagnostics to ISO9000/ISO 14000 certification), and capacity building for small suppliers. The pilot group of SMEs recorded a 46 percent increase in labor productivity, a 26 percent reduction of inventories, and a 10 percent cost reduction; large buying companies reduced payment periods to small companies by 75 percent and increased the productivity of their purchasing departments by 30 percent.

To achieve those gains, buyers and suppliers relied upon, and adapted to their own needs, the whole gamut of SME assistance programs. Hence a pilot supplier development initiative would provide a powerful impetus to redesign the public enterprise support infrastructure. The initiative would establish a coherent system of supplier development with clear rules of responsibility and accountability for private actors (buying companies, their suppliers, and financial institutions), state governments, and federal agencies. The proposed system combines technical assistance and access to finance components at three levels: the company level, the regional/cluster level, and the national level (see Figure 6.2).

On a company level (microlevel initiatives), interested large buying companies are starting to form institutes of supplier development as a technical assistance vehicle, and/or Fideocomisos AAA (company-level trust funds to finance suppliers). The proposed initiative would not finance the private institutes, but it would

Figure 6.2 *National Supplier Development Program*

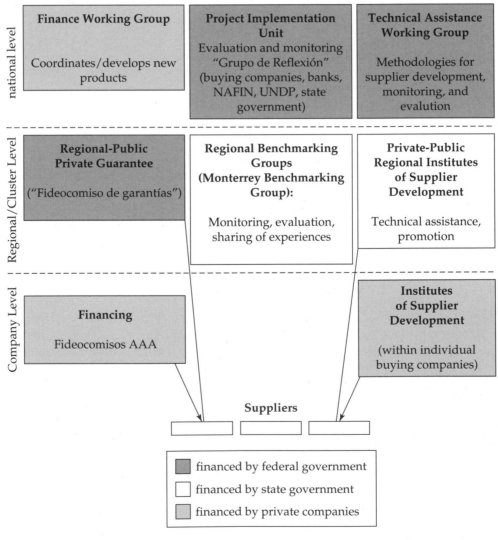

Source: World Bank staff.

provide assistance to help redesign and fine-tune company-level supplier development efforts.

On a cluster/regional level, large buying companies, in collaboration with Secretaries of Economic Development of state governments, would form small, private sector–managed cluster institutes for supplier development (in the auto parts and furniture sector, for instance) to serve the collective needs of a cluster. State governments and buying companies would provide financing for the institutes.

On a national level, knowledge creation and the dissemination of policy knowledge would be provided as a public good. Two technical working groups (finance and technical assistance) would be formed to coordinate development and testing of new products, and to monitor and evaluate the outcomes and impacts. The initiative would have an Internet-based monitoring and evaluation module to facilitate documentation of private and social gains from supplier development efforts and sharing of experiences. As documented experience of supplier development initiatives accumulates, a Private-Public Advisory Council, consisting of top private and public leaders, would be formed to provide strategic direction to supplier development.

National vision and leadership are key, but they cannot be constructed overnight. The concluding chapter of this book explores Mexico's regional diversity as an advantage to be explored in the country's transition to a knowledge economy.

7

Regional Leadership in the Transition to a Knowledge Economy

This chapter shows how regional dynamics can become an entry point for a transition to knowledge-based economy. A taxonomy of Mexico's regions is presented, and policy agendas are offered for each of the four types of states: advanced states (also described in the chapter as fragile leaders), emerging leaders, lagging states, and "dormant potential" states. In conclusion, the chapter outlines a new system for promoting subnational initiatives to enhance knowledge-based competitiveness.

Mexican States and Their Policy Agendas

To capture diverse regional agendas that lay out transitions to a knowledge-based economy, we performed a modified knowledge assessment and constructed a knowledge economy index for each state.

The knowledge assessment methodology and a construction of an aggregate index follow the national methodology of a four pillar framework. It is based on 30 variables such as adult literacy and secondary enrollment for the education pillar; patents per 1,000 people for innovation pillar; and telephones lines per 1,000 people for the ICT pillar. Yet it differs from it in two features. We omitted the incentive regime pillar mainly because we lacked relevant data. We added the economic performance pillar that includes such variables as GDP, FDI per capita, human development index, manufacturing productivity, and number of businesses per 1,000 people. As in national knowledge assessment methodology, variables are not weighted. Annex 6 provides a more detailed description of the variables.

The knowledge economy index is closely correlated to a state's GDP (see Figure 7.1). Figure 7.2 shows Mexican states divided (somewhat arbitrarily) into four groups:

- The most advanced states (by the level of the index) in central and northern Mexico;
- "Emerging leaders," central states with less-developed knowledge infrastructures but advancing rapidly;
- Lagging states, southern states that are the worst three performers; and
- "Dormant potential" states that are below average but higher than the lagging states.

Below we outline four regional policy agendas (see Table 7.1). All four agendas agree on the need to marshal existing knowledge assets (such as universities and research centers) to develop technology and technical assistance for addressing local needs and opportunities.

Figure 7.1 *Mexico: Regional Knowledge Index and GDP per Capita*

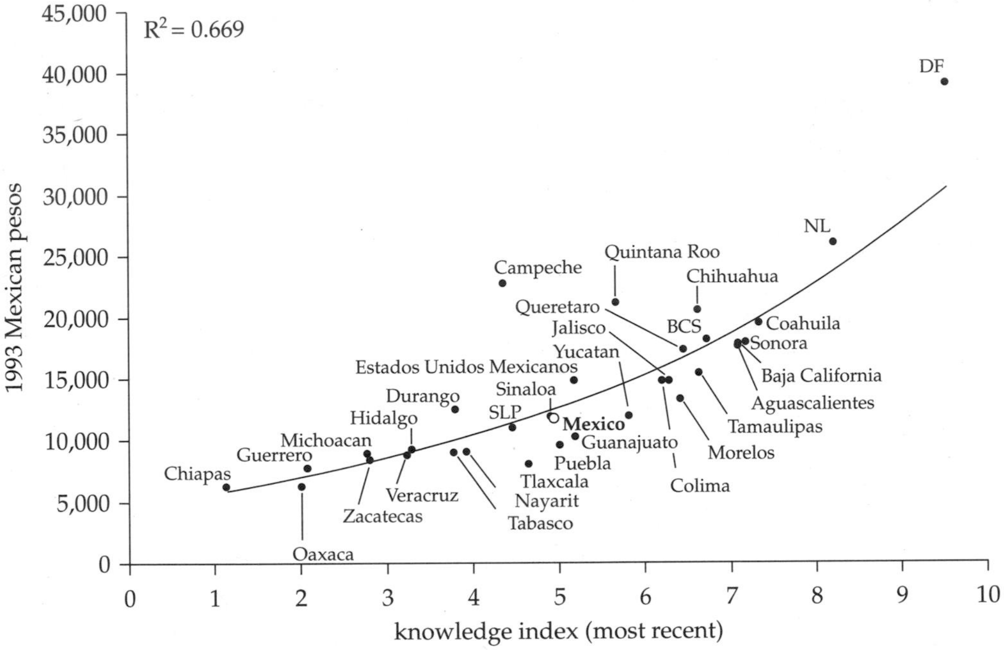

Source: World Bank staff.
Note: BCS—Baja California Sur, DF—Distrito Federal, NL—Nuevo Leon, SLP—San Luis Potossi.

Fragile Leaders

Growth during the past 10 years has come from firms taking advantage of NAFTA, using Mexico as an export base to sell to the North American market. However, Mexico has been losing its preferential trade status vis-à-vis other low-labor-cost countries. As a result, many of the firms, particularly in the electronics and garment sectors, have been emigrating to countries with lower costs. Fragile leaders (mostly northern states and Distrito Federal) face the challenge of reinventing themselves in the context of growing global competition (see Box 7.1 for an illustration). They have the most advanced knowledge endowments of any states in Mexico, but some of them are losing their competitive edge. Border states have grown on the basis of low labor costs and proximity to the United States. As the result of growth, they face congestion and higher wages. The exodus of maquilas to China signifies erosion of traditional competitive advantages and calls for a two-pronged approach:

- Take advantage of geography (proximity to the United States and Canada) by improving infrastructure and decreasing logistics costs; and
- Increase the knowledge content of exports by developing effective educational, innovation, and enterprise upgrading institutions.

Employment and growth have been generated by two quite different types of agents. The first is national big business (with its capital in Monterrey), concentrated mostly in *mature* industries. Multinationals and maquilas comprise the second type of agent. The issue with multinationals and maquilas is low local content and (with very few exceptions, such as Delphi Engineering Center) a virtual absence of innovative activities. To increase local sourcing, there is a need for more

Figure 7.2 *Knowledge Index by Mexican States*

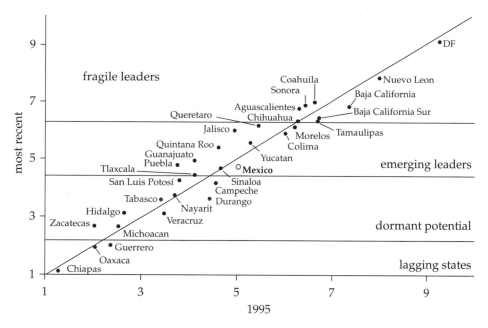

Source: World Bank, "Knowledge Assessment Methodology," http://www.worldbank.org/kam.
Note: The countries or regions plotted below the 45 degree line exhibited a decline in performance during the given time interval, while those plotted above the line showed improvement. There are two possible explanations for a decline: the country may actually have lost ground in absolute terms, or may have improved more slowly than its comparators.

active dialogue with multinationals to create supplier development programs. Well-designed supplier development programs put the private sector in the driver's seat and can overcome numerous constraints faced by private business. Ireland is a paragon of developing efficient private sector–driven national linkage programs (see Chapter 3, Box 3.5).

Monterrey—the industrial, financial, educational, and technological capital of northern Mexico—symbolizes that region's increasingly fragile success and is the key to its future. Monterrey is home to national big business, Mexico's largest private university (Technologico de Monterrey), and many other important institutions. Local business people with national influence and an international perspective have spurred growth. The global expansion of CEMEX and the Latin American expansion of FEMSA (Fomento Economico Mexicano) became examples of how to put knowledge to work in mature industries. Yet other mature industries (glass, steel, textiles, and petrochemicals) face significant challenges in transitioning to a knowledge-based economy. A point of departure in this transformation is that Monterrey has many links to the United States, and especially to Texas. In this context, the government of Nuevo León is developing a project of regional integration of Nuevo Leon with Texas and with the northeastern Mexican states of Coahuila, Tamaulipas, and Chihuahua.

At the center of the program is *Monterrey: Knowledge Technopolis,* an initiative designed to take advantage of the intellectual capital of eight of the best higher education schools and research centers located in the city. Among these are the Tecnológico de Monterrey and the Universidad Autónoma de Nuevo León. Together, these institutions can foster the development of networks and intellectual capital,

Table 7.1 *Four Types of States in Mexico and Four Policy Agendas*

Type of state	Source of growth	Promising features	Major issue or threat	Policy recommendations	Entry points
Fragile leaders (mostly northern states and distrito federal)	National big business concentrated in mature industries; *maquila* industry and multinationals	Monterrey as an industrial hub of Mexico Monterrey Institute of Technology as a model of private sector–driven higher education and lifelong learning	A threat from low-cost countries: exodus of footloose businesses	Two-pronged strategy: to take advantage of geography (proximity to the United States and Canada); improve infrastructure and decrease logistics costs; increase the knowledge content of exports by developing effective educational, innovation and enterprise upgrading institutions	Develop Monterrey as a knowledge technopolis Promote supplier development program with big national business and multinationals
Emerging leaders (central and central-northern states)	Major multinationals and their value chains; emerging knowledge- and service-intensive clusters	Guadalajara as education, culture, and manufacturing center of Mexico Technology development centers of General Motors in Toluca, IBM in Guadalajara, GE in Queretaro, and Motorola in Puebla	Exhaustion of cost-based FDI: transition to cluster-based growth	Make a major stride in coverage and quality of higher education Accelerate cluster processes by enhancing academia-industry linkages and efficient "bridge" organizations	Deepen and strengthen knowledge-based clusters

Table 7.1 (Continued)

Type of state	Source of growth	Promising features	Major issue or threat	Policy recommendations	Entry points
"Dormant potential" states (Zacatecas, Michoacán, Hidalgo, Campeche, Veracruz, San Luis Potosi, Tabasco, Nayarit, Durang)	Natural resources (in particular, mineral wealth)	"Transformando Campeche" as a private-public effort to move up value chains and bring knowledge-intensive business	Volatility and (in states such as Zacatecas) decline associated with the reliance on mineral resources Little pressure to grow and reform: migration of reasonably educated labor to the United States	Diversify the economy and increase value added of natural resources by improving investment climate and engaging in investment promotion and linkage promotion initiatives	Develop infrastructure for a retirement community (health services and leisure industry) Utilize remittances for community infrastructure and micro-enterprise development
Lagging states (Chiapas, Oaxaca, Guerrero)	Tourism; isolated industry enclaves	Tourism development Fondo Chiapas as a controversial but promising attempt at concerted action	Increasingly disintegrating from the rest of Mexico	Four-pronged strategy: strengthen the rule of law and increase credibility of a public sector; strengthen local public institutions through training and twinning arrangements; improve quality of basic education and reduce rezago educativo; accelerate local pockets of vitality through careful private sector–driven interventions	Develop viable local suppliers for public sector and large private firms; support ecotourism based on cultural heritage and natural beauty endowments; exploit the potential of countercyclical tropical agriculture

Source: World Bank staff.

Box 7.1 *Transition to Knowledge Economy: Example of Aguas Calientes*

A nationwide agenda of transition can be illustrated by the example of Aguas Calientes. Aguas Calientes went through three quite distinct periods of growth:

- *1970s.* Mexico made the best of import substitution during the 1970s. It provided physical infrastructure to attract national firms, and the first multinational (Texas Instruments) arrived in 1979.
- *1980s and 1990s.* Mexico sought good quality education and labor stability. Following passage of the North American Free Trade Agreement (NAFTA) in 1994, a major expansion of multinationals occurred in Aguas Calientes.
- *Early 2000s.* Emergence of knowledge-based NAFTA agenda: promotion of linkages, cluster, and supplier development (See Figure 7.3).

Figure 7.3 *Timeline of Transition to Knowledge-Based Economy in Aguas Calientes*

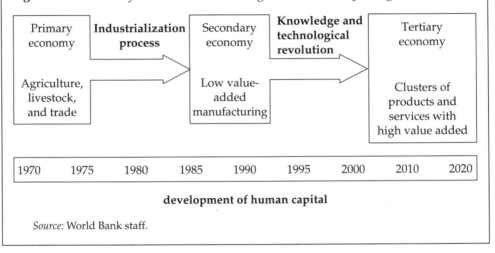

Source: World Bank staff.

---

and thereby serve as the state's innovation system. The aim is to eventually develop a Latin American Route 128. This transformation will require concerted action by economic groups, technology and educational organizations, and the government. This is not an easy task, yet the transformation of Monterrey is a litmus test for the whole of Mexico. Mexico's industrial transformation at the turn of the twentieth century started in Monterrey; now, at the beginning of the twenty-first century Monterrey can become a springboard for transformation to a knowledge-based economy.

Emerging Leaders

The states categorized as emerging leaders fall into two categories. The states in the first category, such as Jalisco, Guanajuato, Puebla, and Queretaro are located in the center and center-north of Mexico. They are characterized by high education and knowledge endowment, yet they face a lower level of industrial and urban congestion than do the northern states. The emerging leaders signal Mexico's future, as exemplified by the technology development centers of major multinational corporations: General Motors in Toluca, IBM in Guadalajara, GE in Queretaro, and Motorola in Puebla. To take advantage of the presence of these MNCs, the govern-

---

Box 7.2 *Adoption of Organizational Knowledge: Innovative Supplier Development Program*

In 1996, 11 large companies in Guadalajara (domestic and multinational) signed a two-year voluntary agreement with Mexico's *Secretaria de Medio Ambiente, Recursos Naturales y Pesca.* The agreement was to mentor small suppliers in implementing environmental management systems (EMS). Each company invited two or three small suppliers to participate in the pilot. The large companies and the World Bank provided the SMEs with funding for EMS training and implementation support. A team of consultants—from two local universities and a foreign environmental management consulting firm—delivered the services. The aim was to adapt for SMEs the ISO 14001 environmental management systems model originally designed for large firms; and evaluate the applicability of the model and the sustainability and replication of the pilot partnership.

By late 1998, virtually all participating SMEs had made major advances in the implementation of ISO 14001, in the reduction of pollutants, and in their ability to use general management systems. Based on this experience, the national government has begun to consider new environmental protection legislation.

The success of this supplier development program can be attributed to four principal factors. First, the invitation to participate usually came from the mentor company rather than from the government or university. Most SMEs indicated that this was a vital source of motivation and cooperation. While all participating firms had some sense of ownership in the project, the presence of a large company "champion" provided important assurance that their dedication was not misplaced. Second, the use of the consultant network provided resources otherwise unavailable to SMEs and even to many large firms. The network in effect provided a rapid response system; a diverse group of experts drew on one another's skills and knowledge to resolve local issues. Third, representatives of local and national environmental authorities, although they attended the pilot's sessions mainly as observers, contributed to the success of the program. They focused managers' attention on the program, and prompted many of them to learn about the benefits and drawbacks of different standards and enforcement actions. Fourth, beyond the training in technical issues, the use of benchmarks and an iterative, collaborative review process was beneficial. It demonstrated new forms of cooperation to participants at all levels and improved the information basis on which they could build the next round of efforts.

Source: World Bank staff.

---

ment should put at the forefront of the policy agenda the facilitation of innovation clusters. This implies major advances in the coverage and quality of higher education, and the enhancement of academia-industry linkages and efficient bridging organizations. Cooperation is at the center of the art and craft of facilitating innovation clusters. The emerging leaders have already demonstrated their capability for collective action, particularly under the guidance of experienced tutors (see Box 7.2). The priority now is to strengthen networks of technology development organizations that are efficient and demand driven. We refer here to incubators to promote university-industry linkages, sectoral and industry technology development centers, and the venture capital industry.

The second category is states such as Quintana Roo, Yucatan, and Morelos, which have both relatively high educational level and significant natural endowments. Those states were able to capitalize on their endowments by attracting investments into the service sector (tourism), agricultural processing, and maquila investments.

Dormant Potential States

Dormant potential states depend almost exclusively on low value-added natural resources. The resources can be abundant, and the states relatively prosperous (such as Tabasco, Campeche, and Veracruz), or in decline (such as mining in Zacatecas). As a consequence of their relative decline, Zacatecas and Michoacan are characterized by very high labor migration to the United States and very high per capita remittances. Diversification of local economies to move to higher value-added exploitation of natural resources, services, and manufacturing is a main policy objective in those states. Knowledge-based services such as higher brand tourism (Box 7.3) can provide new employment possibilities for the labor force that currently emigrates to the United States.

Some of dormant potential states are characterized by the vicious circle of low expectations, low demand for institutional change, and thus low investments and outcomes. To break this pattern from the private sector side, first movers—firms that enter new markets and do things differently—are paramount. Traditional top-down industrial policies to attract investments have a decidedly mixed record. In contrast, successful "light touch," bottom-up interventions (in countries as diverse as Brazil and EU latecomers) suggest the following entry points:

- Investment promotion (which includes promotion of entry of new national and global players).
- Supplier development (particularly in states with natural resource wealth, such as Campeche and Tabsaco).
- Promotion of microbusiness.

Box 7.3 *Culture as a Key Intangible: Potential of High Value-Added Tourism*

Mexico has made significant progress in exploring its tourist potential, although it still lags significantly behind countries such as Spain, France, and Italy. From a knowledge economy perspective, it is important to note that tourists come to those countries not only to see a new destination but to taste and immerse themselves in a unique culture and history. Following those examples, Mexico needs to move to higher value-added tourism, which is mainly about intangibles: reputation, exploration of local culture and history, and sophisticated marketing capabilities on a global scale. Creation of a "sense of belonging"— ties to an ethnic, cultural, or religious community—is an important motivation for participating in such tours.

For instance, local history tours can be developed in the states of Michoacan and Zacatecas. The way history is packaged into tourism in Annapolis, Maryland, is one example. Such tours (along with tequila tasting and other higher value-added services) can be developed jointly and marketed first to Mexican migrants in the United States. The U.S.-born children of Mexican migrants may prove to be a sizeable entry point for "nostalgia tourism." Favorable conditions for the expansion of North American retirement communities already exist in San Miguel de Allende and Cuernavaca. Engineering a resurgence of Mexico's once famous movie industry is yet another opportunity.

As always, private actors will need to assume major risks in exploring commercial opportunities related to such intangibles, but the state has a role to play in enhancing a favorable investment climate and bringing in international expertise to convert opportunities in commercial services.

Source: World Bank staff.

- Facilitation of rural-urban linkages.
- Facilitation of demand-driven business development services for SMEs.
- Public procurements as a means to develop local SMEs.
- Efforts to improve investment climate.

Some of the states are starting to move decisively in these directions. Transformando Campeche is a promising private-public effort to develop high value-added services and manufacturing. Innovative programs to leverage donations of migrants' clubs in the United States have become best practice all over the world. (The clubs collect for community infrastructure development in the home communities.) In three-for-one programs, for instance, every peso of these collective remittances is matched by one peso of federal and one peso of state contributions. Hence, every peso of a migrant generates three pesos of investment. There are many promising beginnings. The challenge is to transform promising pilots into a sustained effort to improve public service delivery, education, and the investment climate.

Lagging States

Analysis of knowledge endowments shows three southern states (Oaxaca, Guerrero, and Chiapas) to clearly be lagging states. The states face the most basic agenda of building robust institutions. To that end the following four-pronged strategy is recommended:

- Strengthen the rule of law and increase the credibility of the public sector;
- Strengthen local public institutions through training and twinning arrangements;
- Improve the quality of basic education and reduce the rezago educativo (educational gap); and
- Accelerate local pockets of vitality through careful private sector–driven interventions.

In these states, the issue of leadership, both private and public, looms as the most significant challenge. Entry points to unleash private sector dynamism and to demonstrate tangible results are paramount, but they require patience and careful monitoring to transform good intentions into robust institutions. Many initiatives in the past (such as Fondo Chiapas) were well conceived and showed substantial promise, but because of weak management and poor monitoring by stakeholders, the promise was never realized. As entry points for the lagging states, one can suggest the development of viable local suppliers for public sector firms and large private firms as well as ecotourism based on cultural heritage and natural beauty endowments.

Other countries under similarly adverse circumstances have demonstrated tangible improvements in areas traditionally believed to have little promise. The key to successful programs is clear leadership, capable of breaking the grip of entrenched interests, and governance structures that can unleash bottom-up initiatives. Chiapas has recently developed a number of initiatives to strengthen local government capacity, such as a network of e-government kiosks to speed the delivery of public services and reduce corruption. These initiatives need to be evaluated and expanded.

Institutional Design of a National System to Promote Transition to a Knowledge-Based Economy

A diversity of innovative local initiatives exists in Mexico. Many of them have been described in preceding chapters. What is sorely needed is a robust mechanism to facilitate, monitor, and scale up these initiatives as a new role for federal government. The challenge of such new governance structures is not unique for Mexico. All countries, including OECD economies, face it quite acutely. OECD economies such as Ireland, Finland, or the Republic of Korea, and emerging economies such as China, have become examples of so-called pragmatic agendas that put innovations in governance at the center of policy making and implementation. A favorable climate for institutional innovation is one pillar of the new pragmatism, which entails, inter alia, the capability for evaluation, and in particular, the ability to distinguish between successes and failures, and the ability to scale up successes.

Designing a system of new institutions consistent with the knowledge-driven NAFTA agenda is an open-ended process based on a diversity of institutional innovations. Every detail of the second-generation NAFTA institutional architecture cannot be planned now. The details can be discovered only through careful, and carefully monitored, experiments.

A national system to promote local initiatives is likely to rely on the following building blocks:

- A federal private-public governance council that endorses proposals to promote knowledge-based competitiveness of states and firms;
- A network of top-notch managerial teams that design and manage competitiveness programs, and first-rate managers similar in caliber to the technocrats who negotiated NAFTA;
- A mechanism to scale up and diffuse good projects;
- Allocation of resources contingent on the results of evaluation and continuous monitoring; and
- Technical assistance, particularly to weak actors (less-developed states and SMEs), to prepare knowledge-based projects.

The basic institutional architecture of a national system to facilitate, evaluate, and scale up local innovations may take various forms but should comprise these elements:

- A distinct regulator and financier at the national level;
- An independent management unit; and
- A diverse array of national and international service providers.

A National Advisory Council

A distinct regulator and financier at the national level are needed. Ideally, a private-public council with substantial private sector participation would define the rules of the game (in a statement of policies and operating procedures) and ensure the satisfactory functioning of those procedures. A national institution with a leadership mandate in this area, such as the Secretary of Economy, could help by pooling experience, so that successful innovations are rapidly identified and failures are quickly exposed; it would provide the common infrastructure needed by all

> **Box 7.4** *Scan Globally, Experiment Locally: Developing Managerial Capability*
>
> Transition to a knowledge-based economy needs to be supported by a corps of men and women, comparable in terms of talent, training, and dedication to those who directed opening to trade, privatization, deregulation, and the negotiation of international treaties with the United States and the European Community. The nucleus of the group would be people who have already emerged from states such as Jalisco and Chihuahua, which pioneered the process of concerted problem solving. This nucleus would be supplemented with new recruits drawn from recent university graduates, Mexican nationals working in international agencies, and those with master's degrees and PhDs returning from study abroad. The salary scale and reward structure should be competitive with the private sector, and for the nucleus of experienced state officials they should be paid an amount on a par with the salary for the position they presently hold.
>
> Initial training for this group could follow the model Harvard University has developed for the orientation of newly elected representatives and senators in the U.S. Congress. That model is used to train the newly appointed staff of international agencies (for example, the director general of the International Labor Organization). A four-week program organized and led by a Mexican university is envisaged. While the program would draw primarily on Mexican university faculty, it might be supplemented by guest lectures by business leaders, government officials, and foreign experts. The Harvard model focuses on classroom training in economics and management. The Mexican model should also include direct exposure in the field to operating programs in several different states—and in at least one developed country, such as in the United States, and one developing country, such as Chile. The training of recruits should expose them to this valuable international experience.
>
> *Source:* World Bank staff.

regional economies. Major organizations such as Bancomext, Consejo Nacional de Ciencia y Tecnologia (CONACYT), Nacional Financiera (NAFIN), and Secretaria del Trabajo y Prevision Social (STPS) would be represented on the council to help ensure, among other things, that distinct public entities do not offer similar programs with differing subsidy rates. Private sector participation is essential to ensure transparency, with conflicts to be resolved by the presidency. The council would accelerate the formation of champions and managers to create new programs and organizations (see Box 7.4).

To allocate funds among the states, the National Advisory Council could rely on matching grants from the federal government, implement a ranking system based on measures of economic performance, or encourage competition for open-ended projects.

MATCHING GRANTS   Under the current matching grants program, the federal government agrees to match every peso, up to a certain limit, that state governments dedicate to economic development projects. Those projects are decided in collaboration with private actors, on the condition that the actors match the state contribution as well. The idea is simply that if the regional government and economic actors are willing to put their own money at risk to finance the projects they define together, then the federal government can assume that their choices are well considered, and add its backing as well. The advantage of this method is that it imposes some discipline on project selection, with almost no increase in red tape.

The economic actors, public and private, at the regional level are given an incentive to sort through their priorities and start looking for potential problems; and the federal government limits itself to ratifying their provisional decisions as they emerge.

One shortcoming of the program is that it foresees little sharing of experience at the national level. The lack of formalization of experiences weakens decision making on projects. Word of success presumably gets around, but the process of deliberation about prospective projects and projects that are, in fact, working remains a black box from the official point of view. Political and bureaucratic meddling is discouraged, but at the price of a kind of willful ignorance concerning what the actors might be learning. The second drawback of the matching grants approach is that it funds those who are on the verge of funding themselves. It thus comes close to violating the fairness requirement, even though its operation is nothing but evenhanded in the way it treats like contenders for funds.

THE BUSINESS CLIMATE RANKING SYSTEM   The second framework for allocating funds among the states also imposes discipline on project selection while holding bureaucracy and the politics of clientelism in check. However, it does this not by ratifying the actors' decisions, but by providing information on economic performance that causes actors to reflect on the possibilities in new ways.

The crucial idea could be the creation of a league of regional economic performance. Projects would be ranked based on these benchmarks of performance:

1. Business registration—cost (for all areas, cost includes time and formal and informal types of payments and contributions, including bribes), procedures required, and delays;
2. Business licensing—numbers and types required, cost, time, and payments required;
3. Obtaining business premises—procedure, costs, constraints, delays;
4. Import and export regulation, customs procedures, costs, delays;
5. Product inputs and equipment certification—types, incidence, procedures, costs, delays;
6. Tax administration—requirements, constraints, costs, and number of taxes and forms; and
7. Business inspections—types (and agency responsible), costs, number, and process followed.

COMPETITION FOR OPEN-ENDED PROJECTS   This third framework uses benchmarking to select projects and to force discussion about the criteria of project selection. Very generally, it operates on two levels. At the top level, a committee of the relevant government entities and qualified private actors, domestic and foreign, collaborates with potential users to establish the criteria for participation and the initial metrics by which applications are to be ranked. At the bottom level, project groups compete to present projects that score highly under the emergent criteria. After each round of projects, the selection criteria and benchmarks are adjusted to reflect improved measures of performance and a richer understanding of success. At least two variants are imaginable, depending on whether projects concern states or other broad jurisdictions of government on the one hand, or groups of firms typically operating in many different political jurisdictions on the other.

Consider, as an illustration of the first possibility, a national program to improve the business environment along the seven dimensions listed above. As the states, by their particular regulations and practices, define distinct business environments, the collaborative elaboration of benchmarks and selection criteria will necessarily entail a joint effort by representatives of the states, national institutions, and private sector. Project funds are then allocated to states according to the criteria and actual rankings; states will allocate the funds they have received to individual projects, applying the national procedures and criteria where appropriate, and augmenting them with local ones, as required. Competition for funds drives efforts to improve. States that do not rank well initially—and projects within high-ranking states that fare poorly in early selection rounds—will be eligible for technical assistance according to criteria established, again, through national and local collaboration. The types of technical assistance, and the level of funding, will be adjusted in a rhythm synchronized with the revisions of the performance metrics and selection criteria.

The disadvantage of this open-ended program regards governance. The criteria selection committee creates opportunities for abuse that are avoided in both the matching grant and business climate benchmark schemes. The dangers can be mitigated, in part, by emphasizing procedures: making the use of transparent methods for selecting program officers and project members a formal criterion for selection, and then using the information that these procedures produce to identify suspect operations. Again, the nature of the projects themselves, and the information they produce about interim results, reduce the threat of corruption or cronyism. The active involvement of outsiders with incentives to denounce collusion can help as well.

An Independent Management Unit

To ensure that there is no conflict of interest in funding decisions, the unit responsible for administering resources and intermediating between supply and demand ideally should be independent and follow transparent operating procedures for resource allocation. The resource allocation procedures should be designed to minimize any tendency toward corruption and clientelism. The procedures could follow the principle of first come first served, to attempt to lessen discretion in the allocation of subsidies, or they could stipulate a more elaborate contest where entrants (enterprises and associated public and private service providers) would have to explain their accomplishments to date and how they could become stronger through activities they propose.

The management unit also might actively promote the benefits of utilizing support services and offer advice (for example, on how to decide the type of service that would be most beneficial). Currently, there are at least two management unit models in Latin America: (i) an externally hired contracting company under a management service agreement (usually backed up by the resources and reputation of an international consultancy) and (ii) an independent local institution with complete financial and operational autonomy from the government. We envision a somewhat different model, which stresses the redirection of existing institutions. The local management unit could be a committee composed of representatives of existing service organizations, potential new entrants, and qualified representatives of private firms (such as the director of the purchasing department of a multinational, with long experience in new supplier relations).

National and International Service Providers

National and international service providers are usually private sector consultants, but they could be service providers from the public sector, as long as they charge for their services and compete on an equal basis with private providers. To ensure that any service provided to the enterprises is relevant and needed, enterprises should contribute a strong share of the financing themselves, typically at least 50 percent, toward the cost of fees and expenses associated with external support services.

Conclusion

Although stakeholders may agree that certain characteristics, such as a decentralized and demand-driven mechanisms, are desirable, different approaches in different localities under one umbrella demonstration program should be tested. (For example, using an existing or restructured institution as the management unit could be tested and compared to using an external contractor as the management unit.) Following preparatory discussions in various localities, Caintra may be determined an appropriate choice as a management unit in Monterrey. On the other hand, in a region with weak local institutions, the independent management unit might be a private contractor from a foreign country. (It then would progressively substitute local staff for foreign staff as knowledge is transmitted.) As a general rule, institutional creativity is the name of the game. A transitional scheme may be required to gradually transfer financing and service provision from the federal level to the subnational level and to independent service providers.

Many elements of the proposed mechanism already exist. *Fondos mixtos y sectoriales* promote local initiatives. CONACYT, the Ministry of Economy, and other federal agencies reach out to movers and shakers in the private sector.

The transition to a system of new capabilities and institutions, consistent with the knowledge-driven "NAFTA plus" agenda, is an open-ended process. It involves diverse institutional innovations designed to generate credible commitments among stakeholders. It would be impossible to describe every detail of the architecture of the knowledge-driven NAFTA. An exciting if pragmatic agenda lies ahead for Mexico. Such an agenda can only be developed by Mexico itself. Our objective was to provide input to the evolving debate by calling attention to the stakes, the issues, and the accomplishments to date. The challenge now is to transform many promising discrete initiatives into a critical mass of changes that will trigger Mexico's rapid transition to a knowledge-based economy.

Annex 1

Theoretical Framework for Growth Projections

Decomposition of Economic Growth

Theoretical Framework

In this total factor productivity (TFP) decomposition exercise, we consider a neo-classical aggregate production function that accounts for the quality of labor. For simplicity, we assume a human-capital augmented version of the Cobb-Douglas production function along with perfect competition and constant returns to scale:

$$Y = AK^{\alpha}(HL)^{1-\alpha}$$

where

- Y is the level of aggregate output
- K is the level of the capital stock
- H is the level of the human capital stock
- L is the size of the labor force
- A is total factor productivity
- α is the share of capital in national income.

Taking logs and time derivatives and rearranging, leads to the estimate of growth rate of total factor productivity with human-capital augmentation:

$$\hat{A} = \hat{Y} - \alpha\hat{K} - (1-\alpha)(\hat{H} + \hat{L})$$

where

$\hat{X}$ represents the growth rate of variable X.

Following Woessmann (2000), we specify human capital stock to have the Mincer specification with the simplest form being:

$$H = e^{rs}$$

where

- r is the market returns to education
- s is the average years of schooling.

Data Sources

Real GDP (in constant 1995 US$) and labor force figures were taken from the World Development Indicators 2003.

The capital stock was constructed using gross capital formation (in constant 1995 US$) obtained from the World Development Indicators 2003. The perpetual inventory method was used with an assumed depreciation rate of 5 percent. To calculate the initial value of the capital stock, we used the average growth rate of gross capital formation for the first five years and applied the formula for the sum of an infinite geometric progressive series.

Estimates for the returns to education for Ireland, Korea, and Mexico were taken from Bils and Klenow (2000). In the case of Finland, there are no available data on the returns to education. As such, we used as a proxy the average of 17 high-income countries for which there were available data provided in Psacharopoulos (1994). As for the average years of schooling, we used the simple average of the estimates obtained from Barro and Lee (2001) and Cohen and Soto (2001). Note that given that data for the average years of schooling were available only on a decade basis, we used interpolation by growth rates to obtain annual estimates of the average years of schooling in order to construct the human capital stock on an annual basis.

The estimates for the labor shares in national income for Korea and Finland were taken from Gollin (2001), while those for Ireland and Mexico were taken from Bernanke and Gürkaynak (2001).[1]

Results

Table A1.1 presents the results of the TFP decomposition. Our annual growth rates of TFP were averaged to produce decade averages[2].

Table A1.1 *Annual Growth Rates of Total Factor Productivity (in percent)*

	Ireland	Finland	Korea, Rep. of	Mexico
1961–1970		2.8691	0.5301	0.2922
1971–1980	2.8346	1.3350	–0.1400	0.4048
1981–1990	2.2632	0.9824	2.8704	–2.5922
1991–2000	4.2404	1.5278	1.8207	–0.1286

Source: Author's calculations.

Projections

In this section, we produce some projections for real GDP per capita for Mexico for the years 2001 to 2020 using different assumptions for the growth rate of TFP.

With reference to Figure A1.1, *Projection 1* plots the path Mexico's real GDP per capita would take if the TFP growth rate were to take its 1991–2000 average value, that is, –0.13 percent per annum. *Projection 2* plots the path Mexico's real GDP per capita would take if the TFP growth rate were to take 2 percent annum, which is close to the 1991–2000 decade average for Korea. *Projection 3* plots the path Mexico's real GDP per capita would take if the TFP growth rate were to take 3 percent annum, which is close to the 1961–1970 decade average for Finland. Lastly, *projection 4* plots the path Mexico's real GDP per capita would take if the TFP growth rate were to take 4.25 percent per annum, which is the approximate value of the 1991–2000 decade average for Ireland.

---

[1] The estimate for labor share for Ireland, Korea, Finland, and Mexico was 0.750, 0.796, 0.680, and 0.59, respectively. The capital shares were obtained by taking 1 and subtracting the respective labor shares.

[2] Note that for Ireland, gross capital formation data were not available prior to 1971. As such, the average annual growth rate of TFP for the period 1971 to 1980 for Ireland in the above table is in fact the average for 1972–1980.

Figure A1.1 *Mexico: Real GDP per Capita—Alternative Projections 2001–2020*

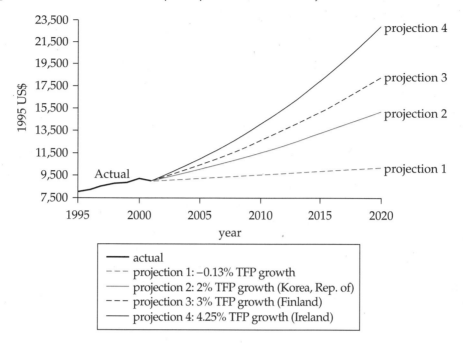

Note that for all 4 projections, capital, labor, and human capital were all assumed to grow at their 1991–2000 average growth rates for Mexico, which are 3.32 percent, 2.75 percent, and 0.92 percent, respectively.

Alternative Methodology

An alternative methodology for computing TFP involves not explicitly accounting for the contribution of human capital as a separate factor of production. This implies that the effects of human capital are aggregated into total factor productivity. From a conceptual standpoint, this methodology is more consistent with the knowledge economy framework, which asserts that the contribution of knowledge to economic growth encompasses the contributions from economic and institutional regime, innovation and technological adoption, ICT infrastructure, and human capital.

As in the first methodology, we consider a standard neoclassical aggregate production function that assumes a Cobb-Douglas specification together with perfect competition and constant returns to scale:

$$Y = AK^{\alpha}L^{1-\alpha}$$

TFP is then derived as the residual after accounting for the contribution of labor and capital to aggregate output. More specifically,

$$A = \frac{Y}{K^{\alpha}L^{1-\alpha}}$$

Next by taking logs and time derivatives, and then rearranging, we obtained the estimate of growth rate of total factor productivity:

$$\hat{A} = \hat{Y} - \alpha\hat{K} - (1-\alpha)\hat{L}$$

where

$\hat{X}$ represents the growth rate of variable X

Table A1.2 below presents the estimates of the growth rates of TFP resulting from this second growth decomposition exercise. The annual growth rates of TFP were again averaged to produce decade averages.[3]

Table A1.2 *Annual Growth Rates of Total Factor Productivity (in percent)*

	Ireland	Finland	Korea, Rep. of	Mexico
1961–1970		3.03	2.08	1.01
1971–1980	3.15	1.86	1.48	0.90
1981–1990	2.74	1.68	4.28	−1.69
1991–2000	4.48	1.58	2.36	0.22
2001–2004		1.42	2.49	−1.41
1991–2004		1.54	2.39	−0.24

Box A1.1 below summarizes results of productivity estimates of other authors (see general bibliography for references).

---

[3] For this second decomposition exercise, recently updated data from the World Development Indicators 2005 were used. Real GDP was in constant 2000 U.S. dollars, whereas in the first decomposition exercise real GDP was in constant 1995 U.S. dollars. Also, the capital stock here was constructed using gross fixed capital formation (in constant 2000 U.S. dollars), which excludes net inventories as a part of investment, making it a more appropriate series for the construction of capital stock.

Box A1.1 *Explanations of Total Factor Productivity Decline in Mexico*

Source	Key findings
Bergoeing et al. (2002)	— TFP in Mexico and Chile dropped during the 1980s. Output in Chile returned to a growth path, but Mexico never recovered, and two decades later it still is 30 percent below the trend for Latin America. — Comparative evidence does not support the notion that this recovery was due to exports or to large external debt. — The differences in economic performance in Mexico and Chile can be explained by the different timing of structural reforms in the two countries. — The crucial difference in performance is explained by the reform of banking and bankruptcy laws.
Bosworth (1998)	—The economic collapse in Mexico of the early 1980s created a persistent disequilibrium situation in which large portions of the labor force are effectively underemployed. —After 1988 the growth in output was barely adequate to match the expansion of factor inputs, and there was little or no increase of capital. — Despite an enormous expansion of foreign borrowing, Mexico has been unable to generate an expansion of capital stock commensurate with the growth in the labor force. — TFP reflects greatly increased allocative inefficiencies; an excess supply of workers has pushed workers into jobs below their normal skill levels since the 1980s. — There has been a failure of investment despite reform measures; Mexico needs a much higher level of investment if it is to provide the future capacity to sustain growth. — Mexico needs ways to smooth the flow of jobs from the informal sector (low technology) to the formal sector.
Fajinzyber and Lederman (1997)	— TFP growth was faster when Mexico was "reformed;" in fact, average TFP growth has been negative in the periods of no reform, possibly due to the fact that recessions have been frequent during this time. — Measured growth in productivity is subject to the effect of short-term fluctuations, which can obscure the impact of reforms on long-run economic performance.
Hallberg, Tan, and Koryukin (2000)	— For the manufacturing sector as a whole, TFP growth accelerated between 1993 and 1995, from an annualized growth rate of 0.6 percent to 13.8 percent. Subsequently, TFP growth rates declined, to 1.3 percent in 1995–1996, and turned negative in 1996–1997. — Nonexporters had less TFP growth than exporters during this period. — Learning through exporting is taking place. While the immediate productivity gains from exporting are modest, sustained productivity gains accrue as experience accumulates. Overall, firms learn and improve productivity through experience with exporting, specifically with years of experience as suppliers. — Firm-level productivity is improved by investments in worker training and implementation of quality control practices.

(continued on next page)

Box A1.1 *(continued)*

Source	Key findings
López-Córdoba (2002)	— Mexico's total factor productivity performance from the early 1980s through the mid-1990s was rather disappointing, with average annual growth between –1 and –2 percent. — Exporting does not have a positive effect on TFP growth; in fact, being an exporter appeared to be negatively correlated with productivity growth. — There is strong support for the view that trade competition fosters improvements in productivity, but there is at best scant evidence that improved access to more and better intermediate inputs translates into productivity growth. — Foreign capital participation reduces productivity, but FDI in industries in which a plant has backward or forward linkages has a significant and positive effect.
Acevedo (2002)	— The source considers only labor productivity. — Schooling has a high impact on wages and productivity; the slow growth in labor productivity in Mexico could be the result of the low education level. — Investment in human capital magnifies technology-driven productivity gains, but Mexico has not invested enough in human capital. — Findings suggest that training obtained outside of firms increases productivity, but Mexico has underinvested in outside training, as can be seen by the high percentage of in-house training.

Annex 2

Knowledge Assessment Methodology (KAM)

The KAM is a user-friendly tool designed by the World Bank Institute to help client countries assess their ability to compete in the global knowledge economy (World Bank 2006). It estimates a country's preparedness to compete in the knowledge economy through a series of relevant and widely available measures. A set of 76 structural and qualitative variables (available for 121 countries) benchmarks how an economy compares with other countries. The KAM helps to identify the problems and opportunities that a country faces, and where it may need to focus policy attention or future investments. The unique strength of the Knowledge for Development (K4D) methodology is its cross-sector approach that enables the user to take a holistic view of a wide range of relevant factors rather than focus only on one area.

The 76 variables serve as proxies for the four areas (pillars) that are critical to the development of a knowledge-based economy: economic and institutional regime, education, innovation, and information and communications technologies (ICTs). Also included within the 76 variables are several measures that track the overall performance of the economy.

Normalization Procedure for the KAM

1. The raw data (u) is collected from World Bank datasets and international literature for 76 variables and 121 countries.
2. Ranks are allocated to countries based on the absolute values (raw data) that describe each and every one of the 76 variables (rank u). Countries with the same performance are allocated the same rank. Therefore, the rank equals 1 for a country that performs the best among the 121 countries in our sample on a particular variable (that is, it has the highest score), the rank equals to 2 for a country that performs second best, and so on.
3. The number of countries with worse rank (Nw) is calculated for each country.
4. The following formula is used in order to normalize the scores for every country on every variable according to their ranking and in relation to the total number of countries in the sample (Nc) with available data: Normalized (u) = 10*(Nw/Nc).
5. The above formula allocates a normalized score from 0 to 10 for each of the 121 countries with available data on the 76 variables. Ten is the top score for the top performers and 0 the worst score for the lagging economies. The top 10 percent of performers receive a normalized score between 9 and 10, the second best 10 percent receive allocated normalized scores between 8 and 9, and so on. As mentioned earlier, more than one country can be allocated either the best or worst normalized scores. The 0–10 scale describes the performance of each country on each variable relative to the performance of the rest of the country sample.

More information on the KAM, its functionalities, technical notes, data sources, and a user guide are available on its Web site: www.worldbank.org/kam.

Annex 3

Comparator Scorecards for Mexico, United States, the Republic of Korea, China, Ireland, and Spain

Mexico

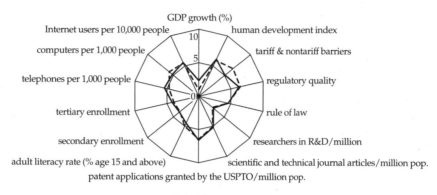

United States

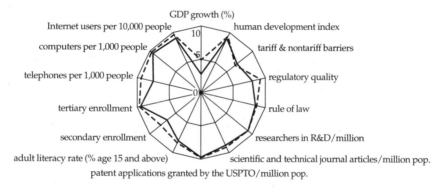

Korea, Rep. of

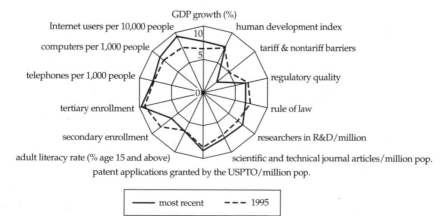

—— most recent   - - - - 1995

Source: World Bank, "Knowledge Assessment Methodology," http://www.worldbank.org/kam.
Note: Each of the 127 variables in the KAM is normalized on a scale of 0 to 10. The fuller the scorecard, the better poised a country is to embrace the knowledge economy. But an economy should not necessarily aim for a perfect score of 10 on all variables because the scorecards may be shaped by the particular structural characteristics of an economy or by trade-offs that characterize different development strategies.

China

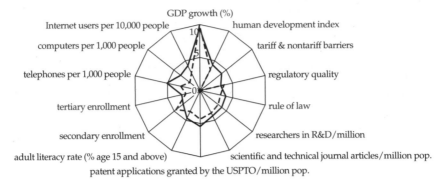

Ireland

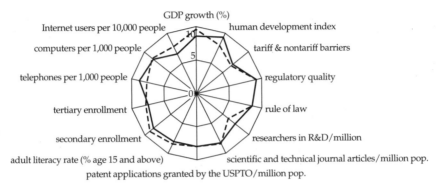

Spain

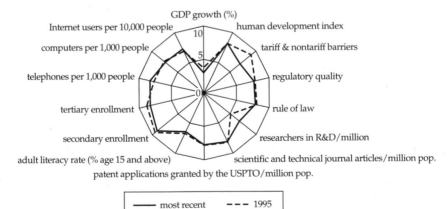

| —— most recent | - - - 1995 |

Source: World Bank, "Knowledge Assessment Methodology," http://www.worldbank.org/kam.
Note: Each of the 127 variables in the KAM is normalized on a scale of 0 to 10. The fuller the scorecard, the better poised a country is to embrace the knowledge economy. But an economy should not necessarily aim for a perfect score of 10 on all variables because the scorecards may be shaped by the particular structural characteristics of an economy or by trade-offs that characterize different development strategies.

Annex 4

Data for Scorecards for Mexico, United States,
Republic of Korea, China, Ireland, and Spain

Variable	Mexico Most recent (actual/normalized)	Mexico 1995 (actual/normalized)	United States Most recent (actual/normalized)	United States 1995 (actual/normalized)	Korea, Rep. of Most recent (actual/normalized)	Korea, Rep. of 1995 (actual/normalized)	China Most recent (actual/normalized)	China 1995 (actual/normalized)	Ireland Most recent (actual/normalized)	Ireland 1995 (actual/normalized)	Spain Most recent (actual/normalized)	Spain 1995 (actual/normalized)
GDP growth (%)	2.40/ 3.15	0.30/ 1.02	2.70/ 3.46	3.80/ 4.80	6.40/ 9.21	4.70/ 6.77	7.90/ 9.69	9.90/ 9.84	7.10/ 9.45	8.70/ 9.76	3.10/ 4.09	3.20/ 3.54
Human development index	0.80/ 6.27	0.77/ 6.10	0.94/ 9.37	0.93/ 9.51	0.89/ 7.70	0.85/ 7.56	0.75/ 4.21	0.68/ 3.41	0.94/ 9.05	0.89/ 8.21	0.92/ 8.41	0.90/ 8.29
Tariff & nontariff barriers	8.00/ 6.59	6.00/ 5.68	8.00/ 6.59	8.00/ 6.96	4.00/ 1.75	6.00/ 5.68	2.00/ 0.00	2.00/ 0.00	8.00/ 6.59	8.00/ 6.96	8.00/ 6.59	8.00/ 6.96
Regulatory quality	0.49/ 6.22	0.46/ 6.54	1.51/ 8.66	1.31/ 9.37	0.86/ 7.01	0.55/ 7.01	-0.41/ 3.07	-0.1/ 3.7	1.64/ 9.13	1.33/ 9.45	1.41/ 8.35	0.96/ 7.95
Rule of law	-0.22/ 4.57	-0.11/ 4.84	1.70/ 8.66	1.70/ 8.89	0.88/ 7.40	0.77/ 7.54	-0.22/ 4.57	-0.43/ 3.17	1.72/ 8.74	1.67/ 8.65	1.15/ 8.03	1.16/ 8.02
Researchers in R&D/million	226.49/ 3.00	213.00/ 3.40	4,048.33/ 9.22	3,636.00/ 9.47	2,882.39/ 8.22	2,205.00/ 7.66	583.88/ 4.56	464.00/ 4.47	2,191.20/ 7.33	1,889.00/ 7.13	1,948.44/ 6.89	1,317.00/ 5.96
Scientific and technical journal articles/mil pop.	23.73/ 5.20	17.73/ 4.88	586.80/ 9.13	676.17/ 9.29	143.19/ 7.48	71.72/ 7.01	9.31/ 4.17	5.81/ 3.70	329.69/ 8.43	292.62/ 8.43	305.68/ 8.27	251.72/ 8.27
Patent applications granted by the USPTO/mil pop.	0.90/ 5.82	0.49/ 5.96	338.78/ 9.91	243.62/ 9.91	86.25/ 8.64	27.50/ 8.17	0.33/ 4.55	0.05/ 3.67	47.34/ 7.91	16.39/ 7.80	8.71/ 7.55	4.28/ 7.52
Adult literacy rate (% age 15 and above)	91.60/ 4.72	89.80/ 5.08	100.00/ 8.19	100.00/ 8.49	97.90/ 6.69	97.00/ 6.51	90.92/ 4.65	80.80/ 3.57	100.00/ 8.19	100.00/ 8.49	97.81/ 6.61	97.10/ 6.67
Secondary enrollment	73.49/ 4.06	61.00/ 3.98	94.09/ 6.95	97.40/ 8.05	94.17/ 7.03	100.90/ 8.44	68.25/ 3.28	65.80/ 4.77	109.08/ 8.98	116.00/ 9.22	114.20/ 9.30	122.00/ 9.53
Tertiary enrollment	20.47/ 4.49	15.30/ 4.14	70.67/ 9.69	80.90/ 9.84	82.03/ 9.84	52.00/ 9.38	12.68/ 3.31	5.30/ 2.11	47.31/ 7.56	39.60/ 8.05	56.84/ 8.35	47.80/ 8.98
Telephones per 1,000 people	401.20/ 5.23	101.00/ 4.92	1,164.30/ 7.73	736.00/ 9.61	1,166.10/ 7.81	448.00/ 8.05	423.20/ 5.31	36.00/ 3.05	1,330.40/ 8.67	407.00/ 7.89	1,345.20/ 8.75	409.00/ 7.97
Computers per 1,000 people	82.00/ 5.58	25.59/ 6.08	658.90/ 9.83	328.09/ 9.83	551.40/ 9.33	107.69/ 8.08	27.60/ 3.58	2.27/ 2.08	420.80/ 8.67	183.04/ 8.75	196.00/ 7.50	61.21/ 7.58
Internet users per 10,000 people	984.82/ 5.70	10.00/ 5.63	5,513.77/ 9.69	755.00/ 9.77	6,034.20/ 9.84	81.00/ 7.73	632.48/ 4.61	0.00/ 0.00	3,130.20/ 7.73	111.00/ 8.05	2,391.08/ 7.19	38.00/ 6.95

Source: Knowledge Assessment Methodology. http://www.worldbank.org/kam.

Note: Average annual GDP growth (most recent) is the average annual GDP growth for the period 1999–2003. Average annual GDP growth (1995) is the average GDP growth for the period 1993–1997.

Annex 5

Performance, Economic Incentive Regime, Governance, Education, Innovation, and Information Communication Technologies: Scorecards for Mexico, United States, Republic of Korea, China, Ireland, and Spain

Performance

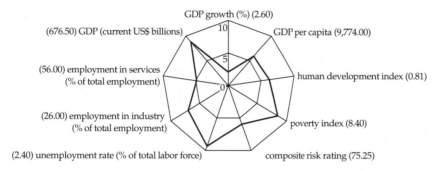

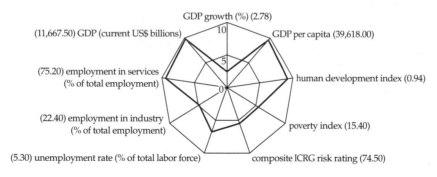

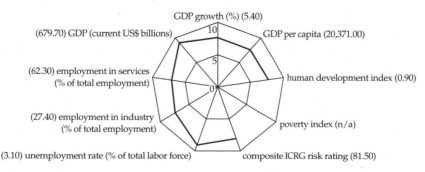

Source: World Bank, "Knowledge Assessment Methodology," http://www.worldbank.org/kam.
   Note: Values in parenthesis denote actual values for the particular country for the most recent period for which data are available. Each of the 127 variables in the KAM is normalized on a scale of 0 to 10. The fuller the scorecard, the better poised a country is to embrace the knowledge economy. But an economy should not necessarily aim for a perfect score of 10 on all variables because the scorecards may be shaped by the particular structural characteristics of an economy or by trade-offs that characterize different development strategies.

Performance

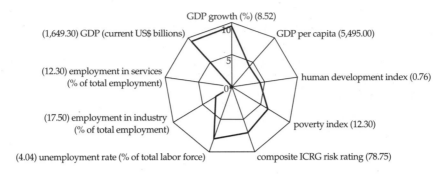

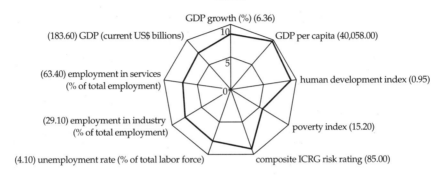

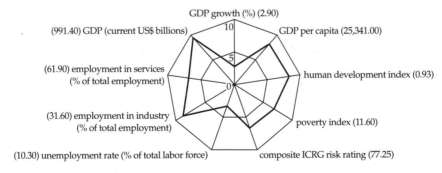

Source: World Bank, "Knowledge Assessment Methodology," http://www.worldbank.org/kam.
Note: Values in parenthesis denote actual values for the particular country for the most recent period for which data are available. Each of the 127 variables in the KAM is normalized on a scale of 0 to 10. The fuller the scorecard, the better poised a country is to embrace the knowledge economy. But an economy should not necessarily aim for a perfect score of 10 on all variables because the scorecards may be shaped by the particular structural characteristics of an economy or by trade-offs that characterize different development strategies.

Economic Incentive Regime

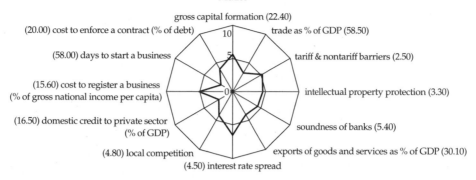

Mexico

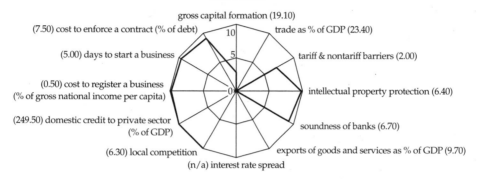

United States

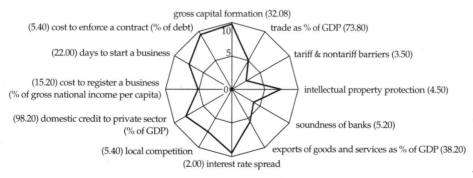

Korea, Rep. of

Source: World Bank, "Knowledge Assessment Methodology," http://www.worldbank.org/kam.
Note: Values in parenthesis denote actual values for the particular country for the most recent period for which data are available. Each of the 127 variables in the KAM is normalized on a scale of 0 to 10. The fuller the scorecard, the better poised a country is to embrace the knowledge economy. But an economy should not necessarily aim for a perfect score of 10 on all variables because the scorecards may be shaped by the particular structural characteristics of an economy or by trade-offs that characterize different development strategies.

Economic Incentive Regime

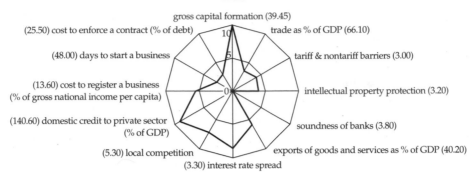

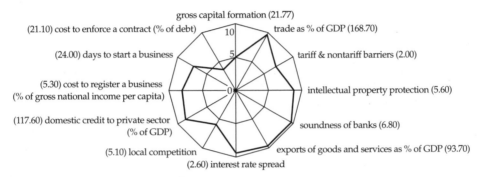

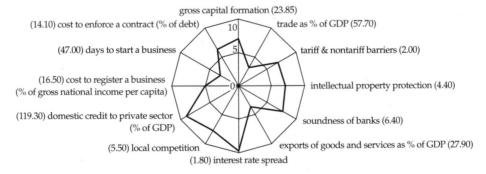

Source: World Bank, "Knowledge Assessment Methodology," http://www.worldbank.org/kam.
Note: Values in parenthesis denote actual values for the particular country for the most recent period for which data are available. Each of the 127 variables in the KAM is normalized on a scale of 0 to 10. The fuller the scorecard, the better poised a country is to embrace the knowledge economy. But an economy should not necessarily aim for a perfect score of 10 on all variables because the scorecards may be shaped by the particular structural characteristics of an economy or by trade-offs that characterize different development strategies.

Governance

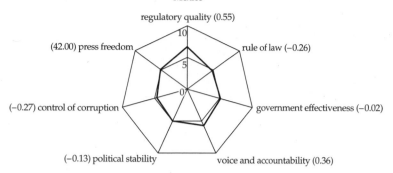

Mexico

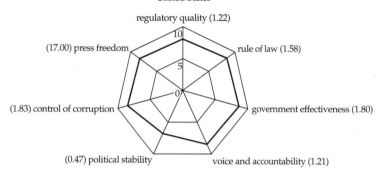

United States

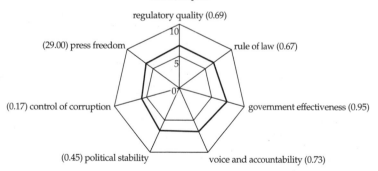

Korea, Rep. of

Source: World Bank, "Knowledge Assessment Methodology," http://www.worldbank.org/kam.
    Note: Values in parenthesis denote actual values for the particular country for the most recent period for which data are available. Each of the 127 variables in the KAM is normalized on a scale of 0 to 10. The fuller the scorecard, the better poised a country is to embrace the knowledge economy. But an economy should not necessarily aim for a perfect score of 10 on all variables because the scorecards may be shaped by the particular structural characteristics of an economy or by trade-offs that characterize different development strategies.

Governance

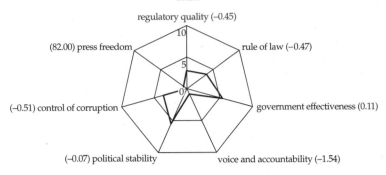

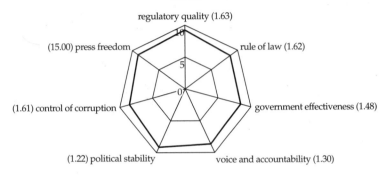

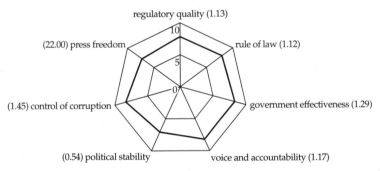

Source: World Bank, "Knowledge Assessment Methodology," http://www.worldbank.org/kam.
   Note: Values in parenthesis denote actual values for the particular country for the most recent period for which data are available. Each of the 127 variables in the KAM is normalized on a scale of 0 to 10. The fuller the scorecard, the better poised a country is to embrace the knowledge economy. But an economy should not necessarily aim for a perfect score of 10 on all variables because the scorecards may be shaped by the particular structural characteristics of an economy or by trade-offs that characterize different development strategies.

Education

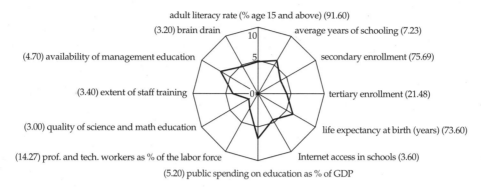

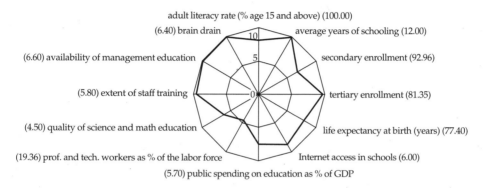

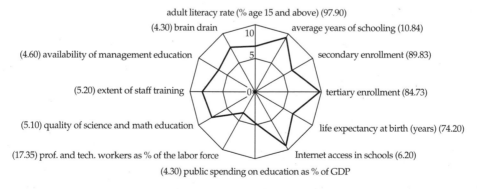

Source: World Bank, "Knowledge Assessment Methodology," http://www.worldbank.org/kam.
Note: Values in parenthesis denote actual values for the particular country for the most recent period for which data are available. Each of the 127 variables in the KAM is normalized on a scale of 0 to 10. The fuller the scorecard, the better poised a country is to embrace the knowledge economy. But an economy should not necessarily aim for a perfect score of 10 on all variables because the scorecards may be shaped by the particular structural characteristics of an economy or by trade-offs that characterize different development strategies.

Education

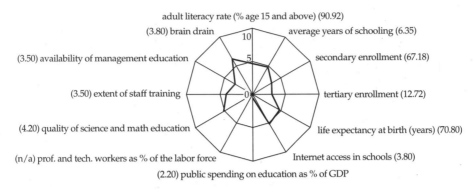

China

adult literacy rate (% age 15 and above) (90.92)

(3.80) brain drain — average years of schooling (6.35)

(3.50) availability of management education — secondary enrollment (67.18)

(3.50) extent of staff training — tertiary enrollment (12.72)

(4.20) quality of science and math education — life expectancy at birth (years) (70.80)

(n/a) prof. and tech. workers as % of the labor force — Internet access in schools (3.80)

(2.20) public spending on education as % of GDP

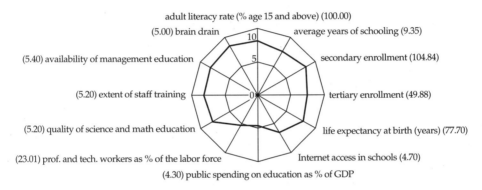

Ireland

adult literacy rate (% age 15 and above) (100.00)

(5.00) brain drain — average years of schooling (9.35)

(5.40) availability of management education — secondary enrollment (104.84)

(5.20) extent of staff training — tertiary enrollment (49.88)

(5.20) quality of science and math education — life expectancy at birth (years) (77.70)

(23.01) prof. and tech. workers as % of the labor force — Internet access in schools (4.70)

(4.30) public spending on education as % of GDP

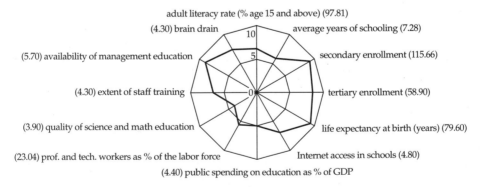

Spain

adult literacy rate (% age 15 and above) (97.81)

(4.30) brain drain — average years of schooling (7.28)

(5.70) availability of management education — secondary enrollment (115.66)

(4.30) extent of staff training — tertiary enrollment (58.90)

(3.90) quality of science and math education — life expectancy at birth (years) (79.60)

(23.04) prof. and tech. workers as % of the labor force — Internet access in schools (4.80)

(4.40) public spending on education as % of GDP

Source: World Bank, "Knowledge Assessment Methodology," http://www.worldbank.org/kam.
Note: Values in parenthesis denote actual values for the particular country for the most recent period for which data are available. Each of the 127 variables in the KAM is normalized on a scale of 0 to 10. The fuller the scorecard, the better poised a country is to embrace the knowledge economy. But an economy should not necessarily aim for a perfect score of 10 on all variables because the scorecards may be shaped by the particular structural characteristics of an economy or by trade-offs that characterize different development strategies.

Innovation

Mexico

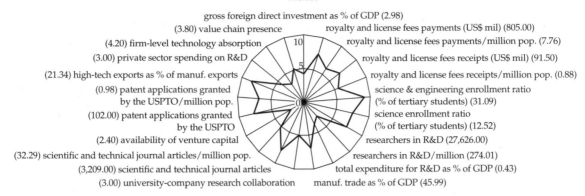

gross foreign direct investment as % of GDP (2.98)
(3.80) value chain presence
(4.20) firm-level technology absorption
(3.00) private sector spending on R&D
(21.34) high-tech exports as % of manuf. exports
(0.98) patent applications granted by the USPTO/million pop.
(102.00) patent applications granted by the USPTO
(2.40) availability of venture capital
(32.29) scientific and technical journal articles/million pop.
(3,209.00) scientific and technical journal articles
(3.00) university-company research collaboration
royalty and license fees payments (US$ mil) (805.00)
royalty and license fees payments/million pop. (7.76)
royalty and license fees receipts (US$ mil) (91.50)
royalty and license fees receipts/million pop. (0.88)
science & engineering enrollment ratio (% of tertiary students) (31.09)
science enrollment ratio (% of tertiary students) (12.52)
researchers in R&D (27,626.00)
researchers in R&D/million (274.01)
total expenditure for R&D as % of GDP (0.43)
manuf. trade as % of GDP (45.99)

United States

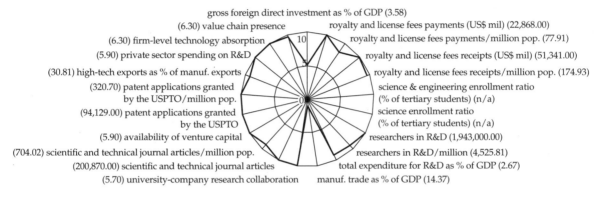

gross foreign direct investment as % of GDP (3.58)
(6.30) value chain presence
(6.30) firm-level technology absorption
(5.90) private sector spending on R&D
(30.81) high-tech exports as % of manuf. exports
(320.70) patent applications granted by the USPTO/million pop.
(94,129.00) patent applications granted by the USPTO
(5.90) availability of venture capital
(704.02) scientific and technical journal articles/million pop.
(200,870.00) scientific and technical journal articles
(5.70) university-company research collaboration
royalty and license fees payments (US$ mil) (22,868.00)
royalty and license fees payments/million pop. (77.91)
royalty and license fees receipts (US$ mil) (51,341.00)
royalty and license fees receipts/million pop. (174.93)
science & engineering enrollment ratio (% of tertiary students) (n/a)
science enrollment ratio (% of tertiary students) (n/a)
researchers in R&D (1,943,000.00)
researchers in R&D/million (4,525.81)
total expenditure for R&D as % of GDP (2.67)
manuf. trade as % of GDP (14.37)

Korea, Rep. of

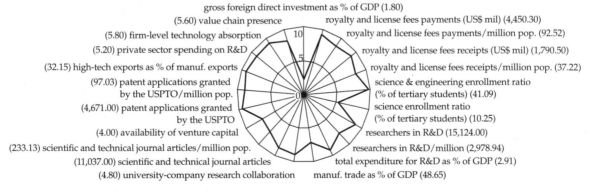

gross foreign direct investment as % of GDP (1.80)
(5.60) value chain presence
(5.80) firm-level technology absorption
(5.20) private sector spending on R&D
(32.15) high-tech exports as % of manuf. exports
(97.03) patent applications granted by the USPTO/million pop.
(4,671.00) patent applications granted by the USPTO
(4.00) availability of venture capital
(233.13) scientific and technical journal articles/million pop.
(11,037.00) scientific and technical journal articles
(4.80) university-company research collaboration
royalty and license fees payments (US$ mil) (4,450.30)
royalty and license fees payments/million pop. (92.52)
royalty and license fees receipts (US$ mil) (1,790.50)
royalty and license fees receipts/million pop. (37.22)
science & engineering enrollment ratio (% of tertiary students) (41.09)
science enrollment ratio (% of tertiary students) (10.25)
researchers in R&D (15,124.00)
researchers in R&D/million (2,978.94)
total expenditure for R&D as % of GDP (2.91)
manuf. trade as % of GDP (48.65)

Source: World Bank, "Knowledge Assessment Methodology," http://www.worldbank.org/kam.
Note: Values in parenthesis denote actual values for the particular country for the most recent period for which data are available. Each of the 127 variables in the KAM is normalized on a scale of 0 to 10. The fuller the scorecard, the better poised a country is to embrace the knowledge economy. But an economy should not necessarily aim for a perfect score of 10 on all variables because the scorecards may be shaped by the particular structural characteristics of an economy or by trade-offs that characterize different development strategies.

Innovation

China

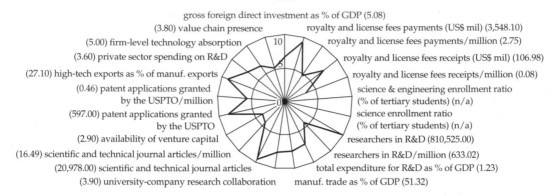

gross foreign direct investment as % of GDP (5.08)
(3.80) value chain presence
(5.00) firm-level technology absorption
(3.60) private sector spending on R&D
(27.10) high-tech exports as % of manuf. exports
(0.46) patent applications granted by the USPTO/million
(597.00) patent applications granted by the USPTO
(2.90) availability of venture capital
(16.49) scientific and technical journal articles/million
(20,978.00) scientific and technical journal articles
(3.90) university-company research collaboration

royalty and license fees payments (US$ mil) (3,548.10)
royalty and license fees payments/million (2.75)
royalty and license fees receipts (US$ mil) (106.98)
royalty and license fees receipts/million (0.08)
science & engineering enrollment ratio (% of tertiary students) (n/a)
science enrollment ratio (% of tertiary students) (n/a)
researchers in R&D (810,525.00)
researchers in R&D/million (633.02)
total expenditure for R&D as % of GDP (1.23)
manuf. trade as % of GDP (51.32)

Ireland

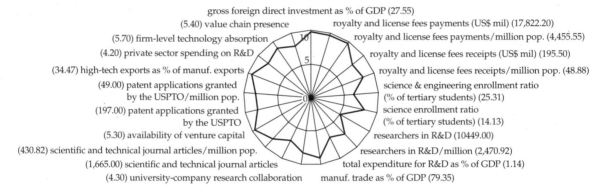

gross foreign direct investment as % of GDP (27.55)
(5.40) value chain presence
(5.70) firm-level technology absorption
(4.20) private sector spending on R&D
(34.47) high-tech exports as % of manuf. exports
(49.00) patent applications granted by the USPTO/million pop.
(197.00) patent applications granted by the USPTO
(5.30) availability of venture capital
(430.82) scientific and technical journal articles/million pop.
(1,665.00) scientific and technical journal articles
(4.30) university-company research collaboration

royalty and license fees payments (US$ mil) (17,822.20)
royalty and license fees payments/million pop. (4,455.55)
royalty and license fees receipts (US$ mil) (195.50)
royalty and license fees receipts/million pop. (48.88)
science & engineering enrollment ratio (% of tertiary students) (25.31)
science enrollment ratio (% of tertiary students) (14.13)
researchers in R&D (10449.00)
researchers in R&D/million (2,470.92)
total expenditure for R&D as % of GDP (1.14)
manuf. trade as % of GDP (79.35)

Spain

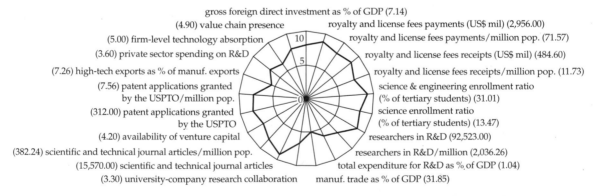

gross foreign direct investment as % of GDP (7.14)
(4.90) value chain presence
(5.00) firm-level technology absorption
(3.60) private sector spending on R&D
(7.26) high-tech exports as % of manuf. exports
(7.56) patent applications granted by the USPTO/million pop.
(312.00) patent applications granted by the USPTO
(4.20) availability of venture capital
(382.24) scientific and technical journal articles/million pop.
(15,570.00) scientific and technical journal articles
(3.30) university-company research collaboration

royalty and license fees payments (US$ mil) (2,956.00)
royalty and license fees payments/million pop. (71.57)
royalty and license fees receipts (US$ mil) (484.60)
royalty and license fees receipts/million pop. (11.73)
science & engineering enrollment ratio (% of tertiary students) (31.01)
science enrollment ratio (% of tertiary students) (13.47)
researchers in R&D (92,523.00)
researchers in R&D/million (2,036.26)
total expenditure for R&D as % of GDP (1.04)
manuf. trade as % of GDP (31.85)

Source: World Bank, "Knowledge Assessment Methodology," http://www.worldbank.org/kam.
Note: Values in parenthesis denote actual values for the particular country for the most recent period for which data are available. Each of the 127 variables in the KAM is normalized on a scale of 0 to 10. The fuller the scorecard, the better poised a country is to embrace the knowledge economy. But an economy should not necessarily aim for a perfect score of 10 on all variables because the scorecards may be shaped by the particular structural characteristics of an economy or by trade-offs that characterize different development strategies.

Information Infrastructure

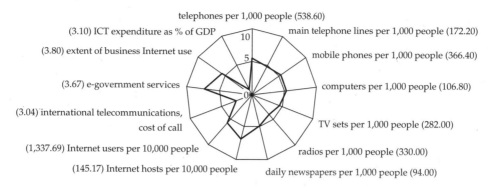

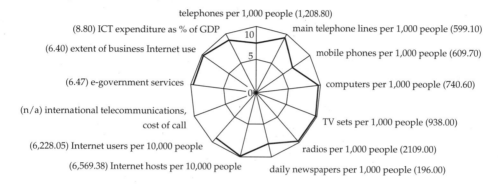

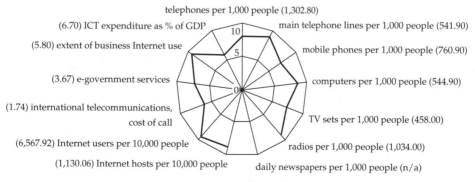

Source: World Bank, "Knowledge Assessment Methodology," http://www.worldbank.org/kam.
Note: Values in parenthesis denote actual values for the particular country for the most recent period for which data are available. Each of the 127 variables in the KAM is normalized on a scale of 0 to 10. The fuller the scorecard, the better poised a country is to embrace the knowledge economy. But an economy should not necessarily aim for a perfect score of 10 on all variables because the scorecards may be shaped by the particular structural characteristics of an economy or by trade-offs that characterize different development strategies.

Information Infrastructure

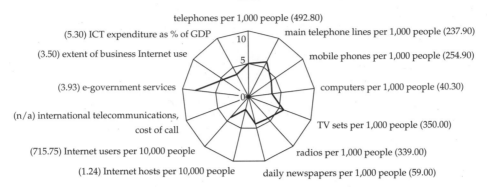

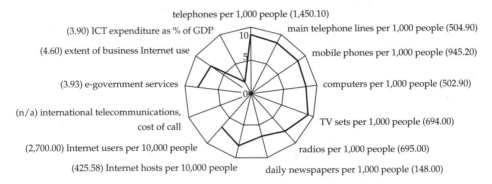

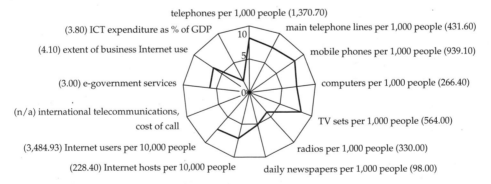

Source: World Bank, "Knowledge Assessment Methodology," http://www.worldbank.org/kam.
Note: Values in parenthesis denote actual values for the particular country for the most recent period for which data are available. Each of the 127 variables in the KAM is normalized on a scale of 0 to 10. The fuller the scorecard, the better poised a country is to embrace the knowledge economy. But an economy should not necessarily aim for a perfect score of 10 on all variables because the scorecards may be shaped by the particular structural characteristics of an economy or by trade-offs that characterize different development strategies.

Annex 6

Variables for Regional Knowledge Assessment

Variable	Beginning year	Last year available
GDP growth SIMA (%)	1995	2002
Regulation index	1999	2001
Strikes per thousands employment	1993	1998
Public debt/GDP (flows annual)	1993	1998
Invesment public/GDP	1995	1999
Patents per 1,000 people	1995	2000
Researchers in R&D per 1,000 people	1999	2001
FDI/GDP	1995	2001
Adult literacy rate (% age 15 and above)	1995	2000
Secondary enrollment	1995	2000
Tertiary enrollment	1995	2000
Average years of schooling	1990	2000
Educational expenditure % from GDP local	1999	2001
Expenditure on ICT/GDP	1999	2001
Telephones lines per 1,000 people	1995	2001
Nonagricultural business (assets/GDPI)	1993	1998
Nonagricultural business (value added/GDP)	1993	1998
Loan portfolio/number of business	1995	1999
HDI (human development index)	1995	2000
GDP per capita	1995	2002
Maquiladora industry (value added/GDP)	1995	1999
Manufacturing/GDP	1993	1998
ITC busines by state/total business	1993	1998
Comunications and transport/GDP	1995	2002
Value added on ITC/GDP	1993	1998
Graduates in science and technology and engineering/total student graduates	1995	2000
Manufacturing productivity (value added/employment)	1993	1998
Business by state/1,000 people	1993	1998
GDP financial services/GDP	1995	2002
Local taxes/GDP	1995	2000

Bibliography

Acevedo, L. G. 2002. "Mexico—Technology, Wages, and Employment. Technology and Firm Performance in Mexico." World Bank, Washington, DC.

Acevedo, L. G. and H. Tan. 2002. "Mexico: In-Firm Training for the Knowledge Economy." Processed.

Amsden, H. Alice, and Takashi Hikino. 1994. "Project Execution Capability, Organizational Know-How and Conglomerate Corporate Growth in Late Industrialization." *Industrial and Corporate Change* 3 (1): 149–172.

Aoki, M., H. K. Kim, and M. Okuno-Fujiwara. 1997. *The Role of Government in East Asian Economic Development, Comparative Institutional Analysis*. Oxford: Clarendon Press.

Aroca, P., M. Bosch, and William F. Maloney. 2003. "Is NAFTA Polarizing Mexico? Or *Existe Tambien el Sur?* Spatial Dimensions of Mexico's Post-Liberalization Growth." World Bank, Washington, DC.

Barro, Robert J., and Jong-Wha Lee. 2001. "International Data on Educational Attainment: Updates and Implications." *Oxford Economic Papers* 3: 541–63.

Batra, G., and H. Tan. 2000. "Technology and Firm Size—Wage Differentials in Colombia, Mexico, and Taiwan (China)." *The World Bank Economic Review* 11 (1): 59–83.

Bergoeing R., P. Kehoe, T. Kehoe, and R. Soto. 2001. "A Decade Lost and Found: Mexico and Chile in the 1980s." NBER Working Paper 8520, National Bureau of Economic Research, Cambridge, MA.

———. 2002. "Policy-Driven Productivity in Chile and Mexico in the 1980s and 1990s." NBER Working Paper 8892, National Bureau of Economic Research, Cambridge, MA.

Bernanke, Ben S., and Refet S. Gürkaynak. 2001. "Is Growth Exogenous? Taking Mankiw, Romer and Weil Seriously." NBER Working Paper 8365, National Bureau of Economic Research, Cambridge, MA.

Bils, Mark, and Peter J. Klenow. 2000. "Does Schooling Cause Growth?" *American Economic Review* 90 (5): 1160–83.

Boston College. 2003. "Trends in International Mathematics and Science Study (TIMSS)." http://timss.bc.edu/timss2003.html (accessed November 16, 2005).

Bosworth, B. 1998. "Productivity Growth in Mexico." Country Economic Memorandum, Report 17392-ME, World Bank, Washington, DC.

Camhi, Rosita, and Rosana Latuf. 2000. "Evaluación del sistema de ayudas estudiantiles a la educación superior." Working paper, Instituto Libertad y Desarrollo, Santiago, Chile.

Carrillo, J., and A. Hualde. 1997. "Maquiladoras de tercera generación, el caso de Delphi-General Motors." *Revista comercio exterior* (September): 127–139.

Casanueva, C. 2001. "The Acquisition of Firm Technological Capabilities in Mexico's Open Economy, the Case of Vitro." *Technological Forecasting and Social Change* 66 (1): 237–242.

Casas, Rosalba, Rebeca De Gortari, and Maria Josefa Santos. 1997. "The Structure and Dynamics of Knowledge in New Technology Fields in Mexico." UNAM (Universidad Autonma de Mexico), Mexico City.

CEE (Consej Coordinador Emresarial). 2000. "Fases de la prospectiva." Presentation for UNIDO (United Nations Industrial Development Organization), Mexico City, October 16.

Ciecon (Centro de Investigación sobre Economía Laboral y Gestión del Conocimiento). 2001. "The Incidence of Training in Mexico." Background paper for *Mexico: Training Mechanisms.* World Bank, Washington, DC.

Cohen, Daniel, and Marcelo Soto. 2001. "Growth and Human Capital: Good Data, Good Results." Technical Paper 179, OECD Development Centre, Paris.

Comisión Federal de Telecomunicaciones. 2002 . *Informe de labores 2001.* Mexico City.

———. 2003. "Indice de producción del sector telecomunicaciones, ITEL, tercer trimestre 2002 (cifras preliminares)." Mexico City.

———. 2005. Cofetel statistics. www.cft.gov.mx (accessed November 17, 2005).

CONACYT (Consejo Nacional de Ciencia y tecnología). 2000a. *Indicadores de actividades científicas y tecnológicas Mexico.* Mexico City.

———. 2000b. CONACYT and PECYT *Programa especial de ciencia y tecnología.* 2001. Programa especial de ciencia y tecnología 2001–2006, México D.F., 2001 (Mexico City).

———. 2002. *Informe general del estado de la ciencia y la tecnología 2002.* Mexico City

CONAFE (Confederacion de Asociaciones de Frisona Espanola). 2003. http://www.conafe.edu.mx/menu.html (accessed June 6, 2003).

Constantino, R., and A. Lara. 2000. "The Automobile Sector." In *Developing Innovation Systems,* ed. M. Cimoli. London: Continuum.

Dalgaard, Thomas. 2000. "The Tax System in Mexico. A Need for Strengthening the Revenue-Raising Capacity." Organisation for Economic Co-operation and Development, Paris.

Dar, A., F. Fluitman, and I. S. Gill. 2000. *Vocational Education and Training Reform.* Washington, DC: Oxford University Press and World Bank.

de Ferranti, David, Guillermo E. Perry, Indermit Gill, J. Luis Guasch, William E. Maloney, Carolina Sánchez-Páramo, and Norbert Schady. 2003. *Closing the Gap in Education and Technology.* Washington, DC: World Bank.

Deichmann, U., ed. 2002. *Economic Structure, Productivity, and Infrastructure Quality in Southern Mexico.* Washington, DC: World Bank.

Duran, Clemente. 1998. "Technological Learning in Mexico." World Bank, Washington, DC.

Dutta, S., B. Lauvin, and F. Paua, eds. 2004. *Global Information Technology Report* 2003–2004. Oxford University Press. www.weforum.org.

Dutrenit, G. 2000. "Strategies and Technological Capabilities in a Multinational Mexican Firm." In *Developing Innovation Systems*, ed. M. Cimoli, 229–45. London: Continuum, London.

Easterly, W., N. Loayza, and Peter Montiel. 1996. *Has Latin America's Post-Reform Growth Been Disapointing?* Washington, DC: World Bank.

Edwards, A. 1993. "Teacher Compensation in Developing Countries." In *Teachers in Developing Countries: Improving Effectiveness and Managing Costs,* ed. Joseph P. Farrell and Joao B. Oliveira, EDI Seminar Series. Washington, DC: World Bank.

Encuesta Nacional de Ingresos y Gastos de los Hogares. 2000. INEGI, Mexico City.

Esquivel, G., D. Lederman, M. Messmacher, and R. Villoro. 2002. "Why NAFTA Did Not Reach the South." World Bank, Washington, DC.

Esquivel, G., and Miguel Messmacher. 2002. "Sources of Regional (Non) Convergence in Mexico." El Colegio de México y Banco de Mexico, Mexico City.

Estache, A., M. Manacorda, and T. Valletti. 2002. "Telecommunication Reforms, Access Regulation, and Internet Adoption in Latin America." Policy Research Working Paper 2802, World Bank, Washington, DC.

Fajnzylber, P., and D. Lederman. 1997. "Economic Reforms and Total Factor Productivity Growth in Latin America and the Caribbean, 1950–95: An Empirical Note." World Bank, Washington, DC.

Fundación Chile. 1997. *Annual Report.* Santiago, Chile.

Gibbons, M. 1998. *Higher Education Relevance in the 21st Century.* Washington, DC: World Bank.

Giugale, M. M., O. Lafourcade, and V. H. Nguyen, eds. 2001. *Mexico: A Comprehensive Development Agenda for the New Era.* Washington, DC: World Bank.

Giugale, M. M., and S. B. Webb, eds. 2000. *Achievements and Challenges of Fiscal Decentralization, Lessons from Mexico.* Washington, DC: World Bank.

Gollin, Douglas. 2001. "Getting Income Shares Right." Working Paper, Williams College, Williamstown, Massachussets.

Hallberg, K., H. Tan, and L. Koryukin. 2000. "Exporting Dynamics and Productivity: Analysis of Mexican Manufacturing in the 1990s." Report 19864-ME, Mexico Country Department, World Bank, Washington, DC.

INEGI. 1999. "Micro, pequeña, mediana y gran empresas." Censos Económicos, INEGI, Mexico City.

———. 2000. "Censo Nacional de Población y Vivienda." INEGI, Mexico City.

———. 2001a. "La producción, salarios, empleo y productividad de la industria maquiladora de exportación, total nacional, 1988–2000." INEGI, Mexico City.

———. 2001b. CensusCenso 2000. www.inegi.gob.mx (accessed April 2, 2003).

Intarakumnerd, Patarapong, Pun-arj, Chairatana, and Tipawan Tangchitpiboon. 2002. "National Innovation Systems in Less Successful Developing Countries: The Case Study of Thailand." *Research Policy* 31 (8–9): 1445–1457.

International Labour Organisation. 2005. http://www.ilo.org/ (accessed April 3, 2005).

ITU (International Telecommunications Union). 2004. *Yearbook of Statistics Telecommunications Services Chronological Time Series 1988–1997* and *ITU Americas Telecommunications Indicators 2000*. http://www.itu.int/ITU-D/ict/statistics/ (accessed October 6, 2004).

Lall, V. S., and S. Ghosh. 2002. "Learning by Dining. Informal Networks and Productivity in Mexican Industry." World Bank, Washington, DC.

Lall, S. 2002. "Foreign Direct Investment, Technology Development and Competitiveness: Issues and Evidence." Queen Elizabeth House, Oxford.

Lederman, D. and William F. Maloney (2002). "Innovation in Mexico: NAFTA Is Not Enough." World Bank, Washington, DC.

Lederman, D. 2003. "Lessons from NAFTA." World Bank, Washington, DC.

Liang, X. 1999. "Teacher Pay in 12 Latin American Countries: How Does Teacher Pay Compare to Other Professions, What Determines Teacher Pay, and Who Are the Teachers?" World Bank, Washington, DC.

Loayza, N., P. Fajnzylber, and C. Calderón. 2002. "Economic Growth in Latin America and the Caribbean: Stylized Facts, Explanations, and Forecasts." World Bank Latin American Regional Studies Program, Washington, DC.

Lomnitz, Heriberta Castanos. 1998. "The Brain Drain from Mexico: The Experience of Scientists." *Science and Public Policy* 25 (4).

López-Córdoba, J. E. 2002. "NAFTA and Mexico's Manufacturing Productivity: An Empirical Investigation Using Micro-Level Data." Inter-American Development Bank, Washington, DC.

Luna, Matilde, and Ricardo Tirado. 1998. "The New Role of Universities and Business Associations in Local Development in Mexico." Proecssed, Mexico City.

Maloney, William F. 2001. "Labor Markets." *In Mexico: A Comprehensive Development Agenda for the New Era*, ed. M. M. Guigale, O. Lafourcade, and V. H. Nguyen, 511–536. Washington, DC: World Bank.

Matthews, L., and J. Sargent. 1995. "Enterprise Training in Developing Countries: Incidence, Productivity Effects, and Policy Implications." Competition and Strategy Unit, Private Sector Development Department, World Bank, Washington, DC.

Mayer, D., and Andrew Foster. 2002. "Scale, Technological Change, and Human Capital: Manufacturing and Development in Mexico." World Bank, Washington, DC.

México, Presidencia de la Republica. 2003. *Contigo un México para Todos*. Mexico City.

Middleton, J., Van Adams, and A. Ziderman. 1993. "Skills for Productivity: Vocational Education and Training in Developing Countries." World Bank, Washington, DC.

Nadal, Alejandro. 1995. "Harnessing the Politics of Science and Technology Policy in Mexico." In *Politics of Technology in Latin America,* ed. Maria Ines Bastos and Charles Cooper. London: Routledge.

Najmabadi, F., and S. Lall. 1995. "Developing Industrial Technology Lessons for Policy and Practice." Operations Evaluation Department, World Bank, Washington, DC.

Naranjo, M. A. 2002. "The Impact of NAFTA on Foreign Direct Investment Flows in Mexico and the Excluded Countries." Department of Economics, Northwestern University. Chicago, IL.

National Science Foundation, Division of Science Resources Studies. 2000. "Latin America: R&D Spending Jumps in Brazil, Mexico, and Costa Rica." NSF 00-316. Arlington, VA.

OECD (Organisation for Economic Co-operation and Development). 1998. *Technology, Productivity, and Job Creation.* Paris.

————. 2000. Science, Technology, and Industry Outlook. Paris.

————. 2001a. "Knowledge and Skills for Life: Results from PISA 2000." Paris.

————. 2001b. "STI Outlook: Mexico." Paris.

————. 2002a. "Economic Survey: Mexico. Assessment and Recommendations." Paris.

————. 2002b. "Education at a Glance 2002." www.oecd.org/els/education/eag2002a (accessed October 17, 2003).

————. 2002c. "Science, Technology and Industry Outlook." Paris.

————. 2003a. "Economic Survey: Mexico, 2003." Paris.

————. 2003b. "Education at a Glance, 2003." http://www.oecd.org/document/34/0,2340,en_2825_495609_14152482_1_1_1_1,00.html (accessed March 5, 2004).

————. 2004. "Mexico: Competition Law and Policy in 2003." Paris.

Oxenham, John. 2002. "Skills and Literacy Training for Better Livelihoods: A Review of Approaches and Experiences." World Bank, Washington, DC.

Parker, Susan W., and Carla Pederzini. 2000. "Gender Differences in Education in Mexico." World Bank, Washington, DC.

Patrinos, Harry Anthony, Joseph Shapiro, and Jorge Trevino Moreno. 2004. "Education for All: Compensating for Disadvantage in Mexico." web.worldbank.org/WBSITE/EXTERNAL/TOPICS/EXTEDUCATION/0,,contentMDK:20263851~menuPK:534136~pagePK:148956~... - 141k.

Psacharopoulos, George. 1994. *World Development* 22 (9): 1325–1343.

Pyramid Research, Benchmarks. 2001. "Latin America: Liberalization in Progress, an Interconnection Update, 2Q 2001."

Radosevic, S. 1999. "International Technology Transfer and Catch-Up in Economic Development." Science and Technology Policy Research, University of Sussex, United Kingdom.

RAND Europe. 2002. "Technology Use and Productivity in Mexico: A Feasibility Study." Proposal submitted to the World Bank, Washington, DC.

Robertson, R. 2002. "Did NAFTA Increase Labor Market Integration between the United States and Mexico?" Department of Economics, Macalester College.

Santamaria, Mauricio, and Gladys López-Acevedo. 2003. "Labor Reform in Mexico. Analysis of a Proposal Drafted by Employers and Employees." World Bank, Washington, DC.

Santaella, A. J. 1998. "Economic Growth in Mexico. Searching for Clues to Its Slowdown." Departamento Académico de Economía, Instituto Tecnológico Autónomo de México, Mexico City.

Scott, J. 2003. "Public Spending and Inequality of Opportunities in Mexico." World Bank, Washington, DC.

SCT (Secretaria de Transporte y Comunicaciones). 2001. *Plan y estrategia 2000–2006.* Mexico City.

———. 2003. *Plan y estrategia anual 2002.* Mexico City, Mexico.

SEDEC (Secretaria de Desarollo Economico). 2001. *The Industrial Policy, Vision 2020.* Rubén Camarillo.

SEDESOL (Secretaria de Desarrollo Social). 2003. Jóvenes con oportunidades." http://www.oportunidades.gob.mx (accessed June 4, 2004).

SEP (Secretaria de Educación Publica). 2001. "Estadística básica de educación superior." Inicio de Cursos 2000–2001. http://www.sep.gob.mx/work/appsite/pubsup00/index.htm (accessed November 18, 2003).

———. 2001. *Programa Nacional de Educación 2001–2006.* Mexico City.

———. 2002. "Carrera magisterial." http://www.sep.gob.mx/wb2/sep/sep_3121_carrera_magisterial (accessed May 18, 2003).

Select Corporation. 2003 "Servicio de banda ancha en México, 1er semestre 2002." Mexico City.

Shaiken, Harley. 1994. "Advanced Manufacturing in Mexico: A New International Division of Labor." *Latin American Research Review* 29 (2).

Stuart, Donald, and J. Tuset. 2002. "Internet Services in Mexico." Operational Management Report, DPRO-90790, Gartner Research, Mexico City.

Tan, H. 2000. "Technological Change and Skills Demand: Panel Evidence from Malaysian Manufacturing." Working Paper, World Bank Institute, Washington, DC.

Tan, Hong and Gladys Lopez-Acevedo. 2005. "Evaluating Training Programs for Small and Medium Enterprises: Lessons from Mexico." World Bank Policy Research Working Paper No. 3760. http://ssrn.com/abstract=844864.

Taylor, J. E., and Antonio Yunez-Naude. 1999. "Education, Migration and Productivity. An Analytical Approach and Evidence from Rural Mexico." OECD, Paris.

Telegeography. 2005. *Global Traffic Statistics* and *Commentary*. Mexico City.

TELEMEX. Annual Report 2004. Mexico City.

Tendler, Judith. 1997. *Good Government in the Tropics*. Baltimore: Johns Hopkins University Press.

UNCTAD. United Nations Conference on Trade and Development. 2000. *World Investment Report 2000*. Geneva, Switzeland.

UNIDO. United Nations Industrial Development Organization. 2000. "Inventario y plan de acción para el programa de prospectiva tecnológica en México." Paper presented at the Seminario Regional del Programa de Prospectiva Tecnológica para América Latina y el Caribe, Montevideo, Uruguay, December 4–5.

USPTO. United States Patent and Trademark Office. http://www.uspto.gov/ (accessed 16 April 2004).

United States Trade Representative to the World Trade Organization. 2002. "Mexico—Measures Affecting Telecommunications Services." WT/DS204. Geneva, Switzeland.

U.S. Department of Commerce, International Trade Administration. 2002. "Export IT Mexico." Washington, DC.

U.S. Department of Education. 1999. "Schooling in Mexico: A Brief Guide for U.S. Educators." Office of Education Research and Improvement (ERIC), http://www.ael.org/ERIC/digests/edorc02-5.pdf (accessed October 3, 2003).

Verner, D. 1999. "Are Wages and Productivity in Zimbabwe Affected by Human Capital Investment and International Trade?" Working Paper, World Bank Institute, Washington, DC.

Vidal, Eloy. 2002. "Mexico Southern States Development Strategy. Rural Infrastructure Telecommunications Sector." World Bank, Washington, DC.

Wagner, C., S. Popper, and E. Horling. 2003. "Technology Use and Productivity in Mexico: A Feasibility Study." RAND Europe.

Wellenius, B., and Gregory Staple. 1996. "Beyond Privatization: The Second Wave of Telecommunications Reforms in Mexico." Discussion Paper 341, World Bank, Washington, DC.

West, Darrell. 2002a. "Global E-Government 2001." Center for Policy Research, Brown University, Providence, RI.

———.2002b. "Global E-Government 2002." Center for Policy Research, Brown University, Providence, RI.

Woessmann, Ludger. 2000. "Specifying Human Capital: A Review, Some Extensions and Development Effects." Working Paper 1007, Kiel Institute of World Economics, Kiel, Germany.

World Bank. 1995. *Priorities and Strategies for Education: World Bank Review.* Washington, DC.

————. 1998a. "Mexico Country Economic Memorandum: Enhancing Factor Productivity Growth." Report 17392-ME. Washington, DC.

————. 1998b. "Mexico: Enhancing Factor Productivity Growth." Country Economic Memorandum, Latin America and the Caribbean Region, Washington, DC.

————. 1999a. "Advancing Educational Equity and Productivity in the Context of Decentralization." Report No. 19283 ME.

————. 1999b. *Knowledge for Development*. New York: Oxford University Press.

————. 1999–2003. *World Development Reports*. Washington, DC.

————. 1999–2006. "World Development Indicators 1999–2006." http://devdata.worldbank.org/edstats/cd.asp (accessed April 3, 2007).

————. 2000a. "Mexico: Export Dynamics and Productivity. Analysis of Mexican Manufacturing in the 1990s." Report 19864-ME, Latin America and the Caribbean Region, Washington, DC.

————. 2000b. "Mexico: Transforming Schools into Effective and Efficient Learning Centers." Report 20593-ME, Latin America and the Caribbean Region, Washington, DC.

————. 2001a. *Mexico Technology Wages and Employment*. 2 vols. Technical Papers, Report 22797-ME, Poverty Reduction and Economic Management Unit, Mexico Department, Washington, DC.

————. 2001b. *Think Globally, Act Locally: Decentralized Incentive Framework for Mexico's Private Sector Development*. Report No. 22643, Latin American and the Caribbean Region, Washington, DC.

————. 2002a. *Constructing Knowledge Societies: New Challenges for Tertiary Education*. Washington, DC.

————. 2002b. *Knowledge in Latin America and the Caribbean: Reconsidering Education, Training, and Technology Policies*. LAC Regional Study, Latin American and the Caribbean Region. Washington, DC.

World Bank and Public-Private Infrastructure Advisory Facility (PPIAF). 2002c. "Private Solutions of Infrastructure in Mexico. A Country Framework Report."Washington, DC.

————. 2003. *Lifelong Learning in the Global Knowledge Economy: Challenges for Developing Countries*. Washington, DC.

————. 2004. Edstats database. http://www1.worldbank.org/education/edstats/ (accessed July 11, 2005).

————. 2005. Statistical Information Management and Analysis (SIMA) – Replaced by Development Data Platform starting July 1, 2005 http://DDPTimeseries.worldbank.org (accessed April 2, 2007).

————. 2006. "Knowledge Assessment Methodology (KAM), Knowledge for Development Program (K4D)." World Bank Institute, Washington, DC.